Energy from the Sea

Energy from the Sea

An International Law Perspective on Ocean Energy

Edited by

Nigel Bankes
Seline Trevisanut

TUTA SUB AEGIDE PALLAS · 1683 ·

BRILL
NIJHOFF

LEIDEN | BOSTON

Originally published as Volume 29, No. 4 (2014) of Brill's journal *International Journal of Marine and Coastal Law*.

Cover illustration: Maria das Neves, Polar Pioneer in Tromsø, 2011.

Library of Congress Cataloging-in-Publication Data

Energy from the sea : an international law perspective on ocean energy / edited by Nigel Bankes, Seline Trevisanut.
pages cm
Includes index.
Includes papers presented as a workshop held in Utrecht on 19–20 February, 2014. — ECIP introduction.
"Originally published as Volume 29, No. 4 (2014) of Brill's ESTU."
ISBN 978-90-04-30351-5 (pbk. : alk. paper) — ISBN 978-90-04-30352-2 (e-book) 1. Ocean energy resources—Law and legislation—Congresses. I. Bankes, Nigel, 1956– editor. II. Trevisanut, Seline, editor.

K3997.A6E54 2015
343.09'24—dc23

2015027426

This publication has been typeset in the multilingual "Brill" typeface. With over 5,100 characters covering Latin, IPA, Greek, and Cyrillic, this typeface is especially suitable for use in the humanities.
For more information, please see brill.com/brill-typeface.

ISBN 978-90-04-30351-5 (paperback)
ISBN 978-90-04-30352-2 (e-book)

This book is printed on acid-free paper.

MIX
Paper from responsible sources
FSC® C109576
FSC www.fsc.org

Printed by Printforce, the Netherlands

Contents

Energy from the Sea: Introduction

Nigel Bankes and Seline Trevisanut

One of the main challenges of our time is to be able to guarantee energy supply at a reasonable price. Policy makers, international institutions and the private sector increasingly look to the oceans as a significant source of energy. Consequently, activities at sea multiply and sometimes become riskier. For example, the oil and gas industry is reaching out towards deeper waters and more remote exploration targets. Moreover, energy security and efficiency imperatives, coupled with climate change mitigation mechanisms, push the development of marine renewable energy technologies. These changes may have a significant impact on the marine environment and also on the continuity of traditional maritime uses, such as navigation and fishing.

Several studies have tackled energy issues in recent years, mainly from the viewpoint of international trade and investment law,[1] or within the framework of the climate change regime in relation to the promotion of renewable energy technologies and the control of greenhouse gas emissions.[2] Little has been done so far to put together these different perspectives and to frame the discussion within general international law. This is of particular relevance in relation to energy projects in marine areas, whose planning and operation are subject to the international law of the sea. The law of the sea provides the legal framework

1 See, *inter alia*, M.-C. Cordonier Segger, M.W. Gehring and A. Newcombe (eds), *Sustainable Development in World Investment Law* (Kluwer Law International, Alphen aan de Rijn, 2011); Y. Selivanova (ed.), *Regulation of Energy in International Trade Law, WTO, NAFTA and Energy Charter* (Kluwer Law International, Alphen aan den Rijn, 2011); R.B. Stewart, B. Kingsbury and B. Rudyk (eds), *Climate Finance: Regulatory and Funding Stategies for climate Change and Global Development* (New York University Press, New York, 2009); E. Sussman, 'The Energy Charter Treaty's Investor Protection Provisions: Potential to Foster Solutions to Global Warming and Promote Sustainable Development' (2007–2008) 14 *ILSA Journal of International & Comparative Law* 391–404.

2 See, *inter alia*, S. Bruce, 'Climate Change Mitigation through Energy Efficiency Laws: from International Obligations to Domestic Regualtion' (2013) 31 *Journal of Energy and Natural Resources Law* 313–350; F. Dodds (ed), *Climate Change and Energy Insecurity: The Challenge for Peace, Security and Development* (Earthscan, London, 2009); C. Fräss-Ehrfeld, *Renewable Energy Sources: A Change to Combat Climate Change* (Kluwer Law International, Alphen aan den Rijn, 2009).

 | DOI 10.1163/9789004303522_002

within which any maritime activity is performed, and (tries to) strike(s)[3] a balance between the multiple activities that can take place simultaneously in the same maritime zone. The workshop held in Utrecht on 19–20 February 2014 on "Energy from the Sea: An International Law Perspective"[4] aimed to problematize energy from the oceans by framing it in general international law terms, and within the law of the sea and its interactions with the relevant international legal regimes. The workshop proposed to flag the main legal challenges raised by the expansion of the ocean energy sector and its consequences for the relevant international normative and institutional framework. This volume is the result of that workshop.

The Utrecht workshop ended with a roundtable composed of three commentators: René Lefeber of the Netherlands Ministry of Foreign Affairs, André Nollkaemper of the University of Amsterdam, and Alex Oude Elferink of Utrecht University and the K.G. Jebsen Centre for the Law of the Sea (University of Tromsø). This introduction identifies some of the main issues which emerged from the papers and from the discussion during the workshop. This volume was first published as a special issue of *The International Journal of Marine and Coastal Law*.[5]

Crosscutting Themes of the Volume

Five main themes emerge from the seven contributions which compose this volume: 1) energy sources and the competition for marine space; 2) energy security; 3) private actors and corporate social responsibility;

3 Many of the contributions in this volume highlight how the law of the sea, and specifically the United Nations Convention on the Law of the Sea (LOSC; Montego Bay, 10 December 1982, in force 16 November 1994) 1833 *UNTS* 396) do not always succeed in finding a balance between the multiple maritime uses; see the contributions by Redgwell, chapter 2, Bonfanti and Romanin Jacur, chapter 3 and Trevisanut, chapter 4.

4 The workshop was co-organized by Seline Trevisanut (University of Utrecht), Erik Molenaar (University of Utrecht/ University of Tromsø), and Nigel Bankes (University of Calgary/ University of Tromsø) with the support of the Netherlands Institute for the Law of the Sea (NILOS) / Utrecht Centre for Water, Oceans and Sustainability Law (Utrecht University), the K.G. Jebsen Centre for the Law of the Sea (University of Tromsø), and the Marie Curie Project OFFSHORELAW (FP7-PEOPLE-2011-IEF Project 299703). Further information concerning the workshop is available at http://ucwosl.rebo.uu.nl/en/type-activiteiten/workshop-energy-from-the-sea-an-international-law-perspective-on-ocean-energy/; accessed 17 September 2014.

5 (2014) 29(4) *The International Journal of Marine and Coastal Law.*

4) fragmentation or integration, evolution and reinforcement of international law; and 5) liability.

Energy Sources and the Competition for Marine Space

It is clear that our use of marine spaces for the production and transportation of energy has evolved significantly since the Truman Proclamation of 1945.[6] While at that time coastal States were principally interested in exploiting the potential hydrocarbon resources of the continental shelf, coastal States are now interested in a broader range of resources including wind, tidal resources and gas hydrates. Similarly, we now seek to use the ocean and its seabed for different modes of transportation for energy resources. While vessels and especially tankers and liquid natural gas (LNG) carriers continue to be an important and cheap mode of transportation for hydrocarbons and especially for oil, the networked sectors (natural gas and in particular electricity) seek secure access to the seabed for electrical transmission lines and natural gas pipelines. The need for interconnections is growing as States seek energy security and to balance the intermittent nature of some sources of renewable energy.

All of these new energy uses of ocean space inevitably means that there is increased competition for ocean space, especially when we take into account more traditional uses of the oceans such as navigation and fishing. A number of the authors in this volume address different aspects of this problem. Barnes notes that the functional nature of coastal state jurisdiction based on sovereign rights rather than sovereignty makes it better suited to take account of the interests of multiple uses and users.[7]

Long addresses the need for marine spatial planning, most explicitly emphasizing the need for greater integration between marine special planning and energy and climate policy, especially in the context of the European Union.[8] Thus he suggests the need for a regional approach to the development of offshore wind power—an approach that transcends national boundaries and an approach that is therefore more consistent with the idea of an internal market for energy within the European Union.

On a smaller scale, and dealing with a set of more technical issues, Bankes observes that the framework agreement between the United Kingdom and

6 Reproduced in S.H. Lay, R. Churchill and M. Nordquist (eds), *New Directions in the Law of the Sea*, vol. 1. (Oceana Publications, Dobbs Ferry, NY, 1973) at pp. 106–7.

7 R. Barnes, 'Energy Sovereignty in Marine Spaces' chapter 1, this volume.

8 R. Long, 'Harnessing Offshore Wind Energy: Legal Challenges and Policy Conundrums in the European Union' Spaces' chapter 6, this volume.

Norway on transboundary hydrocarbon resources serves to facilitate the coordinated development of oil and gas resources not only from those reservoirs that straddle the delimitation line between the two state but also from other reservoirs located close to the line.[9] The goal is to ensure that the boundary does not get in the way of the economic exploitation of reserves if the necessary infrastructure can be accessed.

Müller and Roggenkamp highlight the steps which led to some regional coordination of oil and gas activities in the North Sea, and show how past experience in the oil and gas sector can be drawn upon in coordinating another activity in the same regional sea, namely wind farms and the creation of an offshore grid.[10] There is a need here for coordination between the concurrent activities at the different levels of governance, i.e., local, national, and regional.

Lefeber chose to emphasise this point as part of his closing remarks at the workshop and suggested that in order to enhance cooperation and prevent disputes, public participation procedures for energy projects should allow the participation of interested third States and thereby take into consideration a wider spectrum of competing interests in the planning of the energy projects.

Energy Security

The marine zones associated with coastal state jurisdiction offer those States important incremental opportunities to achieve a level of energy security that may not be available simply by resorting to land-based energy resources or energy imports from other jurisdictions. The chief energy security concern is vulnerability to disruption of energy supply and specifically vulnerability to politically motivated disruption: "Political turmoil, armed conflict, terrorism, piracy, natural disasters, nationalism and geo-political rivalry threaten to various degrees to interrupt the everyday trade in oil, natural gas, coal and electricity."[11] The current disturbances in the Ukraine simply serve to illustrate the energy security challenges associated with over-dependence on a single supplier or a single network or both.

---

9 N. Bankes, 'Recent Framework Agreements for the Recognition and Development of Transboundary Hydrocarbon Resources' chapter 5, this volume.

10 M. Roggenkamp and H. Müller, 'Regulating Offshore Energy Sources—Reinventing the Wheel or More Coordination?' chapter 7, this volume.

11 OECD, *Competition, International Investment and Energy Security*, December 2007, at p. 2. Online. Available at http://www.oecd.org/dataoecd/3/19/40699061.pdf; accessed 15 September 2014. For a comment, see G. Coop, 'Preface' to 'The Energy Charter Treaty's Investor Protection Provisions: Potential to Foster Solutions to Global Warming and Promote Sustainable Development', in Cordonier Segger *et al.* (eds), (n 1) 513–517, at p. 513.

While historically it was hydrocarbons from the continental shelf that allowed coastal States to address their energy security needs, marine spaces increasingly provide the locus for wind generation as both Long[12] and Müller and Roggenkamp[13] point out in this volume. The availability of these opportunities to coastal States raises questions about their responsibility to use these resources to address global challenges like climate change. The legal regime of the United Nations Convention on the Law of the Sea (LOSC)[14] distinguishes between the living resources of the exclusive economic zone (EEZ) and the energy resources of the continental shelf. With respect to the former, the coastal state has a duty to make any surplus available to other fishing nations.[15] The energy resources of the continental shelf however are considered to be within the exclusive purview of the coastal state, with, to this point, no obligation to permit others to explore for and develop those resources or indeed to conserve those resources.[16] As several of the authors in this volume point out, other international agreements such as the Energy Charter Treaty[17] and even the regional norms of the EU (e.g. the Hydrocarbons, Renewables and Carbon Capture and Storage Directives)[18] reinforce the discretionary power of coastal States to choose not to develop such energy resources or to allow others to engage in the same. Both Barnes and Long however suggest that such discretionary authority needs to be interrogated. For Barnes, such interrogation would come as part of seeking an appropriate theoretical justification for "energy sovereignty in marine spaces," while for Long, the interrogation would occur within the context of developing an integrated energy, climate change and marine spatial planning policies at least at a regional level and within the legal framework of the European Union.

12 Long (n 8).

13 Roggenkamp and Müller (n 10).

14 See (n 3).

15 Article 62 LOSC (n 3).

16 D. Ong, 'Towards and International Law for the Conservation of Offshore Hydrocarbon Resources within the Continental Shelf?' in D. Freestone, R. Barnes and D. Ong (eds), *Law of the Sea. Progress and Prospects* (Oxford University Press, Oxford, 2006) 93–119.

17 See Barnes (n 7).

18 Respectively, Directive 2013/30 on safety of offshore oil and gas operations, OJ L 178/66, 28 June 2013; Directive 2009/28 on the promotion of the use of energy from renewable sources, OJ L 140/16, 5 June 2009; and Directive 2009/31 on the geological storage of carbon dioxide, OJ L 140/114, 5 June 2009. See Barnes (n 7); Long (n 8); and Roggenkamp and Müller (n 10).

Private Actors and Corporate Social Responsibility

Ocean space is international space. While some zones are subject to full coastal sovereignty (internal waters and territorial seas) and subject to the right of innocent passage, other zones are subject only to coastal state sovereign rights. Still other areas lie beyond the limits of national jurisdiction. International law therefore plays an essential role in regulating activities within this space, albeit mediated though national implementation responsibilities. But the key actors in the energy sector of ocean space are not States but are invariably private actors including oil and gas companies, other energy companies, pipeline operators, transmission line operators, and the shipping sector which both serves the energy industry (e.g., vessel support for drilling operations) and transports its product. Other constituencies are also interested in offshore energy developments including traditional users (fishers and indigenous communities) and non-governmental organizations, especially environmental organizations (ENGOs).

Several of the authors in this volume suggest that this has important implications for the way in which norms are developed in this area and the way in which norms are implemented. Bankes, for example, notes that while there is a significant state interest in the development of transboundary petroleum deposits, as a matter of practice, negotiations over the actual arrangements for unitizing and producing such a deposit will inevitably be led by the licensees who will have a much more intimate knowledge of the geological and other properties of the deposit as well as the possible commercial arrangements for getting production to the market.[19] Thus, the treaty arrangements which provide a legal umbrella for developing transboundary deposits need to recognize a role for these private entities while no doubt reserving to the States the authority to approve any such arrangements between these entities.

Nollkaemper, in his final comments, noticed how States are often the weaker party in the offshore energy sector and that the exclusivity of their jurisdiction is hollow because it relies on the role of other actors. The spectrum of participation of private actors is wide as it includes law-making processes, implementation of international obligations, and also participation and consultation rights under international law. Trevisanut analyses these different aspects in order to first identify who those private actors are, and then to better understand their roles within the offshore energy sector and different models of participation.[20]

---

19 Bankes (n 9).

20 S. Trevisanut, 'The Role of Private Actors in Offshore Energy: Shifting Models of Participation', chapter 4, this volume.

Bonfanti and Romanin Jacur also emphasise the important role played by non-state actors in developing the energy resources of ocean space but they also emphasise the important role that these actors play in developing the applicable norms.[21] They refer for example to the important role played by the industry within organizations such as the International Maritime Organization (IMO) in developing technical norms, but they also refer to the role that marine business operators play in developing corporate social responsibility standards aimed at preventing pollution and environmental disasters and in addressing liability issues.

The participation of private actors in law making processes is also analysed by Trevisanut who highlights the role played in the offshore sector, not only by the individual companies involved in the industry, but also by the relevant professional associations. In the aftermath of the disasters that occurred in the Timor Sea[22] and in the Gulf of Mexico,[23] which poignantly showed the consequences of de-regulation and lack of control, it is important to assess arguments in favour of self-regulation of the industry as well as ideas of co-regulation.[24]

In this regard, Bonfanti and Romanin Jacur analyse the concept of Ocean Corporate Social Responsibility (OCSR), namely the notion of corporate social responsibility as applied to maritime activities, specifically for the protection of the marine environment. They conclude that there is cross-fertilization between LOSC and OCSR instruments and that the latter has become a standard

---

21 A. Bonfanti and F. Romanin Jacur, 'Energy from the Sea and the Protection of the Marine Environment: Treaty-Based Regimes and Ocean Corporate Social Responsibility', chapter 3, this volume.

22 On 21 August 2009, a well of the Montara platform, located in the Australian waters of the Timor Sea, blew out and caused a leak of an estimated rate 400 barrels (approximately 64 tonnes) of crude oil a day. The uncontrolled release continued until 3 November 2009. The blowout caused transboundary pollution damage in the Indonesian exclusive economic zone (see Australian Maritime Safety Authority 'Response to the Montara Wellhead Platform Incident, Report of the Incident Analysis team' (March 2010) at p. 7, available at www.amsa.gov.au; accessed 22 September 2014).

23 The Deepwater Horizon was a mobile offshore drilling unit that was operated at a depth of more than 1500 m in the Gulf of Mexico. Following an explosion in April 2010, killing eleven crewmembers, the rig sank and an oil spill affected more than 1000 km of coastline (R. Abeyratne 'The Deepwater Horizon Disaster—Some Liability Issues' (2010) 35 *Tulane Maritime Law Journal* 125). It severely damaged the environment and caused immense costs for the private economy in the region; 'Deepwater Horizon Oil Spill, Incident Specific Preparedness Review (ISPR)' (2011) available at www.uscg.mil/foia/docs/dwh/bpdwh.pdf; accessed 22 September 2014.

24 See Trevisanut (n 20).

of interpretation for the former. In their view this development strengthens the protection of the marine environment by guaranteeing the greater effectiveness of the treaty-based regimes.

Fragmentation or Coordination, Evolution and Reinforcement

While there is much commentary in the general public international law literature on the so-called problem of fragmentation in international law,[25] the authors in this volume refer instead to the important framework role of the LOSC in integrating, coordinating and reinforcing a dense body of norms to assist in regulating energy-related activities in marine spaces. The framework nature of LOSC has also allowed these norms to evolve and be updated as necessary to meet changing circumstances. Both Redgwell[26] and the contribution of Bonfanti and Romanin Jacur[27] emphasise these points. LOSC facilitates integration though its limited ambition. LOSC did not seek to cover the field in developing norms for all activities that might occur within the oceans and thus, as is well known, it defers to specialized organizations such as the IMO to develop more detailed rules within the framework of the Convention. Much of this occurs through multiple references in LOSC to generally accepted international rules and standards (GAIRS). In addition, LOSC also encourages regional cooperation, and this has allowed considerable normative development at the energy\oceans interface, consistent with LOSC standards, in a number of regions, especially the OSPAR region of the northeast Atlantic and in the Mediterranean.[28]

A particularly interesting normative development that both Bonfanti and Romanin Jacur,[29] and Redgwell[30] refer to in this context is the capacity of the law-making technique known as "incorporation by reference" to generate norms within other fora (such as the IMO), that become binding on parties to the LOSC even if those parties did not participate in (or even dissented from) those rule-making exercises. Given the difficulty of amending LOSC

25 Report of the International Law Commission, *Conclusions of the Work of the Study Group on the Fragmentation of International Law: Difficulties Arising from the Diversification and Expansion of International Law* (2006). Available at http://legal.un.org/ilc/texts/instruments/english/draft%20articles/1_9_2006.pdf; accessed 18 September 2014.

26 C. Redgwell, 'Mind the Gap in the GAIRS: The Role of Other Instruments in LOSC Regime Implementation in the Offshore Energy Sector', chapter 2, this volume.

27 Bonfanti and Romanin Jacur (n 21).

28 See Roggenkamp and Müller (10); Trevisanut (n 20).

29 Bonfanti and Romanin Jacur (n 21).

30 Redgwell (n 26).

these features of the regime have allowed it to evolve and adapt to changing circumstances and demands. Thus, the picture of the law of the sea that emerges in this volume is a picture of coordination and integration and mutual recognition and reinforcement rather than a picture of fragmentation and disintegration.

Many problems still remain to be solved. As Redgwell reminds us, the United Nations General Assembly, in its annual review of the state of the oceans and the law of the sea in 2006, called generally for "an integrated, interdisciplinary and intersectoral approach"[31] to maritime activities. This approach concerns not only the law-making processes but also implementation and enforcement mechanisms. This leads to a more general reflection on the institutional machinery created by LOSC and on the institutional stratification which characterizes the law of the sea. Most of the contributions of this issue show how a multiplicity of institutional actors contribute to the shape of the relevant legal framework applicable to the offshore energy sector.

In April 2012, the UN General Assembly emphasized

> the need to strengthen the ability of competent international organizations to contribute, at the global, regional, subregional and bilateral levels, through cooperation programmes with Governments, to the development of national capacity in marine science and the sustainable management of the oceans and their resources.[32]

The considerable number of international bureaucracies involved in ocean affairs might hamper the application of any holistic approach to ocean governance. The offshore energy sector highlights some of these difficulties. In his remarks, Nollkamper took the view that the jurisdictional rules of LOSC do not need to be reformed because concurrent jurisdiction is the normal state of affairs in the law of the sea. This of course has consequences for the applicable law and the implementation of obligations. For Oude Elferink, this means that there is a pressing need to identify the deficiencies of the general regulatory framework, and that we should ask what we expect from that framework. Many of the authors in this volume try to tackle this question and offer some interesting, sometimes diverging, viewpoints.

31 UNGA resolution 60/30, 8 March 2006, at p. 2.

32 UNGA res. RES/66/231, 5 April 2012, at p. 2.

Liability

The exploitation of energy resources in marine areas and their subsequent transportation raises concerns as to the risk of environmental harm. The legitimacy of these concerns is confirmed by the infamous roll call of incidents triggered both by oil tankers (Torrey Canyon, Amoco Cadiz, Erica, and the Prestige) and by blowouts from drilling installations (Montara in the Timor Sea and Deepwater Horizon in the Gulf of Mexico). For lawyers, this raises questions about the duty to prevent harm and the design of effective measure, including vessel design, equipment and crewing standards, and best practice rules in relation to blowout preventers. But it also raises questions about liability and compensation and in particular the creation of effective regimes to ensure that victims have access to adequate compensation in a timely manner.

While the IMO has played a leading role in developing rules to deal with both prevention[33] and (civil) liability[34] in the context of vessels and especially tankers, the authors of the chapters in this volume note that there is no similar *comprehensive* effort to address these issues in the context of offshore oil and gas exploration and production.[35] That said, there are important regional, issue specific, and non-state actor initiatives that address some of these issues in the context of the upstream oil and gas sector. For example, at the regional level, Redgwell refers to OSPAR Decision 98\3 on the removal of offshore production installations[36] as well as to the 1994 Protocol to the Barcelona Convention for the Protection of the Mediterranean Sea against Pollution;[37] Bonfanti and Romanin Jacur make similar references. Both sets of authors note that this same issue has also attracted the attention of the IMO through its Guidelines

33 See the International Convention for the Prevention of Pollution from Ships (MARPOL Convention), (London, 2 November 1973) amended by the 1978 Protocol (London, 1 June 1978) 1340 *UNTS* 184.

34 See the International Convention on Civil Liability for Oil Pollution Damage (1992 CLC Convention), (Brussels, 29 November 1969) as amended by the 1992 Protocol (London, 27 November 1992, in force 30 May 1996) 1956 *UNTS* 255.

35 See Bonfanti and Romanin Jacur (n 21); Trevisanut (n 20).

36 OSPAR 98/14/1-E, 22–23 July 1998, Annex 33.

37 Protocol for the Protection of the Mediterranean Sea against Pollution Resulting from Exploration and Exploitation of the Continental Shelf and the Seabed and its Subsoil to the Convention for the Protection of the Mediterranean Sea Against Pollution (Barcelona Convention), adopted 14 October 1994, entered into force 24 March 2011, UNEP(OCA)/MED IG.4/4.

and Standards for the Removal of Offshore Installations and Structures.[38] Clearly the IMO is competent to address this because of the nexus between such installations and shipping and navigational interests. It is more difficult for it to claim competence in relation to pollution and liability issues associated with offshore exploration and production. It is perhaps therefore not surprising that to the extent that these issues have been addressed they have been addressed by non-state actors and associations of regulators developing guideline and best practices but also in one limited case a compensation regime in the form of the Offshore Pollution Liability Agreement (OPOL), an agreement between a limited number of operators working principally (but no longer exclusively) in the North Sea.[39] This topic will demand further attention in the coming years.

Conclusions

It clearly emerges from the contributions to this special volume that the private sector plays a crucial role in the development of offshore energy sources. The private sector participates in law-making processes and also in the implementation of the relevant obligations; it has the technological knowledge and financial resources to engage. But States are still the granting authority. No activity can take place without the authorisation of the coastal State under which jurisdiction the project will be realized. We can thus conclude that there is a 'diffuse authority' in the energy sector: the authority, and the rights and obligations related thereto, are shared between different actors (mainly States and private actors) at different level of governance (local, national, regional, international, etc.). This 'diffuse authority' has some advantages, such as the continuous update of the applicable legal framework thanks to the integration of the technological and regulatory developments which occur in practice.[40] The participation of non-state actors is fundamental in this regard, both in the law-making and in the implementation phases. But, of course, 'diffuse authority' has also disadvantages. It may cause States to rely on private actors

38 Guidelines and Standards for the Removal of Offshore Installations and Structures on the Continental Shelf and in the Exclusive Economic Zone, Resolution A.672(16) of 19 October 1989, IMO Assembly, Sixteenth Session, *Resolutions and Other Decisions*, at p. 293.

39 For the text of the agreement and the background see http://www.opol.org.uk/ accessed 20 September 2014 and for comment, see Bonfanti and Romanin Jacur (n 21) and Trevisanut (n 20).

40 See Bonfanti and Romanin Jacur (n 21), and Redgwell (n 26).

and to fail to see the urgency of intervening at the regulatory level. It may also mean that the interests of the non-state actors might prevail to the detriment of more 'public' interests, such as the protection of the marine environment. It must also mean, as Nollkaemper has reminded us in some of his writings, that we need to develop a more sophisticated understanding of the concept of shared responsibility in international law.[41]

---

41 For more detailed discussion of ideas of shared responsibility involving both States and private actors see A. Nollkaemper and D. Jacobs, 'Shared Responsibility in International Law: A Conceptual Framework' (2013) 34 *Michigan Journal of International Law* 359–438. Nollkaemper and Jacobs see the need to develop ideas of shared responsibility in response to five drivers: (1) the increased interdependence of international society, (2) the increased 'moralization' of international society involving a paradigm based on the rights of the individual, (3) the heterogeneity of modern international society involving a multiplicity of actors, (4) the permeability of different normative orders, and (5) (at pp. 430–432) the increased judicialization of the international legal order.

CHAPTER 1

Energy Sovereignty in Marine Spaces

Richard Barnes
Professor of International Law, Law School,
University of Hull, Hull, HU6 7RX, UK

Abstract

The term "energy sovereignty" is used with differing emphases to describe a State's rights or assertions over energy resources and supplies. Given the importance of offshore energy developments, particularly in the field of renewables, this chapter explores the meaning of energy sovereignty, arguing that more complex, cooperative approaches towards sovereignty are required in order to adapt to the nature of energy and energy demands. This approach is particularly important in the context of marine resources, where there is shown to be a carefully crafted balancing of interests between coastal States, third States and community interests. The chapter further suggests that in order to help explain energy sovereignty against this complex background, recourse may be had to theories of justification of ownership of resources. The example of natural rights-based approaches is used to show how this can inform the direction that legal regimes might take.

Keywords

energy – sovereignty – sovereign rights – marine renewables

Introduction

Significant deposits of oil and gas are known to exist under the world's oceans. New deposits are still being discovered or rendered accessible through new or more efficient technologies. More recently, the oceans have become the principal focus for developments in the field of renewable energy with the growth in offshore wind farms. Invariably, energy resources will be shipped by sea, or transmitted through undersea pipelines and cables. The exploration, production and supply of energy from the sea have had an impact on all other ocean activities. This means that marine spaces are at the heart of debates about

 | DOI 10.1163/9789004303522_003

meeting the world's energy demands, and that international law of the sea is at the heart of debates about how such demands are met and balanced against other ocean uses. Much of this debate is framed in terms of energy sovereignty, which raises questions about the extent to which States, both individually and collectively, can and should be able to secure their energy supply needs, and how this will operate in practice. This chapter explores some of the preliminary issues that arise from claims about energy sovereignty in respect of marine resources. This is important because as calls for energy sovereignty grow in frequency and force, they must be reconciled with well-established rules and values concerning the way in which sovereignty operates, and must adapt to the particular physical conditions in which marine energy resources are located.

The chapter begins by analysing the meaning of "energy sovereignty", breaking it down into its component parts: energy and sovereignty. It argues that if we are to regulate energy, then this must accord with the physical properties of energy, and in particular adapt to a more nuanced understanding of the distinction between energy resources and energy use. A fuller understanding of energy opens up opportunities to re-imagine the way we regulate energy, or at least properly conceptualise the way in which we regulate energy. This is particularly important in the context of marine renewables (wind/tidal energy), where the resource is not exclusive, or spatially located, but is subject to uncontrolled natural variables, all of which present challenges for existing legal approaches. The chapter then considers how sovereignty can be conceptualised, and suggests that relative accounts of sovereignty are better suited to the realities of energy use and the practice of States. This analysis of energy and sovereignty is then put into context in the next part, which outlines how debates about energy sovereignty have developed. The chapter shows that multilateral agreements do not appear to say much, at least directly, about energy sovereignty as it pertains to the complexities of energy supply and use. However, a broader network of international rights and obligations directly and indirectly affects energy use, and constrains more self-interested approaches towards the control of energy resources. Indeed, in some marine spaces States exercise sovereign rights or jurisdiction which are forms of authority more heavily qualified by requirements to exercise due regard to the interests of other States. This suggests that it is difficult to sustain claims to energy sovereignty based purely upon securing national interests. If a more nuanced approach to energy sovereignty is adopted, then this will require further analysis. The final part of the chapter begins this analysis by exploring the more fundamental justifications for control over resources. Typically, such justifications are framed in terms of good order or as calls for the redistribution of wealth. This compares poorly to justifications of property. Since energy sovereignty is essentially concerned with questions of who can control energy resources and supplies, the extent of such authority and any limits on this, i.e., exclusive control, justifications framed in terms of ownership might better inform debates about the meaning of energy sovereignty. Some of the implications of this approach are highlighted through examples drawn from natural rights-based approaches to property. The questions that even one such approach might generate suggest that much more research is needed to develop a meaningful understanding of "energy sovereignty".

Defining Energy and Sovereignty

Energy

If we are to talk meaningfully about energy sovereignty then it is necessary to understand the object of sovereignty. What is energy? This is not an easy question to answer, especially for a non-scientist. It can be regarded as an abstract scientific construct used to interpret aspects of reality. Yet it may also be observed and measured. In either case, there are aspects of energy that are not fully understood or explicable. As a noted physicist has observed: "It is important to realize that in physics today, we have no knowledge of what energy *is*."[1] A provocative remark: it should signal the fact that knowledge is contingent and changeable, and this needs to be factored into regulatory regimes.

To help frame the present discussion, energy can be defined as the power derived from the utilisation of physical or chemical resources. It is a property that a system possesses and can be used to do work. This is done by transferring energy from one object or system to another, for example, by burning fuel to produce heat, or converting kinetic energy from water into electricity. Scientists tell us that energy may take a variety of forms: electrical, light, elastic, kinetic, sound, thermal, chemical, gravitational and nuclear. These are generally reduced to potential or kinetic forms of energy. Each of these forms of energy may be stored, accessed and used in different ways depending upon its physical properties, location and the state of technology. Since energy has properties that determine how it can be used, these factors must be taken into account in the design of any regulatory regime. This applies to both specific rules and broad principles, such as sovereignty. Thus if a particular resource or form of energy is not exclusively located within a State, then it is generally not susceptible to claims of sovereignty.

1 R.P. Feynman, R.B. Leighton and M. Sands, *The Feynman Lectures on Physics* (Basic Books, New York, 2011) vol. 1, sections 4-1–4-8.

The physical properties of an energy resource determine how it may be regulated. For example, sunlight (solar energy) is ubiquitous and results in approximately 170,000 terawatts of energy being delivered to the earth each day.[2] To highlight its potential for meeting energy demands, the International Energy Agency (IEA) reports that it "takes the sun one hour and 25 minutes to send us the amount of energy we currently consume in a year."[3] It is fungible, non-exclusive and intangible. It warms the earth to levels that are conducive to life. It is essential to the sustenance of life through photosynthesis. It provides a source of renewable energy. As a general category or source of energy, these factors render it a common resource; it cannot be possessed or rendered excludable, either by way of sovereign claims or individual ownership. This would be not only physically impossible, but also morally objectionable, because it would deprive non-owners or persons without access of the means to obtain an essential good. Of course this general proposition admits qualifications, since some limited absence of light may result from other factors, such as building shade.[4]

Another example is wind energy. Wind is the movement of air across the surface of the earth as denser cool air moves to fill space in low-pressure areas that is occupied by warm air. This movement is the product of differences or changes in air pressure, which are in turn the result of thermal changes and the rotation of the Earth. Wind stores kinetic energy which may be captured through wind turbines, which convert the energy into electrical or mechanical energy. Global potential for wind energy is estimated to be around 72 terawatts.[5] Wind performs a critical function in natural weather systems. It provides a renewable source of energy. It is also intangible, fungible and non-exclusive; so, like sunlight, it is a common pool resource. In the case of sunlight and wind, the energy may be captured at fixed points and this takes energy out of the natural system. This may allow for regulation under the "law of capture" within

---

2 D.J. Rose, *Learning about Energy* (Plenum Press, New York, 1986) at p. 71.

3 International Energy Agency, *Solar Energy Perspectives* (IEA Publications, Pairs, 2011) at p. 32.

4 Most legal systems have developed local rules concerning rights to light in this context. See the Law Commission, *Rights to Light*. Law Commission Consultation Paper 210 (2013). Available at http://lawcommission.justice.gov.uk/docs/cp210_rights_to_light_version-web.pdf.

5 C.L. Archer and M.Z. Jacobsen, 'Evaluation of Global Wind Power' (2005) 110 *Journal of Geophysical Research* Atmospheres D12110 1–20. However, such figures are subject to considerable debate. See C. de Castro, M. Mediavilla, L.J. Miguel and F. Frechosa, 'Global Wind Power Potential: Physical and Technological Limits' (2011) 39 *Energy Policy* 6677–6682.

individual States.[6] However, this may fail to account for important externalities. In the case of wind energy, capture subtracts energy from downstream users.[7] Wind flow is distorted or reduced when passing through a turbine, leaving less kinetic energy for capture by other users.[8] Accordingly, some element of collective or cooperative regulation between States will be required.

The examples of renewable energy may be contrasted with spatially fixed, tangible, finite sources of energy, such as coal or oil.[9] These are excludable and frequently reduced to State or private ownership, at least when located exclusively within a single State. However, even in these cases, the use of such resources will produce externalities (e.g., transboundary pollution) that entail some degree of collective regulation.

The physical attributes of energy may also affect the way in which it is regulated in less obvious, but equally important ways. It is a fundamental law of physics that energy cannot be created from nothing or destroyed. Energy can only be transformed from one state to another. This is known as the law of the conservation of energy (or the first law of thermodynamics) and it raises some interesting questions about the nature of energy and our use of it. First, it may be observed that energy production is focused on the generation of high-quality energy (energy that can do meaningful work). As such, we are concerned with transforming energy resources into particular types of energy (e.g., electrical energy). Second, this in turn raises questions about whether or not it is meaningful to talk in terms of "energy sovereignty". It is a fact of nature that we cannot control energy absolutely, but merely its potential at certain points in time or space. And even this is technologically contingent. If energy is not consumed, but merely changes state, then is it possible to exert sovereignty over energy *per se*? Rather it seems more useful to talk about control not of energy, but of control over the opportunities to change its state. At the very least, this attribute of energy suggests that its use will generate consequences beyond the scope of an individual agent's ability to control. Such externalities

6 See generally, T. Daintith, 'The Rule of Capture. The Least Worst Property Rule for Oil and Gas' in A. McHarg, B. Barton, A. Bradbrook and L. Godden (eds), *Property and the Law in Energy and Natural Resources* (Oxford University Press, Oxford, 2010) 140–159.

7 See Y. Lifshitz-Goldberg, 'Gone with the Wind? The Potential Tragedy of the Common Wind' (2010) 28 *UCLA Journal of Environmental Law and Policy* 435–71, at pp. 455–61.

8 This has already been the subject of litigation in Norway. See Norwegian Supreme Court decision of 27 May 2011. *Norsk Retstidende* 2011, p. 780, reported in K. Lilleholt, 'Wind Power, Ownership, and Neighbours' (2012) 20 *European Review of Private Law* 1159–63.

9 The contrast with oil is perhaps more equivocal, given the rule of capture. See Daintith (n 6).

might include the uncontrolled dissipation of energy from industrial power generation, or the creation of by-products which the State is unable to handle, or pecuniary costs by others that suffer the consequences of an energy-use activity. If this is true, then sovereignty, narrowly construed in terms of exclusive power over a resource, seems to be a limited framework for control. Instead we ought to consider control over energy as being defined in much more nuanced terms that reflect its natural qualities and consequences of its use.

A second factor—the location of an energy resource—may determine aspects of its regulation. For example, fossil fuels are physically located in fixed positions in the ground or seabed. Their fixed location determines the spatial parameters for extraction activities and may determine which States(s) can control extraction. On land, such resources are normally subsumed within the doctrine of territorial sovereignty and are at the host State's disposal, at least when they are located wholly within that State's territory. As indicated above, transboundary deposits of oil and gas require cooperative arrangements in order to facilitate exploitation, since they cannot be exploited without affecting other States' territorial rights.[10] Deposits of oil or gas within marine areas are subject to a degree of exclusive control when located in the exclusive economic zone (EEZ) or continental shelf. However, such spaces are subject to additional restrictions that protect the interests of other States or the international community.[11] Location is important to questions of energy supply and transmission. Since energy resources are unevenly distributed and frequently located far from places where the resources are needed, energy or raw materials must be transported around the world. Raw materials for energy production (coal and oil) must be transported to centres of industry, often by sea. Gas must be piped from production facilities to storage sites and end users. Again this may be through undersea pipelines. The same applies to the transmission of electricity through power lines that link energy generators and users. This requires the creation of resilient energy systems or networks that can ensure supplies of energy. Such networks cannot be created by individual States, but require the cooperation of supply-States, user-States and States of

10 See W.T. Onorato, 'Apportionment of an International Common Petroleum Deposit' (1967) 17 *International and Comparative Law Quarterly* (ICLQ) 85–102, and 'Apportionment of an International Common Petroleum Deposit' (1977) 26 *ICLQ* 324–337; D. Ong, 'Joint Development of Common Offshore Oil and Gas Deposits: "Mere" State Practice or Customary International Law?' (1999) 93 *American Journal of International Law* (AJIL) 771–804.

11 See below at pp. 27–35, especially pp. 30–32.

transit—hence the priority afforded to energy transit in the Energy Charter Treaty.[12] These regimes require laws that facilitate the creation and maintenance of energy supplies. Thus, location reinforces the point that more nuanced versions of sovereignty or control are required to adapt to the essential attributes of different energy resources.

The third factor influencing energy regulation is the state of technology. Technology affects our ability to access and use certain resources. For example, offshore oil and gas exploration only emerged in the 20th century with the development of technology that allowed oil and gas to be captured. Prior to this, international law had limited concern for the question of control over offshore mineral resources. However, as the capacity to engage in offshore oil and gas activities pushed out to sea and could occur at greater depths, so the law had to adapt to this new reality. Accordingly, the regime of the continental shelf emerged. This function of technology was explicitly acknowledged in the reference to exploitability in determining the outer limits of the legal continental shelf.[13] The outward reach of energy activities will continue with the vast potential of methane hydrate deposits on the deep seabed likely to generate new regulatory challenges in the Area.[14] In the context of wind energy, limitations in storage technology present the most significant obstacles to renewable energy development. Electricity generated can be directed into electricity grids but cannot readily be conserved for use on demand. It must either be rejected or diverted. More sophisticated networks may allow for the diversion of surplus energy between States, but will require cooperation between States to manage fluctuations in supply and demand.[15]

In summary, if we are concerned with the regulation of energy, then we should be concerned with both the control of the sources of energy and the processes whereby energy is transformed from one state to another. We also need to be aware of the way in which the nature of energy resources and their use shapes regulation. As will be demonstrated in the next section, a narrow view of sovereignty, drawn in terms of exclusive control over energy

12 See Energy Charter Treaty (Lisbon, 17 December 1994, entry into force 16 April 1998), reproduced in (1995) 33 *ILM* 360. See below at pp. 592–593.

13 Article 1 of the 1958 Convention on the Continental Shelf (Geneva, 29 April 1958, entry into force 10 June 1964) 499 *UNTS* 311.

14 See R.S. Santos, T. Morato and F.J.A.S. Barriga, 'Increasing Pressure at the Bottom of the Ocean' in A. Mendonca, A. Cunha and R. Chakrabarti (eds), *Natural Resources, Sustainability and Humanity. A Comprehensive View* (Springer, Dordrecht, 2012) 69–81 at p. 75.

15 See T. Ackermann (ed), *Wind Power in Power Systems* (Wiley, Chichester, 2012), chapters 21 and 22.

resources, does appear to be suited to these essential considerations. This suggests that questions of energy-resource control and use require more nuanced accounts of sovereignty. Or in other words, it supports a functional approach to sovereignty.[16] As discussed below, there is some recognition of the different qualities of energy in legal instruments, such as the reference to "energy cycle" and transit provisions in the Energy Charter Treaty. Indeed, a quick survey of such international instruments supports the point that cooperative and nuanced approaches to sovereignty are required to address questions of energy use.

Observations on Sovereignty

It is trite but nonetheless true to observe that sovereignty is a controversial and contested principle. It is an intellectual construct that may be analysed from a variety of perspectives: historical, economic, political, legal and so on. Each perspective permeates the others. Even within the more limited field of international law, discussions of sovereignty diverge considerably and generate fierce debate.[17] It is not possible to survey and unpack part, never mind all, of this material, but some of its lineaments may be remarked upon in order to help us understand how the notion of sovereignty might apply to energy resources. Two approaches to sovereignty (focusing on its territory or natural resources) are provided in order to illustrate the way in which narrow and broad conceptions of sovereignty might accommodate questions about control over energy. This reaffirms the position advanced that only more nuanced constructions of sovereignty can be used to deal with energy resources.

In perhaps the most general terms, sovereignty refers to the locus of authority within a system. For international law, as a decentralised system of states, that locus is normally considered to be the State. This is reflected in positive international legal doctrine. Thus Judge Huber described sovereignty as independence: "Independence in regard to a portion of the globe is the right to exercise therein, to the exclusion of any other State, the functions of a State".[18]

16 This echoes Gavouneli's view of jurisdiction in the law of the sea. M. Gavouneli, *Functional Jurisdiction in the Law of the Sea* (Martinus Nijhoff, Leiden, 2007).

17 See J. Bartleson, *A Genealogy of Sovereignty* (Cambridge University Press, Cambridge, 1995); S.D. Krasner, *Sovereignty: Organised Hypocrisy* (Princeton University Press, Princeton, 1999); N. Walker, *Sovereignty in Transition* (Hart, Oxford, 2003); M. Koskenniemi, *From Apology to Utopia* (Cambridge University Press, Cambridge, 2005) chapter 4; J. Bartelson, 'The Concept of Sovereignty Revisited' (2006) 17 *European Journal of International Law* (*EJIL*) 463–74; R. Jackson, *Sovereignty: Evolution of an Idea* (Polity Press, Cambridge, 2007).

18 *Island of Palmas* case (1928) 2 RIAA 829, at p. 838.

Authority in this view is framed spatially, and is sometimes referred to as "territorial sovereignty". Here sovereignty is exclusionary within the spatial limits of the State, wherein the State may exercise plenary authority. This view of territorial sovereignty is often associated with an absolutist view of sovereignty: the State is either sovereign or it is not.[19] This approach seems to provide a conceptual basis for strong State control of resources; see, e.g., the idea of energy nationalism as discussed by authors such as Böhme.[20] There is some support for this, since this approach to the allocation of authority to States in this way is often regarded as fundamental to the structure of international law.[21]

The general view is that sovereignty over natural resources entitles the State to freely determine how such resources are dealt with under domestic property and regulatory regimes.[22] As an intellectual construct, sovereignty does not demand a particular definition or content. Understood thus, the absolutist view is in no way necessary, although it may be regarded as desirable as a means of facilitating good order. It provides a simplified, yet compelling account of a complex world, by carving up the world into non-overlapping territorial units with authority to regulate internal matters, subject to a duty not to harm or interfere in the authority of other States.[23] The actions of other actors, such as individuals, corporations and non-governmental organisations (NGOs), are then linked to these centres of authority. International law rules of attribution and accountability structure the legal relationships outwards from the central hub of sovereignty. This view is reflected in certain rules of international law that retain strong normative influence. Thus Article 2(4) of the United Nations Charter requires States to refrain from the threat or use of force against the territorial integrity or political independence of other States, and Article 2(7) provides that

19 G. Elian, *The Principle of Sovereignty over Natural Resources* (Sijthoff and Noordhoff, Alphen aan den Rijn, 1979) at pp. 1–10; K.J. Holsti, *Taming the Sovereigns* (Cambridge University Press, Cambridge, 2004) at p. 114.

20 D. Böhme, *EU-Russia Energy Relations: What Chance for Solutions? A Focus on the Natural Gas Sector* (Universitätsverlag, Potsdam, 2011) at pp. 46–8.

21 J.L. Brierly, *The Law of Nations* 6th ed. (Oxford University Press, Oxford, 1963) at p. 162; M. Shaw, 'Territorial Administration by Non-territorial Sovereigns' in T. Broude and Y. Shany (eds), *The Shifting Allocation of Authority in International Law* (Hart, Oxford, 2008) 369–415, at pp. 369–370.

22 See for example, Y. Omorogbe and P. Oniemola, 'Property Rights in Oil and Gas under Domanial Regimes' in McHarg, *et al.* (eds) (n 6) 115–139, at p. 115.

23 B. Kingsbury, 'Sovereignty and Inequality' (1998) 9 *EJIL* 599–625, at pp. 610–11.

> [n]othing contained in the present Charter shall authorize the United Nations to intervene in matters which are essentially within the domestic jurisdiction of any state or shall require the Members to submit such matters to settlement under the present Charter . . .[24]

Despite the existence of specific rules that echo an absolutist approach to sovereignty, this approach is considered by most commentators to bear little resemblance to reality. For example, Slaughter notes two deficiencies with this view of sovereignty: the ineffectiveness challenge, which highlights that States cannot pursue their objectives without some degree of political or economic support from other States, and the interference challenge, which recognises that the exclusive domestic jurisdiction of States is frequently infringed in practice.[25] These arguments challenge the exclusionary idea of sovereignty. Even those holding to the classical positivist position accept that sovereignty has limits and so it is described as the "fullest rights over territory *known to the law*".[26] Thus the law necessarily delimits the scope of sovereignty, and the door is quickly open to relative accounts of sovereignty. Indeed, absolute sovereignty is under increasing challenge from those that regard sovereignty as a variable or relative concept, or who advocate a view of sovereignty as a status realised through participation in the international system.[27] Here (external) sovereignty is regarded as contingent on the existence of an (international) society and it is from this society that authority is drawn.[28] At present, it seems that relative explanations of sovereignty are in the ascendancy.[29]

---

24 United Nations Charter (San Francisco, 26 June 1945, entry into force 26 October 1945) 892 *UNTS* 119.

25 A.M. Slaughter, 'Sovereignty and Power in a Networked World Order' (2004) 40 *Stanford Journal of International Law* 283–327 at pp. 284–5.

26 Brierly (n 21) at p. 162 (emphasis added).

27 A. Chayes and A.H. Chayes, *The New Sovereignty. Compliance with International Regulatory Agreements* (Harvard University Press, Harvard, 1998) at p. 27.

28 Admittedly, this pithy observation glosses over considerably more complexities than space permits addressing here. Here it suffices to observe that law is viewed as socially contingent, and so society rather than the individual State is the source of legal authority. See Judge Anzilotti in the *Customs Regime between Germany and Austria* (1931) PCIL, Se. A/B, No. 41, 57. On the basis of authority, see further P. Allott, 'Mare Nostrum: A New International Law of the Sea' (1992) 86 *AJIL* 764–87. See also some of the observations in J. d'Aspremont, *Formalism and the Sources of International Law—A Theory of the Ascertainment of Legal Rules* (Oxford University Press, Oxford, 2011) chapter 1.1.

29 See the discussion by G. Simpson, *Great Powers and Outlaw States. Unequal Sovereigns in the International Legal Order* (Cambridge University Press, Cambridge, 2004) chapter 2.

In contrast to the traditional view of sovereignty, within accounts of relative sovereignty, authority is diffuse and manifested through various interactions. Accordingly, it is possible to view the application of sovereignty to natural resources as a series of jural relations concerned with, *inter alia*, the right to possess, use, manage, and enjoy the benefits derived from territory and natural resources therein. And sovereignty is not just about rights; it entails duties. In order to protect the interests of other actors, States are subject to certain duties of non-harmful use or cooperation in respect of territory and natural resources. Sovereignty is meted out and dealt with not in absolute terms, but by way of variable, individual transactions. Territory and the resources therein may be jointly managed by States, subject to trusteeship regimes, or bound by "use-rights" in favour of other States.[30] Foreign investment may be secured by exclusive rights to natural resources, and guaranteed against expropriation.[31] These dealings may limit how authority is exercised temporarily. They may result in the same resource being subject to multiple uses and degrees of control by various actors. A good example of this is the treatment of fisheries under international, European Union (EU) law and domestic law.[32]

Although commenting upon how international law deals with property rights in respect of natural resources, Redgwell's brief survey of international instruments and cases demonstrates how international law structures and limits control of resources in terms analogous to property.[33] This reaffirms the above point that sovereignty over resources is constructed in terms of discrete jural relations. An important element of this is the role played by international human rights law and the protection of property as a human right.[34] Here enjoyment of certain rights is directly opposed to the State, indicating a direct concern with needs or interests of individuals, rather than States. This view of sovereignty permits a more calibrated understanding of the ways in which States act, and more closely resembles how natural resources or energy are regulated. Furthermore, whilst it does not necessarily support the type of conceptualization of energy sovereignty rooted in individual choice and

30 See further R. Barnes, *Property Rights and Natural Resources* (Hart, Oxford, 2009) at 222–8.

31 See M. Sornarajah, *The International Law on Foreign Investment*, 3rd ed. (Cambridge University Press, Cambridge, 2010) chapter 10.

32 See generally, R. Churchill and D. Owen, *The EC Common Fisheries Policy* (Oxford University Press, Oxford, 2010).

33 C. Redgwell, 'Property Law Sources and Analogies in International Law' in McHarg, *et al.* (eds) (n 6), at 100–12.

34 *Ibid.*, at pp. 105–6.

control,[35] it is at least consistent with its goal of securing individual access to essential energy needs.

Traditional conceptions of sovereignty, as exclusive control over a portion of the globe, are simply irreconcilable with the way the world works today. States are increasingly interdependent, socially, politically and economically, and this is reflected in law. Many energy resources are fluid, but part of expensive, complex, and fixed transnational networks. This is particularly the case for marine renewable energy resources, which draw upon components of global systems, and whose use cannot be confined to the territory of single States. The networks necessary to make use of renewable energy need to be resilient and secure. This means that more nuanced notions of sovereignty are required to support and sustain energy use. However, more recent accounts of sovereignty tend to either contest the nature of sovereignty or atomise it, examining it as a series of localised jural relations as manifest in particular contexts. The sophistry of such approaches may be better adapted to reality and more flexible, but this renders it difficult to apprise ourselves of how effectively and fairly access to and use of energy are determined at the global level. It collapses into highly localised relationships. The main problem with an account of energy sovereignty drawn in terms of relative sovereignty is that it may lack coherence. It is then exposed to criticism for being descriptive rather than normative. International law, like any other social system, is a system of informed and patterned behaviour. This indicates the need for principles or points of reference to determine the legitimacy of specific rules that transcend the individual rules. In short, it requires sovereignty to be justified. Before considering how this might be approached, it is helpful to examine how questions of energy sovereignty are approached in the literature and the main legal texts. This tends to support a more flexible approach that can adapt to the nature of energy and its uses.

Energy Sovereignty in Context

Any consideration of energy sovereignty cannot take place in a vacuum. It must acknowledge how policies, laws and debates have evolved, the meaning and relationship of core terms and concepts, and the place of law in shaping any debates. This part examines, first, how the term "energy sovereignty", as well as cognate concepts such as energy security and energy nationalism, is used and how it has developed in the context of questions about access to traditional

35 See discussion at pp. 36–37.

energy resources.[36] Noting the complexity of such matters, it demonstrates the main relevance of international law to debates about control of energy. A review of how specific instruments, including the UN Convention on the Law of the Sea (LOSC) and the Energy Charter Treaty, actually address questions of energy sovereignty, shows how more nuanced approaches to energy sovereignty are either supported or required by international law.

Use and Development of the Concept of Energy Sovereignty

Use of the term "energy sovereignty" is growing, although its precise meaning is not clear, especially when viewed from a legal perspective. Friends of the Earth define the term as "the right of people to have access to energy and to choose sustainable energy sources and consumption patterns that will lead them towards truly sustainable societies."[37] The idea is firmly located in the discourse of rights and associated with similar movements/concepts such as "food sovereignty".[38] It is thus about empowering individuals and ensuring that resources are available to meet needs. In contrast, Böhme uses the phrase to describe the approach of energy-producing countries to secure control over natural resources, and especially to resist exploitation of these resources under free market regimes.[39] This approach is also known as "energy nationalism",[40] and it is closely linked to the more frequently used term "energy security". This seeks to ensure that the State controls access to energy resources.[41] The IEA defines energy security as the "uninterrupted availability of energy sources at

36 The term "energy sovereignty" is preferred since this accommodates a wider range of perspectives than the more commonly used term "energy security".

37 Friends of the Earth International. *Annual Report 2013*, at p. 3, available at http://www.foei.org/wp-content/uploads/2014/06/FoEI-Annual-Report-2013.pdf. This and subsequent online resources were accessed 1 September 2014.

38 N. Bellinger and M. Fakhri, 'The Intersection Between Food Sovereignty and Law' (2013) 28 *Natural Resources and Environment* 45–48; M. Windfuhr and J. Jonsén, *Food Sovereignty: Towards Democracy in Localized Food Systems* (Intermediate Technology Working Group Publishing, Rugby, 2005) at p. 21.

39 Böhme (n 20).

40 D. Bochkarev and G. Austin, *Energy Sovereignty and Security: Restoring Confidence in a Cooperative International System*. East West Institute Policy Paper 01/2007, at p. 2. Available at http://www.ewi.info/idea/energy-sovereignty-and-security-restoring-confidence-cooperative-international-system.

41 See generally, G. Kaft and A. Korin (eds), *Energy Security Challenges for the 21st* Century (Greenwood, Santa Barbara, 2009); R. Youngs, *Energy Security. Europe's New Foreign Policy Challenge* (Routledge, London, 2009); G. Bahgat, *Energy Security and Interdisciplinary Approach* (Wiley, Chichester, 2011).

an affordable price."[42] Similarly, Barton *et al.* define it as "a condition in which a nation and all, or most, of its citizens and businesses have access to sufficient energy resources at reasonable prices for the foreseeable future free from serious risk of major disruption of service".[43] Whilst these approaches do not deny the interests of individuals, they place the State at the centre of debates about ensuring energy security. For present purposes it is not necessary to synthesise a common meaning of energy sovereignty, but merely to note that nuances in any definition of the core concept reflect different views on how to address fundamental questions about who controls energy, and how best to structure such control in order to meet the needs or interests of energy users. It may also be observed that different views of energy sovereignty are susceptible to different accounts of sovereignty, as explored above.

Energy sovereignty is not a new concern. Control of energy resources has been the object of both national/international policy and academic study for much of the twentieth century.[44] This has mainly focused upon the supply of oil as the means of sustaining military machines and industrial development. International lawyers will be familiar with how the desire to secure access to oil supplies provoked the Truman Proclamation of 1945,[45] influenced the development and regulation of oil concessions from the 1950s,[46] and came to the fore of debates about international peace and security with the emergence of the Organization of Petroleum Exporting Countries (OPEC) in the 1970s.[47] The post-World War II process of decolonisation generated considerable literature on questions of sovereignty over natural resources.[48] It also highlighted

42 See: http://www.iea.org/topics/energysecurity/subtopics/whatisenergysecurity/.

43 B. Barton, C. Redgwell, A. Rønne, and D.N. Zillman, 'Introduction' in B. Barton, C. Redgwell, A. Rønne, and D.N. Zillman (eds), *Energy Security. Managing Risk in a Dynamic Legal and Regulatory Environment* (Oxford University Press, Oxford, 2004) 3–14 at p. 5.

44 D.R. Bohi and M.A. Toman, *The Economics of Energy Security* (Kluwer, Dordrecht, 1996); D. Yergin, *The Quest: Energy, Security, and the Remaking of the Modern World* (Penguin, London, 2011).

45 A. Hollick, 'US Oceans Policy. The Truman Proclamation' (1976) 17 *Virginia Journal of International Law* 23–55.

46 M.A. Mughraby, *Permanent Sovereignty over Oil Resources: a study of Middle East oil concessions and change* (Middle East Research and Publications Centre, Beirut, 1966).

47 J.J. Paust and A. Blaustein, 'The Arab Oil Weapon. A Threat to International Peace' (1974) 68 *AJIL* 410–439.

48 See, for example, G. Elian, *The Principle of Sovereignty over Natural Resources* (Sijthoff & Noordhoff, Alphen aan den Rijn, 1979); K. Hossein and S.R. Chowdry, *Permanent Sovereignty over Natural Resources: Principles and Practice* (Pinter, London, 1984); G. Abi-Saab, 'Permanent Sovereignty over Natural Resources and Economic Activities'

the importance of international cooperation in meeting energy supplies, given the dislocation of many energy resources from the main consumers of energy. To a large extent, it is oil (and gas) which have shaped discussions about the regulation of energy supply, and in particular, exploration, production and supply lines, as well as the regulation of oil and gas markets. With increasing dependence on gas and electricity, there is now greater need for cooperation in developing, maintaining and managing resilient energy-supply networks. Unlike oil and coal, gas and electricity are particularly dependent upon fixed and complex networks of cables and pipelines. In recent decades, the regulation of energy has come under increased scrutiny from an environmental perspective, with the realisation of the impacts of global warming and the move towards renewable energy supplies. This has begun to generate a distinct legal literature, and efforts to place energy issues within the broader paradigm of sustainable development.[49] Whilst this has not lessened the importance of traditional concerns about the control of energy resources and supplies, it has demonstrated the increasing complexity of factors that need to be accounted for in energy regulation.

International Law and the Regulation of Energy

The regulation of energy is undoubtedly complex. Typically regulation occurs through technical rules of domestic law which focus on discrete aspects of energy production systems: exploration, exploitation, production and supply. These are overlaid by rules on planning, health and safety, environmental protection, finance and investment, taxation and so on. In part the complexity is a product of the way the domestic law has developed. Thus, it has been observed that energy law has evolved incrementally, instrumentally, and in a disjointed fashion,[50] and that it focuses on adequate supply, rather than on efficient or equitable use or environmental consequences. At the risk of over-simplifying trends in regulation, approaches have evolved (or perhaps revolved) under domestic law from regimes focused upon State-centred control to deregulated

---

in M. Bedjaoui (ed), *International Law: Achievements and Prospects* (Martinus Nijhoff, Dordrecht, 1991) 597–618; N. Schrijver, *Sovereignty over Natural Resources. Balancing Rights and Duties* (Cambridge University Press, Cambridge, 1997).

49 A.J. Bradbrook and R.L. Ottinger (eds), *Energy Law and Sustainable Development* (IUCN, Gland, 2003); R. Lyster and A.J. Bradbrook, *Energy, Law and the Environment* (Cambridge University Press, Cambridge, 2006); H.T. Anker, B.E. Olsen and A. Rønne (eds), *Legal Systems and Wind Energy. A Comparative Perspective* (Kluwer Law International, Alphen aan den Rijn, 2009); R.L. Ottinger, *Renewable Energy Law and Development. Case Study Analysis* (Edward Elgar, Cheltenham, 2013).

50 N.A. Robinson, 'Foreword' in Bradbrook and Ottinger (eds), *ibid.*, vii–xiii at p. vii.

market-based approaches, with more recent efforts that seek to blend public and private regulatory approaches.[51] Domestic regimes and regulatory approaches are dynamic systems, continuously evolving novel and differentiated tools to regulate energy activities.

Leaving aside the complex relationship between domestic and international law, it remains necessary for international law to provide a sufficiently coherent and certain basis for operation of domestic regulatory regimes, whilst also ensuring that such regimes respect necessary limits dictated by international law.[52] More specifically, international law has a central role to play in six aspects of energy regulation. First, it determines, or provides the framework for, how transboundary or common resources are to be utilised. At root these are essentially questions about who controls a non-exclusive resource. Commentators have long been concerned with how international law should deal with common deposits of oil and gas reserves.[53] However, renewable resources may present even more complex problems of international coordination and cooperation. For example, wind and tidal energy are the products of common-pool resources which result from complex natural processes that reach beyond the exclusive control of any State.[54] As such they require coordinated regulation between States in accordance with the natural patterns of the energy system, as well as the consequences of its capture. This is particularly important in the marine environment, where the interplay of States' rights and duties is more complex. Second, international law may constrain the ability of States to control or interfere in energy production activities, particularly through international investment law.[55] Third, international law facilitates

51 B. Barton, L. Barrera-Hernández, A.R. Lucas and A. Rønne, 'Introduction' in B. Barton, L. Barrera-Hernández, A.R. Lucas and A. Rønne, (eds), *Regulating Energy and Natural Resources* (Oxford University Press, Oxford, 2006) 3–10, at pp. 3–6.

52 See further S.W. Schill, 'The interface between international and national energy law' in K. Talus (ed), *Research Handbook on International Energy Law* (Edward Elgar, Cheltenham, 2014) at pp. 44–76; A. Bradbrook, 'The Development of Renewable Energy Technologies and Energy Efficiency Measures through Public International Law' in D. Zilman, C. Redgwell, Y.O. Omorogbe and L.K. Barrera-Hernández (eds), *Beyond the Carbon Economy. Energy Law in Transition* (Oxford University Press, Oxford, 2008) 109–32; C. Redgwell, 'International Energy Security' in Barton, *et al.* (eds), (n 43) 17–47.

53 See Onorato (n 11); and Ong (n 10).

54 On the domestic aspects of this see: Lifshitz-Goldberg (n 7). On the international law aspects of common-pool resources, see Barnes (n 30).

55 See generally R. Dolzer and C. Schreuer, *Principles of International Investment Law* (Oxford University Press, Oxford, 2012); Sornarajah (n 31); S.L. Escarcena, *Indirect Expropriation in International Law* (Edward Elgar, Cheltenham, 2014).

access to and supply of energy resources. Many energy resources are located far from the users of energy and so international networks of supply (pipelines, cables and transport routes) are required to support the transfer of energy and raw materials. Again, this is important in a marine context where the oceans and the seabed provide a medium for such networks. Fourth, international law provides the basic framework for controlling the transboundary consequences of energy use—i.e., transboundary pollution. Fifth, international law coordinates responses to global challenges, and in particular climate change. Last, it may facilitate the coordination of domestic energy law regimes and policies, including finance, technological support and training for developing countries.

In these six categories, international law has much to say on some aspects of energy sovereignty, particularly transboundary pollution[56] and protection of investments from expropriation.[57] In the context of the marine environment, a useful overview of such instruments, as well as domestic measures, is contained in the Report of the UN Secretary-General on *Oceans and Law of the Sea 2012*.[58] More specifically, we may note that the transport of oil and gas resources, which is central to questions of energy sovereignty, is subject to numerous provisions of the LOSC dealing with pollution,[59] as well as MARPOL,[60] regional pollution agreements,[61] and liability regimes.[62] Offshore exploration activities are also addressed through the LOSC,[63] as well as regional pollution regimes. Furthermore, the disposal of energy by-products, such as radioactive waste, is controlled through instruments such as the London Dumping Convention[64]

56 See P. Birnie, A. Boyle and C. Redgwell, *International Law and the Environment* 3rd ed. (Oxford University Press, Oxford, 2009).

57 See for example the authors cited in (n 55).

58 UN Doc. A/67/79, 4 April 2012.

59 United Nations Convention on the Law of the Sea (Montego Bay, 10 December 1982, in force 16 November 1994), 1833 *UNTS* 396. See generally, Part XII and, in particular, Article 211 on ship-source pollution.

60 International Convention for the Prevention of Pollution from Ships, as Modified by the Protocol of 1978 Relating Thereto (London, 2 November 1973 and 17 February 1978, entry into force 2 October 1983), 1340 *UNTS* 62.

61 See for example, Article 4 of the Convention for the Protection of the Marine Environment of the North-East Atlantic 1992 (Paris, 22 September 1992, entry into force 25 March 1998), (1993) 23 *LOSB* 32 (OSPAR Convention).

62 See the Convention on Civil Liability for Oil Pollution Damage 1992 (London, 27 November 1992, entry into force 30 May 1996), 973 *UNTS* 3.

63 See LOSC, Article 194(3)(c).

64 Convention on the Prevention of Marine Pollution by Dumping of Wastes and Other Matter 1972 (London, 29 December 1972, entry into force 30 August 1975), 1046 *UNTS* 138.

or the Basel Convention.[65] However, as indicated below, international law has surprisingly little to say, at least directly, on the meaning of energy sovereignty or sovereignty over energy resources in the marine environment.

Four law of the sea instruments expressly refer to energy in the context of pollution,[66] but of these, only the LOSC directly addresses the issue of sovereignty over energy. Article 56(1)(a), provides that coastal States have: "*sovereign rights* for the purpose of exploring and exploiting, conserving and managing the natural resources, whether living or non-living, of the waters superjacent to the seabed and of the seabed and its subsoil, and with regard to other activities for the economic exploitation and exploration of the (exclusive economic) zone, such as the production of energy from the water, currents and winds".[67] This is, however, qualified by Article 56(2), which requires coastal States to exercise such rights with due regard to the rights and interests of other States, and in a manner compatible with the LOSC. This places a balancing of interests at the heart of any questions about energy sovereignty.[68]

There is some debate over the meaning of sovereign rights. O'Connell has noted the propensity of such rights to consolidate in sovereignty.[69] Although not dealing with the question of sovereignty, Article 60(1) is important since it provides the basis for regulating structures used to access marine energy resources in the EEZ. Coastal States are allocated *exclusive rights* to construct, operate and use such structures.[70] The precise nature of the right is not specified, although it presumably flows from the State's general sovereign rights over resources in the EEZ. Article 60(2) subsequently refers to exclusive jurisdiction

---

65 Convention on the Control of Transboundary Movements of Hazardous Wastes and Their Disposal 1989 (Basel, 22 March 1989, entry into force 5 May 1992), (1989) 28 *ILM* 657.

66 Energy is included within the definition of pollution in four instruments. See Article 2(a) of the Convention for the Protection of the Marine Environment and Coastal Region of the Mediterranean, as amended (Barcelona, 16 February 1976, and amended 10 June 1995, entry into force 12 February 1978 and 9 July 2004, respectively),(1996) 31 LOSB 65; Article 2(1) of the Convention on the Protection of the Marine Environment of the Baltic Sea Area 1992 (Helsinki, 9 April 1992, entry into force 17 January 2000), 2099 *UNTS* 197; Article 1(d) of the OSPAR Convention; Article 1(1)(4) of the United Nations Convention on the Law of the Sea 1982.

67 Similarly, Article 77 on the continental shelf provides coastal States with exclusive sovereign rights as regards natural resources. However, this is focused on mineral resources of the seabed and subsoil, and does not concern renewables.

68 Regard may also be had to Article 59 which requires that conflicts about unattributed rights are resolved on the basis of equity in light of relevant circumstances and the interests of the parties and the international community.

69 D.P. O'Connell, *The International Law of the Sea* (Clarendon Press, Oxford, 1982) at p. 481.

70 Article 60(1). These provisions extend to the continental shelf, according to Article 80.

to regulate such structures, which includes prescriptive and enforcement jurisdiction. Decisions concerning the placement and operation of such structures must take into account navigational concerns, whilst their removal must have due regard to fishing and protection of the marine environment.[71]

The LOSC is silent on the control of energy in the territorial sea. Since this is described as a zone to which the sovereignty of the State extends, sovereignty over energy resources would be treated in the same way as on land territory.[72] In practice, there is no doubting the existence of exclusive coastal State authority over energy resources, either mineral or renewable. This is subject to the preservation of third-State navigational interests through the regime of innocent passage.[73] This does not require sharing or the use of resources in a particular way; merely that the location of extraction/generation facilities does not hamper or deny the right of passage.[74]

Control over energy supply is not directly mentioned in the LOSC, but is covered by Article 79, which provides that "*All* States are entitled to lay submarine cables and pipelines on the continental shelf". This is crucial to the creation and maintenance of energy networks, and as with the above provisions, it also includes a "balancing of interests", which permits the coastal State to take reasonable measures to ensure the enjoyment of its resource-related rights.[75] The freedoms of the high seas include the freedom to lay submarine cables and pipelines and the freedom to establish installations.[76] This would apply to wind turbines and other renewable energy installations. Both freedoms are subject to the provisions of Part VI on the continental shelf, where this extends under the high seas. Thus, only the coastal State may authorise or operate platforms fixed to the seabed of its continental shelf where this extends beyond 200 nm.[77] It is questionable whether or not this includes floating devices used to generate energy. However, technological and economic limitations mean that such devices are not likely to operate in the near future and render questions about their regulation on the highs seas somewhat moot at present.[78] More significant is Article 87(2) which requires both freedoms to

71 Article 60(7) and (3), respectively.

72 See Article 2.

73 Articles 17–19.

74 Article 24.

75 Article 70(2) and (3).

76 Articles 87(c) and (d), respectively.

77 Article 80 cross-references Article 60.

78 Interesting questions arise as to the extent that the provisions on the common heritage of mankind in Part XI, as well as the provisions of the 1994 Implementation Agreement, might apply to renewable projects. See the Agreement Relating to the Implementation

be exercised with due regard to the interests of other States.[79] As in the EEZ, States' rights are subject to an important, if somewhat general, balancing of interests with those of other States.

This brief overview of the LOSC indicates that beyond the territorial sea, any rights in respect of energy resources, or the means for providing energy supplies, are inherently subject to a balancing of interests in light of other States' interests and potentially competing uses of sea space. The exercise of sovereign rights, jurisdiction or "freedoms" is more strongly linked to the interest of other States or the international community. This supports a more cooperative approach towards the regulation of energy resources and supplies in the marine environment. In particular, the requirement of due regard requires States to be aware of and take into account the interests of other States when exercising authority. Furthermore, it may require positive cooperation, and possibly the pursuit of mutually beneficial outcomes.[80] Despite the articulation of concepts that facilitate cooperative approaches, the LOSC offers little guidance as to the way in which such rights are to be exercised in specific contexts concerning energy development activities and further research is required to explore and explain how such a balancing of interests ought to work.

The second main reference to energy sovereignty in a multilateral instrument occurs in the Energy Charter Treaty (ECT). The ECT aims to promote cooperation in the energy field and the development of an efficient energy market throughout Europe.[81] Its remit is generally limited to investment protection, rather than the regulation of sovereignty or the wider range of energy-use activities.[82] The ECT applies to contracting States' territories, including territorial waters and sea and seabed areas where the State exercises sovereign rights and jurisdiction.[83] Article 18 of the ECT declares States to have "sovereignty and sovereign rights over energy resources". This is to be exercised in accordance with and subject to the rules of international law. Although the ECT is committed to the development of energy markets, it does not limit a State's authority and discretion as to how it structures ownership of energy resources.

---

of Part XI of the United Nations Convention on the Law of the Sea of 10 December 1982 (New York, 28 July 1994, entry into force 28 July 1998) 1836 *UNTS* 42.

79 Article 87(2).

80 *Fisheries Jurisdiction case* (United Kingdom v. Iceland) Merits, Judgment [1972] ICJ Reports 3, para. 72.

81 Article 2 of the ECT, and Title I of the Concluding Document of the Hague Conference on the European Energy Charter.

82 See generally, T. Wälde (ed), *The Energy Charter Treaty. An East-West Gateway for Investment and Trade* (Kluwer Law International, London, 1996).

83 Article 1(10).

Although the ECT "promotes access to resources", this hortatory requirement does not trump sovereignty and leaves the ownership of resources unaffected.[84] This is reaffirmed by Article 18(3), which provides that "[e]ach state continues to hold in particular the rights to decide the geographical areas within its Area to be made available for exploration and development of its energy resources, the optimalization [sic] of their recovery and the rate at which they may be depleted or otherwise exploited, to specify and enjoy any taxes, royalties or other financial payments payable by virtue of such exploration and exploitation, and to regulate the environmental and safety aspects of such exploration, development and reclamation within its Area, and to participate in such exploration and exploitation, inter alia, through direct participation by the government or through state enterprises."[85] The ECT pays lip service to environmental concerns with a sweeping list of factors to be taken into account. Article 19 comprises a list of eleven hortatory action points that request parties to "promote", "have regard to" or "take into account" certain environmental matters. For the most part, objectives like public participation, the polluter-pays principle, the use of environmentally sound technologies, and environmental impact assessment, are addressed in greater detail in other instruments.[86]

Following on from the above discussion of the nature of energy, it is to be noted that there is some recognition of the different qualities of energy in the ECT. Thus it refers to the regulation of energy throughout the "energy cycle", meaning from prospecting, though production and consumption, to conversion and supply, and ultimately disposal.[87] However, as noted above, this provision is framed in hortatory terms. If we are to realise a meaningful account of energy sovereignty, then such an account must reflect a broader understanding of the whole energy cycle and its complexities. To some extent the ECT provisions on transit already do this.[88] Thus, States are required to make necessary provisions to facilitate the transit of energy materials and products, which

84 Article 18(2).

85 See also Article 2 of Directive 94/22/EC of the European Parliament and of the Council of 30 May 1994 on the conditions for granting and using authorizations for the prospection, exploration and production of hydrocarbons. OJ L 164, 30 June 1994, 3–8; Article 4 of Directive 2009/31/EC on the geological storage of carbon dioxide and amending Council Directive 85/337/EEC, European Parliament and Council Directives 2000/60/EC, 2001/80/EC, 2004/35/EC, 2006/12/EC, 2008/1/EC and Regulation (EC) No 1013/2006. OJ L 140, 5 June 2009, at pp. 114–135.

86 See further C. Shine, 'Environmental Protection under the Energy Charter Treaty' in Wälde (ed), (n 82) 520–45.

87 Article 19.

88 Article 7.

helps address the concerns re the displacement of the location of energy resources from users. It is also reflected in the broader range of environmental and liability laws that govern human activities. In this sense authority to govern energy is already diffused across the system of international law. This conclusion might not be novel, but it serves to reinforce the interconnectedness of regulatory matters. Energy law cannot be viewed apart from wider and related legal regimes.

Nuclear energy apart, there has been little attention to marine energy generation in multilateral fora. This was noted in the Report of the UN Secretary-General on *Oceans and the Law of the Sea 2012*.[89] At the UN level, ECOSOC established a number of standing committees dealing with aspects of natural resources and renewable energy, although these have since been subsumed within the work of the Commission on Sustainable Development.[90] In 2009, the International Renewable Energy Agency (IRENA) was established with the objective of promoting "the widespread and increased adoption and the sustainable use of all forms of renewable energy."[91] Like the UN bodies, IRENA's mandate is generally limited to facilitating dialogue, promoting research and education, and developing policy recommendations. Perhaps unsurprisingly, most binding international agreements concerned with energy production have emerged in the context of transboundary hydrocarbon exploitation.[92] This seems to be a most fertile area for further research, since these agreements will reveal much about States' perspectives on energy sovereignty. These bilateral treaties do not generally address energy sovereignty directly, but are instead focused on the practical aspects of development, focusing on ensuring the optimal exploitation of resources. Of course, one should be careful about generalising from agreements designed between different parties and in different contexts. However, as Bankes's analysis shows, they are very much designed to provide a secure basis for commercial development. They also provide evidence of an increasing institutionalisation of hydrocarbon development.[93] In practice, this normally entails some degree of compromise

89 Secretary General (n 58) at para. 26.

90 See N. Schrijver, *Development without Destruction. The UN and Global Resource Management* (Indiana University Press, Indiana, 2010) at pp. 141–2.

91 Available online at http://www.irena.org/documents/uploadDocuments/Statute/IRENA_FC_Statute_signed_in_Bonn_26_01_2009_incl_declaration_on_further_authentic_versions.pdf.

92 See further N. Bankes, 'Recent Framework Agreements for the Recognition and Development of Transboundary Hydrocarbon Resources', this volume.

93 *Ibid.*, at p. 122.

by States with claims to the resource, and some limitation on unilateral exploitation, either by way of joint authorisations or, at least, authorisations that follow defined procedures. This reveals that a more nuanced approach to questions of sovereignty or sovereign rights over energy resources prevails in practice.

Justifications of Sovereignty over Marine Energy Resources and Supplies

Justificatory considerations have implications for specific rules on the use of resources, so a fuller appreciation of the various intellectual justifications for control can enrich our understanding of the best way in which energy resources can and should be regulated. The main justification associated with sovereignty is that of order and stability of the system.[94] In the context of resources, and still especially in that part of it dealing with marine resources, much of the literature on the justification of sovereignty over natural resources lacks depth. Typically this focuses on thin justifications based upon redistribution of wealth during and post-decolonisation.[95] This can be contrasted with the depth of the literature on the theoretical justification of property and property rights over natural resources.[96] This literature presents a plurality of justifications for ownership, cast in terms of liberty, natural rights, utility, order, and efficiency, each with different implications for determining entitlement to own and use things.

Given the need to develop a strong normative basis for the control of energy resources, it is suggested that recourse to more fundamental justificatory theories is desirable. The most important questions concerning energy are questions related to control. Which States should control energy? How should States control energy? What are States entitled to do with the energy? Are there any limits on States' use of energy? These are the same sort of questions that we ask about control, or ownership, of any resource by individual or community; should resources be excludable or shared, and if so, why? Therefore, at least for analytical purposes, it is informative to draw upon these justificatory theories. If we cast sovereignty in these terms, we can see how different justifications open up new avenues for answering questions about future resource

94 See Jackson (n 17) at p. 111.

95 See for example Schrijver (n 48) at pp. 20–5.

96 See J.W. Hamilton and N. Bankes, 'Different Views of the Cathedral: The Literature on Property Law' in McHarg, *et al.* (n 6) 19–59 at pp. 46–52. Also, Barnes (n 30) at pp. 29–61.

control and supply. The above justification of sovereignty based upon order is of only partial use in providing an analytical framework for exploring these questions. As a way forward, we should consider alternative justifications of energy sovereignty. To provoke some thoughts on the matter, the final part of the chapter explores a natural rights-based justification for sovereignty and its possible implications for marine energy resources and supplies.

It may be observed, first, that this analytical technique is not antithetical to international law. Natural rights are those rights inherent in a certain agent by virtue of their existence, and which are not contingent on the law or custom or some other forms of positive authority. The idea that certain rights are naturally inherent to States has a long tradition. Thus, Vattel notes that the rights of states are "naturally the same as those of any other state."[97] Later, the

> general and fundamental rule of our duties towards ourselves is, that every moral being ought to live in a manner comfortable to his nature ... A nation is a being determined by its essential attributes, that has its own nature, and can act in conformity with it ... The Law of Nature prescribes it certain duties.[98]

Whilst a natural-rights view of territorial sovereignty is dismissed by Shaw,[99] who explicitly sees it as confusing concepts of property and sovereignty, it is not without its adherents.[100] Natural law-based approaches still retain some currency in explaining the way in which international law works.[101]

The basic justification of sovereignty as a natural right runs thus: States by virtue of their existence as moral agents enjoy exclusive authority over the physical space that constitutes the State. The existence of this authority precedes the existence of any conventional rules governing the status of the State, and entails certain rights and duties that must be recognised within

97 E. de Vattel, *The Law of Nations* (S. & E. Butler, Northampton, MA, 1805), Book I, Chapter I, §. 4.

98 *Ibid.*, at §. 13.

99 M. Shaw, *Title to Territory* (Ashgate, Aldershot, 2005) at p. 17.

100 Nussbaum indicates that early scholars such as Martens viewed states as possessing certain natural rights: territorial sovereignty, independence, equality of treatment. A. Nussbaum, *A Concise History of the Law of Nations* (MacMillan, New York, 1953) at p. 183; also, E. Lauterpacht (ed), *International Law, Being the Collected Papers of Hersch Lauterpacht* vol. 1 (Cambridge University Press, Cambridge, 1970) at p. 76; L. Henkin, *International Law, Politics and Values* (Martinus Nijhoff, Dordrecht, 1995) at p. 40.

101 S. Hall, 'The Persistent Spectre: Natural Law, International Order and the Limits of Legal Positivism' (2001) 12 *EJIL* 269–307.

subsequent conventional rules. What consequences does this justification of sovereignty entail? As noted, a starting point is to regard the physical space of the State as an essential component of its agency. Thus territory and the resources therein, including energy resources, comprise part of the State and should not be separated from it.

At first glance this seems to support the claim of energy sovereignty linked to energy nationalism. The analogy is the agency of individual persons and "ownership" of their body, of which they cannot be deprived.[102] Of course, the analogy is not complete, since States do not necessarily require a particular amount of "physical form" to exist, and so the notion of territory as a fundamental requirement of statehood is notoriously fluid.[103] States are social constructs rather than physical agents, and if some physical capacity or need for energy resources is not a necessary part of this construct, then the claim to ownership or control is broken. Moreover, it ignores the broader and more complex dependency of States on each other to service their needs, only one of which is energy. States need things that may only exist within the "body" of other States, or must be transited through other States. Thus States, or ordinarily their citizens and private companies, necessarily trade in goods and services that cannot be produced locally, or that can be procured more cheaply elsewhere. Arguably, securing transit and trade becomes more, or as important, as the reliance upon rules that allocate control based upon the initial location of energy resources. This belies a special significance attaching to the mere physical components of the State, and suggests that resources can be detached or used apart from the State for good reason, as determined by the needs of the wider community of States. This detachment or rather insertion of collective interests was highlighted in the above discussion of the balancing of interests that is inherent to the exercise of sovereign rights over marine resources, as well as the transit provisions of the ECT.

This basic approach to sovereignty as a natural right presents further difficulties when applied to marine energy resources, because maritime spaces beyond the territorial sea or continental shelf (as a natural prolongation of the

---

102 Another way to conceive of this is to view States as communities of people who require physical space and resources to exist. These basic individual needs are then extrapolated to the level of the State as an organisational body. Of course, this is no longer an account based on natural rights, but rather one based upon need, and raises further questions about why the persons living in a particular space should have their needs met whilst others are not so entitled.

103 'There is ... no rule that the land frontiers of a State must be fully delimited and defined." *North Sea Continental Shelf case* [1969] ICJ Report 4 at p. 22.

landmass)[104] are not part of the State as such, but rather areas within which the State may extend its sovereign rights or jurisdiction. Arguably, this means that the simple natural rights-based justification cannot justify exclusive control over marine renewable energy resources derived from the water column or the wind, or other complex natural systems.[105] One needs to further justify claims to such resources in other terms.

An extension of the natural-rights approach contends that when States vest their efforts in something, they thereby reduce it to their sovereignty. In some ways, this might be conceived of as a rule of capture for States. The analogy is the labour-based justification of property.[106] However, the simple form of this justification as applied to territorial sovereignty generates undesirable consequences, since it essentially justifies a first-occupation view of sovereignty (possibly conquest or annexation). One may note here the controversy generated by Russia's claims to the North Pole.[107] This first-occupation approach is now discredited, but more plausible versions (the so-called labour/desert approach) require the labour to be socially productive. Thus a person's or a State's claim to control of "external" things can be justified, for example, through the introduction of socially productive effort: extraction, regulation, use, transport, transfer of technology and so on. The meaning of "socially productive" is open to debate, but potentially wide in definition. It could include conservation. In part this is reflected in the conservation and management duties of the coastal State over living resources of the EEZ.[108] It is not clear that any such legal requirement of productive use applies to energy resources, and this is something to consider further, especially in the face of increasing pressure on limited energy supplies.[109] This emphasis on socially productive effort provides another interesting avenue to explore, since most productive activities concerning energy capture and use are conducted

---

104 See the Truman Proclamation 1945, reproduced in S.H. Lay, R. Churchill and M. Nordquist (eds), *New Directions in the Law of the Sea*, vol. 1. (Oceana Publications, Dobbs Ferry, NY, 1973) at pp. 106–7.

105 E.g., ocean thermal energy or salinity gradient energy. See IRENA, *Ocean Energy Brief* Nos. 1 and 2. Available online at http://www.irena.org/menu/index.aspx?mnu=Subcat&PriMenuID=36&CatID=141&SubcatID=445.

106 See the discussion of Locke's approach in Barnes (n 30), at p. 30ff.

107 See N. Matz-Luck, 'Planting the Flag in Arctic Waters. Russia's Claim to the North Pole' (2009) 2 *Göttingen Journal of International Law* 235–255.

108 See for example LOSC, Articles 61–2.

109 See D. Ong, 'Towards and International Law for the Conservation of Offshore Hydrocarbon Resources within the Continental Shelf?' in D. Freestone, R. Barnes and D. Ong (eds), *Law of the Sea. Progress and Prospects* (Oxford University Press, Oxford, 2006) 93–119.

by a multiplicity of actors, public and private, and whose actions might be attributed to a range of States, not merely the State hosting the raw materials or production facilities.[110] This may provide a counterpoint to simplistic accounts of "State directed" labour and reward for energy production, and one which justifies a broader stake in the products of offshore energy developments. This is particularly so given that improvements might be the product of efforts beyond a single State, such as the building of networks of supply lines, or the creation of market and regulatory regimes at the international level. If a "reward" is given for socially productive effort, then this might also provide a moral basis for more cooperative approaches to energy use and supply, and shared interests in energy resources. This is highly relevant to marine renewable energy, where complex physical and market networks are required to ensure that energy can be captured when available and then distributed to those with the ability to use it.

This brief outline indicates the potential for analysing questions of energy sovereignty and control of marine resources in terms of property justifications. It does not explore the full implications of this approach, and there are many interesting questions that remain to be asked. For example, one might ask how the Lockean proviso that requires enough and as good be left for others might be applied to claims by some States to exclusive control over globally important energy reserves. Neither does this chapter consider other important justifications, such as liberty, identity, utility or efficiency, good order. Such approaches open up many more questions about how we should allocate control over energy resources, and in what forms, to States (or indeed to other actors). It is clear that if we are to take claims about energy sovereignty seriously, and to consider how these can and should be advanced, much more work is required to frame the terms of the debate.

---

110 On private actors, see further S. Trevisanut, 'The Role of Private Actors in the Offshore Energy Industry: Shifting Models of Participation', this volume.

CHAPTER 2

Mind the Gap in the GAIRS: The Role of Other Instruments in LOSC Regime Implementation in the Offshore Energy Sector

Catherine Redgwell
Chichele Professor of International Law,
All Souls College, Oxford OX1 4AL, UK

Abstract

While the international legal framework for offshore energy activities is anchored in the 1982 Law of the Sea Convention (LOSC), it "is complemented by an array of relevant instruments and measures at the global, regional and national levels". This chapter examines the role of generally accepted international rules and standards (GAIRS) in the implementation of the LOSC in the offshore energy sector, with particular reference to the decommissioning of offshore installations, marine pollution from continental shelf exploration and exploitation, submarine cables and pipelines, and shipping. This analysis reveals that this role has been one of facilitating, strengthening and updating the LOSC in the light of legal and technical developments since its conclusion—a process of normative reinforcement rather than normative conflict. Yet, as highlighted in the conclusion, significant gaps nonetheless remain in the regulation of offshore energy activities.

Keywords

Law of the Sea Convention (LOSC) – generally accepted international rules and standards (GAIRS) – offshore energy sector – decommissioning – marine pollution

Introduction

While the international legal framework for offshore energy activities is anchored in the 1982 Law of the Sea Convention (LOSC),[1] it "is complemented by an array of relevant instruments and measures at the global, regional and national

1 Montego Bay, 10 December 1982, in force 16 November 1994 1833 *United Nations Treaty Series* (*UNTS*) 396.

 | DOI 10.1163/9789004303522_004

levels."[2] The purpose of this contribution is to examine this instrument mix[3] in the implementation of the LOSC in the offshore energy sector. The LOSC recognizes State sovereignty (in the territorial sea) and sovereign rights (in the exclusive economic zone (EEZ) and continental shelf (CS)) over non-living marine resources.[4] Of these, oil and gas are the most important with the most concentrated activity taking place in the Gulf of Mexico, the North Sea, offshore West Africa and South-East Asia.[5] Offshore renewable energy activity is also increasing and production of energy from the oceans (wind, water and waves) is likewise regulated under the EEZ regime of the LOSC.[6] Since these activities occur largely within 200 nautical miles,[7] coastal States are "effectively accorded exclusive responsibility for the management of the majority of non-living resources in the world's oceans".[8] In exercising this responsibility in the implementation of, and compliance with, the LOSC, a persistent theme is the need for financial and technical assistance: whether for conventional offshore oil and gas activities[9] or for more novel techniques for energy production from the oceans.[10]

---

2 Report of the Secretary-General, *Oceans and the law of the sea*, A/67/79, 4 April 2012, para. 27. Available at http://daccess-dds-ny.un.org/doc/UNDOC/GEN/N12/284/79/PDF/N1228479.pdf?OpenElement; accessed 18 August 2014. The report addresses marine renewable energy in particular, although this observation is generally applicable to offshore energy activities.

3 Accordingly, the relationship between the LOSC and customary international law will not be explored here. For general discussion, see J. Harrison, *Making the Law of the Sea: A Study in the Development of International Law* (Cambridge University Press, Cambridge, 2011); and J.A. Roach, 'Today's Customary International Law of the Sea' (2014) 45(3) *Ocean Development and International Law* (*ODIL*) 239–259.

4 See generally C. Redgwell, 'International Energy Law' in M.M. Roggenkamp, C. Redgwell, I. del Guayo and A. Ronne (eds), *Energy Law in Europe* (3rd edn, Oxford University Press, Oxford, in press), section C.

5 'Non-Living Marine Resources' in D. Rothwell and T. Stephens, *The International Law of the Sea* (Hart Publishing, Oxford, 2010) 287–291, at p. 287.

6 Article 56(1)(a); see (n 2).

7 On the energy resources of the deep seabed, see further below.

8 Rothwell and Stephens (n 5), at p. 298.

9 Thus, for example, the World Bank Group has financed a number of offshore oil exploration and development projects in developing States which include seismic and geological studies: Report of the Secretary-General, *Realization of the benefits under the United Nations Convention on the Law of the Sea: Measures undertaken in response to needs of States in regard to development and management of ocean resources, and approaches for further action*, UN Doc A/46/722, 4 December 1991, para. 159; and http://www.worldbank.org/en/topic/energy; accessed 18 August 2014.

10 See, for example, Report of the Secretary-General, *Realization of the benefits under the United Nations Convention on the Law of the Sea: Needs of States in regard to development and management of ocean resources*, UN Doc A/45/712, 16 November 1990, paras. 106–112.

The LOSC also regulates the functional jurisdiction[11] coastal States exercise over the associated exploration and production infrastructure (such as offshore installations and devices, and submarine cables and pipelines) and activities (such as drilling and maritime transport). It is additionally concerned with protection of the marine environment, on which the offshore energy sector has a major impact.[12] Thus, while the LOSC does not limit the extent of the exploitation of non-living energy resources—there is no duty of conservation as there is for living resources under the LOSC,[13] nor any obligation to utilize such resources sustainably—there is an obligation to prevent, reduce and control pollution of the marine environment.[14]

The zonal fragmentation of the LOSC and the functional jurisdiction associated with it has come under increasing criticism in the light of the obstacles it poses to concerted action to address global problems, such as climate change and "sustainable energy for all,"[15] and conservation of marine biodiversity.[16] The United Nations General Assembly, in its annual review of the state of the oceans and the law of the sea, has called generally for "an integrated,

11 See generally M. Gavouneli, *Functional Jurisdiction in the Law of the Sea* (Martinus Nijhoff, Leiden, 2007).

12 This was notable even during the LOSC negotiations. For example, Attard notes that a number of changes were made to the provisions on pollution from vessels following the 1978 *Amoco Cadiz* oil tanker disaster. D. Attard, *The Exclusive Economic Zone in International Law* (Oxford University Press, Oxford, 1987), at p. 96, citing U. Jenisch, 'Law of the Sea Conference before Session 8' (1979) 30 *Aussen Politik* 40–61, at pp. 57 ff.

13 See D. Ong, 'Towards an International Law for the Conservation of Offshore Hydrocarbon Resources within the Continental Shelf?' in D. Freestone, R. Barnes and D. Ong (eds), *The Law of the Sea: Progress and Prospects* (Hart Publishing, Oxford, 2006) 93–119.

14 This includes taking measures "designed to the minimize to the fullest possible extent" pollution from vessels and "from installations and devices used in exploration or exploitation of the natural resources of the sea-bed and subsoil": Article 194(3)(b) and (c).

15 See United Nations Conference on Sustainable Development, *The Future We Want* (2012), para. 127, available at http://www.se4all.org; accessed 18 August 2014. The decade 2014–2024 has been designated the "United Nations Decade of Sustainable Energy for All" in further acknowledgement of the importance of energy issues for sustainable development.

16 P. Sands and J. Peel, *Principles of International Environmental Law 3rd ed.* (Cambridge University Press, Cambridge, 2012), at p. 448 ("complexity of problems affecting the oceans … [requires] holistic solutions"); on protection of marine biological diversity in areas beyond national jurisdiction, see R. Rayfuse and R. Warner, 'Securing a Sustainable Future for the Oceans Beyond National Jurisdiction: The Legal Basis for an Integrated Cross-Sectoral Regime for High Seas Governance for the 21st Century' (2008) 23 *IJMCL* 399–421, at p. 402.

interdisciplinary and intersectoral approach",[17] while others have suggested the specific need for an energy protocol to the LOSC[18] or even a new treaty addressed to the offshore oil and gas sector.[19] Of these the first seems the most likely at the global level, supplemented by regional reinforcement of generally accepted international rules and standards (GAIRS),[20] including those promulgated by international organisations and by industry.[21] This builds on existing processes for the evolution of the LOSC which are explored in the next section, which considers the dynamic nature of GAIRS and their function as benchmarks under the LOSC with the specific offshore energy examples of the decommissioning of offshore installations, marine pollution from continental shelf exploration and exploitation, submarine cables and pipelines, and shipping. This analysis reveals that the role of other instruments has been one of facilitating, strengthening and updating the LOSC in the light of legal and technical developments since its conclusion—a process of normative reinforcement rather than normative conflict.[22] Yet, as highlighted in the conclusion, significant gaps nonetheless remain in the regulation of offshore energy activities.

17 *Oceans and the Law of the Sea*, UNGA Resolution 60/30, 8 March 2006, at p. 2.

18 M. Tsamenyi and M. Herriman, 'Ocean Energy and the Law of the Sea: The Need for a Protocol?' (1998) 29 *ODIL* 3–19. Some go further and suggest wholesale renegotiation of the LOSC: F. Galea, 'A Legal Regime for the Exploration and Exploitation of Offshore Renewable Energy' (2011) 25 *Ocean Yearbook* 101–129.

19 S. Rares, 'An International Convention on offshore hydrocarbon leaks?' (2011) 12 *Lloyd's Maritime and Commercial Law Quarterly* 361–371.

20 Tan identifies the adoption of "new and progressive GAIRS" as one method for meeting increasing coastal State demands for resource and environmental protection "without unravelling the... consensus [reflected in the LOSC]": A. Tan, *Vessel Source Marine Pollution: The Law and Politics of International Regulation* (Cambridge University Press, Cambridge, 2006), at p. 229.

21 See for example Report No. 426 on *Regulators' Use of Standards* produced by the International Association of Oil and Gas Producers in 2010, comparing the use of national, regional and international and industry standards across fourteen key energy jurisdictions, noting, *inter alia*, a rise in reliance on international standards. Available at http://www.ogp.org.uk/pubs/426.pdf; accessed 18 August 2014.

22 Or the 'non-fragmentation' of international law in this sphere: on fragmentation see Report of the International Law Commission, *Conclusions of the work of the Study Group on the Fragmentation of international law: Difficulties arising from the Diversification and Expansion of International Law* (2006). Available at http://legal.un.org/ilc/texts/instruments/english/draft%20articles/1_9_2006.pdf; accessed 18 August 2014.

Dynamic Evolution of the LOSC

Although negotiated as a "package deal,"[23] ostensibly comprehensive in scope and universal in its participation, the LOSC was always intended to be capable of further evolution. Inevitably strategic interests change over time, and "economic and technological developments have increased the ability to access and harvest the [living and non-living] resources of the sea and the seabed."[24] This evolution was envisaged to occur in a number of ways. One is the "normal" pathway of treaty amendment that, in the case of the LOSC, is far from easy.[25] There is no provision in the LOSC for expedited amendment nor a tacit acceptance amendment procedure such as that employed under various International Maritime Organization (IMO) instruments, which in any event are usually applied to technical annexes or appendices.[26] This formal amendment procedure under the LOSC has never been used.[27]

---

23 See H. Caminos and M. Molitor, 'Progressive Development of International Law and the Package Deal' (1985) 79 *American Journal of International Law* (*AJIL*) 871–890; Harrison (n 3); and A. Boyle, 'Further Development of the 1982 Convention on the Law of the Sea: Mechanisms for Change' in Freestone (n 13), 40–62, at pp. 40–41.

24 M.D. Evans, 'The Law of the Sea' in *ibid.* (ed), *International Law* (4th edn., Oxford University Press, Oxford, 2014) 651–687, at p. 652; E. Posner and A. Sykes, 'The Economic Foundations of the Law of the Sea' (2010) 104 *AJIL* 569–596. Tan (n 20), at p. 225, also refers to the GAIRS formula as responsive to the need for flexibility and dynamism shaped by subsequent development of the law.

25 Boyle (n 23), at p. 41; see Articles 312–314. Note that this is either through general amendment, or through *inter se* agreements, with the *caveat* that the latter must be compatible with "the effective execution and object and purpose" of the LOSC: Article 311(3).

26 A pioneer in this regard was the 1973 International Convention for the Prevention of Pollution from Ships and 1978 Protocol (MARPOL 73/78) with its tacit amendment procedure: London, 17 February 1978, in force 2 October 1983, 1340 *UNTS* 62. It is these more dynamic and flexible standards which are amongst the GAIRS incorporated by reference in the LOSC.

27 Articles 312–316 address treaty amendment. The 1994 Implementation Agreement was adopted as an agreed interpretation by the contracting parties of the LOSC in the sense of Article 31(3)(a) of the 1969 Vienna Convention on the Law of Treaties (Vienna, 23 May 1969, in force 27 January 1980, 1155 UNTS 331), which is generally considered reflective of customary international law. See further D.H. Anderson, 'Resolution and Agreement Relating to the Implementation of Part XI of the UN Convention on the Law of the Sea: A General Assessment' (1995) 55(2) *Zeitschrift fur auslaendisches oeffentliches Recht und Voelkerrecht* (*ZaoRV*) 275–289. As Evans points out, the Agreement was "rather

Another method for the evolution of the LOSC, and the principal focus of this contribution, is the incorporation by reference of other GAIRS.[28] This phrase is inherently evolutionary in character, fostering a dynamic interpretation of the relevant LOSC provisions.[29] A further, related, method for the LOSC's evolution is the negotiation of additional global and regional instruments and soft law.[30] In the energy context, "other treaties and soft-law instruments operating in tandem with the LOSC" relevant for offshore energy activities "include instruments that deal with matters such as prevention of pollution,[31] the removal of

euphemistically entitled 'Implementation Agreement' [and] *de facto* amended the Convention so as to make it acceptable to as broad a range of states as possible:" Evans (n 24), at p. 653; Harrison (n 3), at pp. 92–93.

28 Van Reenan calls provisions referring to rules of public international law "rules of reference" which are incorporated in, but do not over-ride, the LOSC. He accepts these may also include non-binding rules incorporated by reference (e.g., recommended practices and procedures), although the analysis is limited to treaty and customary "rules of reference": R. Van Reenen, 'Rules of Reference in the new Convention on the Law of the Sea in particular connection with pollution of the sea by oil from tankers' (1981) XII *Netherlands Yearbook of International Law* 3–44. A number of authors appear to use "rules of reference" synonymously with GAIRS: see, e.g., Tan (n 20), at p. 195; Y. Tanaka, *The International Law of the Sea* (Cambridge University Press, Cambridge, 2012), at pp. 35–36 (referring to both "generally accepted" and "generally applicable" international rules and standards). The LOSC does not explain what GAIRS are, other than occasionally to link these with promulgation by a competent international organization or diplomatic conference, e.g., Article 211(5).

29 As Boyle observes, many of the terms utilised in the LOSC are potentially inherently evolutionary, using the examples, *inter alia*, of "the pollution of the marine environment" and the identification of "generally accepted international rules and standards": A. Boyle, 'Further Development of the Law of the Sea Convention: Mechanisms for Change' (2005) 54(3) *International and Comparative Law Quarterly* (ICLQ) 563–584, at 569.

30 Boyle (n 23), at p. 41. Other methods for the development of the law of the sea, such as by international courts and tribunals, have contributed relatively little to the development of the LOSC. The chief areas have been continental shelf/EEZ delimitation elaborating upon the provisions of Articles 74 and 83, principally in the jurisprudence of the International Court of Justice (ICJ), and the cases on prompt release (usually of fisheries vessels under Article 292) heard by the International Tribunal for the Law of the Sea (ITLOS).

31 See, e.g., the 1994 Protocol for the Protection of the Mediterranean Sea against Pollution [Resulting] from [Exploration and Exploitation of the Continental Shelf and the Seabed and its Subsoil] [Madrid, 14 October 1994, in force 24 March 2011, ECOLEX TRE-001206].

offshore installations and structures,[32] and the protection of such platforms from terrorist attacks and other acts of violence."[33, 34]

External Rules and Standards in the LOSC

This reliance on external rules and standards has led to the description of the LOSC as "framework"[35] in character, particularly in Part XII. This is recognised in several different ways. First, there is an exhortation to co-operate on a global and regional basis in formulating rules and standards for the protection and preservation of the marine environment.[36] This is amplified in particular contexts, such as for vessel-source pollution, where Article 211(1) requires

32 See, e.g., the [IMO's] 1989 Guidelines and Standards for the Removal of Offshore Installations and Structures on the Continental Shelf and in the Exclusive Economic Zone [Resolution A.672(16) of 19 October 1989, IMO Assembly, Sixteenth Session, *Resolutions and Other Decisions*, at p. 293].

33 See, e.g., the 1988 Protocol for the Suppression of Unlawful Acts against the Safety of Fixed Platforms located on the Continental Shelf [Rome, 10 March 1988, in force 1 March 1992, 1678 *UNTS* 304]. The recent *Arctic Sunrise* incident reveals a further gap under the LOSC, which is that there is no express obligation of prompt release of vessels and crew in relation to oil platforms and infringement of their safety zones, though this may be sought as a provisional measure under Article 290: see 'Arctic Sunrise' (*Neth.* v. *Russ.*), ITLOS Case No. 22, Provisional Measures, 22 November 2013, and for comment D. Guilfoyle and C.A. Miles, 'Provisional Measures and the MV *Arctic* Sunrise' (2014) 108(2) *AJIL* 271–287.

34 Rothwell and Stephens (n 5), at p. 289.

35 See Evans (n 24), at p. 653, referring to the need to supplement the LOSC "by a number of other major conventions addressing certain issues in greater detail." Other commentators use "umbrella" to convey the same sense: see e.g., S. Rosenne, 'IMO Interface with the Law of the Sea Convention' in M.H. Nordquist and J.N. Moore (eds), *Current Maritime Issues and the International Maritime Organisation* (Martinus Nijhoff Publishers, The Hague, 1999), at p. 252; and E. Franckx (ed), *Vessel-source Pollution and Coastal State Jurisdiction: The Work of the ILA Committee on Coastal State Jurisdiction relating to Marine Pollution (1991–2000)* (Kluwer Law International, The Hague, 2001), at p. 12. "Framework" is not used here in the classical sense of framework treaties with subsequent protocols and annexes that provide more detailed ('internal') rules and standards, such as MARPOL 73/78, or the 1992 OSPAR Convention for the Protection of the Marine Environment of the North-East Atlantic (Paris, 22 September 1992, in force 25 March 1998, 2354 *UNTS* 67) with its annexes and appendices.

36 See e.g., Article 197. Section 2 of Part XII, Articles 197–201, is addressed to global and regional co-operation, extending beyond the articulation of substantive rules and standards to notification and contingency planning arrangements, as well as to exchange of scientific information and the establishment of appropriate scientific criteria for

States, acting through the competent international organisation or general diplomatic conference, to *establish* international rules and standards to prevent, reduce and control vessel-source marine pollution, to promote the adoption of routeing systems, and in the same manner to *review* those rules and standards periodically.[37] This has been one of the most active areas for GAIRS generation, largely under IMO auspices. This gives continued vitality to such standards. Less positively, the ambiguity surrounding which internationally agreed rules and standards are "generally accepted" and thus incorporated in the LOSC may introduce unwelcome uncertainty into determining, for example, the scope of coastal and flag state jurisdiction under the LOSC.[38]

Second, internationally agreed rules and standards are used as a benchmark under the LOSC for international minimum standards, ranging from the weak "taking into account" for land-based and atmospheric sources of marine pollution, and for the abandonment of offshore installations or structures,[39] to the more robust "no less effective" standard of result for regulation of pollution from sea-bed activities such as drilling, activities in the Area, and dumping,[40] and the high-water mark of "at least have the same effect" obligation of result

---

pollution prevention, reduction and control. Global and regional cooperation is also reinforced in respect of each source of marine pollution in Part XII Section 5.

37 Similar wording for pollution from seabed activities subject to national jurisdiction is found in Article 208(5), with the addition of a reference to regional rules. Here a degree of variation according to the particular circumstances (e.g., particularly sensitive sea areas such as the Baltic; an area of intensive offshore oil and gas activity such as the North Sea) may—indeed, even should—be taken into account. This is made explicit with respect to upward derogation from international rules and standards to prevent marine pollution from vessels in designated areas of the EEZ owing, e.g., to their ecological conditions (Art 211(6)).

38 P. Birnie, A. Boyle and C. Redgwell, *International Law and the Environment* (3rd edn., Oxford University Press, Oxford, 2009), at pp. 389–90; A.E. Boyle, 'Marine pollution under the Law of the Sea Convention' (1985) 79 *AJIL* 347–372, at p. 357.

39 Article 207(1), addressed to pollution from land-based sources; Article 212(1), pollution from or through the atmosphere; and Article 60(3) (abandonment).

40 Article 208(3), addressed to pollution from sea-bed activities; Article 209(2), pollution from activities in the area; and Article 210(6), pollution from dumping. The latter uses the phrase "global rules and standards" which is considered equivalent to "GAIRS": see, e.g., Boyle (n 38), at p. 355. From an extensive literature on this point, Oxman cautions against attributing to any difference in terminology a necessary difference in meaning given the long and complex negotiation of the LOSC: B.H. Oxman, 'The duty to respect generally accepted international standards' (1991) 24 *New York University Journal of International Law & Politics* 109–159, at p. 132, (n 70).

applicable to vessel-source pollution.[41] These are dynamic benchmarks, since these global rules and standards will not—and indeed have not—remained static.

GAIRS and Offshore Energy Activities

Decommissioning of Offshore Installations

This is certainly the case with respect to energy activities. An example is the decommissioning of offshore energy installations and their disposal or reuse. Article 60(3) LOSC provides that:

> Due notice must be given of the construction of such artificial islands, installations or structures, and permanent means for giving warning of their presence must be maintained. Any installations or structures which are abandoned or disused shall be removed to ensure safety of navigation, taking into account any generally accepted international standards established in this regard by the competent international organization. Such removal shall also have due regard to fishing, the protection of the marine environment and the rights and duties of other States. Appropriate publicity shall be given to the depth, position, and dimensions of any installations or structures not entirely removed.[42]

In 1989 the IMO produced a set of non-binding "Guidelines and Standards for the Removal of Offshore Installations and Structures on the Continental Shelf and in the Exclusive Economic Zone."[43] States parties to the LOSC have an

41 Article 211(2). See, generally, B. Vukas, 'Generally accepted international rules and standards' in A.H.A. Soons (ed), *Implementation of the Law of the Sea Convention through International Institutions* (Law of the Sea Institute, Honolulu, 1990), 405–421, at pp. 406–408.

42 For the drafting history of this provision, see S.V. Nandan, S. Rosenne, and N.R. Grandy (eds), *The United Nations Convention on the Law of the Sea 1982: A Commentary*, vol. II (Martinus Nijhoff Publishers, Dordrecht/Boston/London, 1993), at p. 586. The IMO is one such "competent international organization" for the purposes of Art. 60(3); also relevant are global and regional rules and standards on dumping with respect to disposal of the remains. See Division for Ocean Affairs and the Law of the Sea Office of Legal Affairs, *Obligations of States Parties under the United Nations Convention on the Law of the Sea and Complementary Instruments* (United Nations, New York, 2004), at p. 46.

43 See (n 32). These are also annexed to the commentary on Article 60 in Nandan *et al.*, *ibid.*, at pp. 589–693. The IMO is not, of course, an energy organization, its primary focus

obligation under Article 60(3) to take these Guidelines into account when considering the decommissioning of offshore installations. The Guidelines require an evaluation of six factors:

(i) any potential effect on navigation and other users of the sea;
(ii) the rate of deterioration of the material and possible future effects upon the marine environment;
(iii) the potential effects upon the marine environment;
(iv) the risk that the material may shift from its present position over time;
(v) the costs, technical feasibility, and risk to personnel in removing the installation or structure; and
(vi) the other uses to which the installation or structure may be put, or other justifications for leaving it intact, in whole or in part.[44]

The Guidelines further stipulate that lightweight structures (4,000 tonnes or less) in shallower waters (75 metres depth or shallower) must be entirely removed. Where partial remains are left *in situ*, clearance of 55 metres must be provided in the interests of safety of navigation, in particular submarine navigation. Any installations emplaced after 1 January 1998 must be capable of total removal.

Article 60(3) and the IMO Guidelines are further reinforced through implementation in national policy and legislation, and through regional agreements. Thus, for example, the 1992 Convention for the Protection of the Marine Environment of the North-East Atlantic (OSPAR) amplifies these obligations in Annex III, which explicitly addresses a further feature of decommissioning, namely disposal of the remains.[45] With effect from 9 February 1999, a further decision of the OSPAR parties on decommissioning was binding on the parties (Decision 98/3).[46] In general terms, therefore, State practice has followed the lead of the LOSC. For example, the OSPAR Convention provisions, in particular Decision 98/3, provide for exceptions from entire removal, while the 1989

being on shipping and related matters: see Article 1(a), Convention establishing the International Maritime Organization, Geneva, 6 March 1948, in force 17 March 1958, 289 *UNTS* 48.

44 See J. Side, M. Baines, and K. Young, 'Current controls for abandonment and disposal of offshore installations at sea' (1993) 17(5) *Marine Policy* 354–362.

45 OSPAR, Annex III on the Prevention and Elimination of Pollution from Offshore Sources (n 35).

46 OSPAR Decision 98/3 on the Disposal of Disused Offshore Installations, 9 February 1999, Ministerial Meeting of the OSPAR Commission, Sintra, 22–23 July 1998, Summary Record OSPAR 98/14/1, Annex 33.

IMO Guidelines expressly contemplate partial removal. Despite this recognition of partial removal, the OSPAR regime has increasingly restricted exceptions to entire removal and the IMO Guidelines specifically require that any installations emplaced after 1 January 1998 must be capable of entire removal. Article 20 of the 1994 Protocol to the Barcelona Convention for the Protection of the Mediterranean Sea against Pollution[47] also requires total removal of installations. Thus the rules incorporated by reference in the LOSC, even on the weaker "taking into account" end of the scale, may obtain separate binding force through regional treaty arrangements which further clarify, and even extend, the nature and scope of LOSC obligations.

While "taking into account" does not indicate an obligation to comply with such standards *per se*, more robust wording such as "at least the same effect as" and "no less effective than international rules and standards" may well "impose a legal obligation on a state [party to the LOSC] to respect a standard which it would not otherwise be legally bound to respect."[48] This obligation may well be novel either because the generally accepted standard referred to may be expressed in non-binding form[49]—such as the 1989 IMO Guidelines—or the State Party to the LOSC is not a party to the binding instrument containing the rule referred to. In either case any legal obligation flows from the LOSC.

Marine Pollution from Continental Shelf Activities

However, this presupposes that there *are* international rules and standards against which national laws and regulations may be benchmarked as, e.g., "no less effective." Pollution from seabed activities within national jurisdiction under Article 208 is one example of sparse content: (i) the 1990 Oil Pollution Preparedness and Response Convention and Protocol[50] applies to fixed or floating offshore installations or structures engaged in oil and gas exploitation or the loading or unloading of oil, and to oil terminals, pipelines and other handling facilities (Art 2(5)); and (ii) Regulation 39 of MARPOL 73/78 Annex I

47 See (n 31).

48 Oxman (n 40), at p. 144.

49 This was expressly considered by the International Law Commission (ILC) in its commentary to what was to become Article 10 of the 1958 Geneva Convention on the High Seas (Geneva, 29 April 1958, in force 30 September 1962, 450 *UNTS* 82), *viz.*, that "the more general expression 'internationally accepted standards'... also covers regulations which are a product of international co-operation, without necessarily having been confirmed by formal treaties": ILC, Articles concerning the Law of the Sea with Commentary in *Yearbook of the International Law Commission*, 1956, vol. II, at p. 281.

50 London, 30 November 1990, in force 13 May 1995, 1891 *UNTS* 51 (Convention); London, 14 March 2000, in force 14 June 2007 [2003] *ATNIF* 9 (Protocol).

provides special requirements for fixed and floating platforms engaged in seabed activities.[51] Unlike vessel-source pollution, there is no global agreement on operational or accidental pollution from seabed activities[52] with consequent criticism of the general legal regime, and of the LOSC in particular, for failing to protect the marine environment adequately from the harmful effects of oil and gas activities.[53]

Specific regional arrangements, on the other hand, have more thoroughly addressed marine pollution arising from continental shelf exploration and exploitation, particularly in the regional and semi-enclosed seas of the European region. As early as 1969 in the North Sea area there was the Agreement for Co-operation in Dealing with Pollution of the North Sea by Oil, replaced in 1983 by an updated agreement which also extends to harmful substances other than oil, and oil pollution emergencies.[54] Protection of the marine environment, including the regulation of dumping from ships and from installations in the North Sea and the North-East Atlantic, is now regulated by the 1992 OSPAR Convention. In the Mediterranean, there is the 1976 Convention for the Protection of the Mediterranean Sea against Pollution, updated in 1995 with the Convention for the Protection of the Marine Environment and Coastal Region of the Mediterranean, with its 1994 Protocol on pollution from continental shelf exploration and exploitation.[55] The European Union (EU) acceded to the Protocol in 2013 as part of a suite of measures in response to the

---

51 Special rules are also evolving for seabed activities in the Arctic region: see (n 94).

52 There are calls to fill this gap: see (n 91).

53 A. Yankov, 'The Law of the Sea Convention and Agenda 21: Marine Environment Implications' in Freestone (n 13), at pp. 290–291; and M.H. Nordquist, J.N. Moore, A. Chircop, and R. Long (eds), *The Regulation of Continental Shelf Development: Rethinking International Standards* (Brill, Leiden, 2013).

54 Cmnd 4205 (1969); Cmnd 8942 (1983).

55 Barcelona, 16 February 1976, in force 12 February 1978, 1102 *UNTS* 27, and (n 31). To date seven Protocols have been added to the Convention, addressed to integrated coastal management (2008), vessel-source pollution and emergency response (2002); hazardous waste (1996), pollution from continental shelf exploration and exploitation (1994), specially protected areas and biodiversity (1995), land-based pollution (1980), oil and other harmful substances in emergencies (1976), and dumping (1976). The Barcelona Convention has been viewed as a prototype for the other regional seas agreements concluded under UNEP's regional seas programme. See generally P. Sand, *Marine Environment Law in the United Nations Environment Programme: An Emergent Eco-Regime* (London, Tycooly Publishing, 1988); and R.R. Churchill and A.V. Lowe, *The Law of the Sea* (rev edn, Manchester, Manchester University Press, 1999), ch. 15.

Deepwater Horizon blow-out.[56] Article 12 and Annex VI of the 1992 Convention on the Protection of the Marine Environment of the Baltic Sea Area (Helsinki Convention) address prevention and elimination of pollution from seabed activities in the Baltic Sea area.[57] Amongst other things, Annex VI requires the application of best environmental practices (BEP) and best available techniques (BAT) to offshore activities, mandatory prior environmental impact assessment (EIA) and discharge criteria in the exploration and exploitation phases (regulations 4 and 5). As this Baltic example underscores, these additional regional arrangements can fill both substantive and procedural gaps in the implementation of the LOSC in the offshore energy sector.

Submarine Cables and Pipelines

A further example of the paucity of GAIRS external to the LOSC in the offshore energy context is with respect to submarine cables and pipelines, for which the LOSC provides only the general jurisdictional framework. There is no general treaty on the construction and use of pipelines at international law, whether onshore or offshore, nor is there a global treaty on submarine (power) cables.[58] With respect to the latter, in 2010 the UN Secretary-General's Report on the Oceans and the Law of the Sea specifically noted that some States had

---

56 The European Commission conducted a "gap analysis" of offshore practices and the EU legislative framework for offshore energy activities in response to Deepwater Horizon: see 'Facing the challenge of the safety of offshore oil and gas activities', COM(2010) 560 final, adopted 12 October 2010, OJ C/2011/121/54. This accession to the Offshore Protocol, combined with adoption of EU Directive 2013/30/EU on Safety of Offshore Oil and Gas Operations, OJ L 178, 20 June 2013, p. 66, and the establishment in 2012 by Commission Decision (OJ C 18, 21 January 2012, p. 8) of the European Union Offshore Oil and Gas Authorities Group, are intended to plug the identified gaps in risk reduction and emergency response in the sector.

57 Helsinki, 9 April 1992, in force 17 January 2000, 1507 *UNTS* 167.

58 See, generally, D.R. Burnett, 'Submarine Cables on the Continental Shelf' in Nordquist *et al.* (eds) (n 53); D.R. Burnett, R. Beckman and T.M. Davenport (eds), *Submarine Cables: The Handbook of Law and Policy* (Martinus Nijhoff Publishers, Leiden, 2014); D. Nelson, 'Submarine Cables and Pipelines' in R.-J. Dupuy and D. Vignes (eds), *A Handbook on the New Law of the Sea* (Martinus Nijhoff Publishers, Dordrecht, 1991) vol. 2, at p. 987; I.A. Siddiky, 'The international legal instruments for cross-border pipelines' in K. Talus (ed), *Research Handbook on International Energy Law* (Edward Elgar, Cheltenham, 2014) 308–328. For discussion of North Sea practice see, e.g.: M. M. Roggenkamp, 'Petroleum Pipelines in the North Sea: Questions of Jurisdiction and Practical Status' (1998) 16(1) *Journal of Energy and Natural Resources Law* 92–109; V. Roeben, 'Governing Shared Offshore Electricity Infrastructure in the Northern Seas' (2013) 62(4) *ICLQ* 839–864.

expressed the "need to consider gaps in the existing legal regime regarding submarine cables at the international and national levels, in particular in the implementation of article 113 [LOSC]" with the current legal regime viewed as inadequate to address "the operation of, and threats to, submarine cables." One solution suggested is development of "a code of best practices with regard to the laying and repair of submarine cables and the conduct of cable-routing surveys."[59]

For offshore pipelines the general jurisdictional—and marine environmental protection—rules of the LOSC are supplemented by any applicable *lex specialis* such as the Helsinki Convention, for example, which as noted above applies to the whole of the Baltic Sea Area, including the internal waters, territorial sea and EEZ of the nine littoral States. This is the regional sea through which a major submarine gas pipeline, the Nord Stream gas pipeline, transits five Baltic States from the point of departure (Russia) to landing (Germany) via the continental shelves of Finland, Sweden and Denmark.[60] Substantively this Convention applies, *inter alia*, to the prevention of dumping (defined as "deliberate disposal of... man-made structures at sea"), and to prevent pollution from exploration and exploitation of its part of the seabed and subsoil or "from any associated activities thereon." It also requires parties generally to prevent and eliminate pollution of the marine environment of the Baltic Sea Area caused by harmful substances from all sources (including hydrocarbons). It thus provides regional reinforcement, *inter alia*, both of the general marine environmental provisions of the LOSC and of the global prevention of dumping regulation of the 1972 London (Dumping) Convention (as amended).[61] However, what it does not provide is holistic regulation of the

59 Report of the Secretary-General, *Oceans and the law of the sea*, A/65/69, 29 March 2010, para. 71. Available at http://daccess-dds-ny.un.org/doc/UNDOC/GEN/N10/296/54/PDF/N1029654.pdf?OpenElement; accessed 18 August 2014.

60 See E. Zolfagharifard, 'Nord Stream: the world's largest gas pipeline', *The Engineer* 4 May 2010, available at http://www.theengineer.co.uk; accessed 18 August 2014; N. Cho and F. Geelhoed, 'The Nord Stream Pipeline Project—A Brief Overview of its Legal and European Relevance for Supply Security' in M.M. Roggenkamp and U. Hammer (eds), *European Energy Law Report VI*, (Intersentia, Mortsel/Cambridge, 2009) 227–247; and C. Redgwell, 'Contractual and Treaty Arrangements Supporting Large European Transboundary Pipeline Projects: Can Adequate Human Rights and Environmental Protection Be Secured?' in M. Roggenkamp, L. Barrera-Hernandez, D. Zillman and I. del Guayo (eds), *Energy Networks and the Law: Innovative Solutions in Changing Markets* (Oxford University Press, Oxford, 2012) 102–117.

61 The 1996 Protocol to the Convention on the Prevention of Marine Pollution by Dumping of Wastes and Other Matter (36 *ILM* 1 (1997)) was concluded 8 November 1996 and entered

construction, operation and decommissioning of pipelines traversing the continental shelves of the Baltic littoral States but not directly connected or associated with the exploration and exploitation of the offshore energy resources there. Consequently the pipeline is regulated by a mix of national and regional rules and contractual arrangements.

Shipping

GAIRS are more evident in the general shipping context where the LOSC qualifies the power of States to legislate on such matters by reference to international standards.[62] With the extension of coastal State sovereign rights over the EEZ, the jurisdiction exercisable there over environmental matters in particular is explicitly linked with GAIRS "established through the competent international organization or general diplomatic conference."[63] Although not explicitly stated as such, this is a "no more stringent than" requirement of conformity with such GAIRS.[64] As Attard notes, this linkage arose at UNCLOS III because of concerns by maritime States that the proliferation of national EEZ standards would endanger the freedom of shipping.[65] The IMO also has an "approval" role with respect to vessel routeing, safety zones around offshore installations, strait States regulation of navigation in international straits, and in mandatory measures to prevent vessel-source pollution in designated areas of the EEZ.[66]

into force on 24 March 2006. It replaces the 1972 Convention (London, 29 December 1972, in force 30 August 1975, 1046 *ILM* 120) where States are party to both instruments.

62 There are numerous references, including Article 21(2) (no coastal State laws and regulations on the design, construction, manning or equipment of foreign ships unless giving effect to GAIRS) and Article 94(5) (a flag State's regulations must "conform to generally accepted international standards, procedures and practices").

63 Article 211(5); see generally, E.J. Molenaar, *Coastal State Jurisdiction over Vessel-Source Pollution* (Kluwer Law International, The Hague, 1998), at pp. 140–167.

64 E.J. Molenaar, 'Options for Regional Regulation of Merchant Shipping Outside IMO, with Particular Reference to the Arctic Region' (2014) 45(2) *ODIL* 272–298, at p. 274.

65 Attard (n 12), at p. 95. See also Tan (n 20), at p. 199, who notes that "the OPEC-imposed embargo also convinced the oil companies and developed States of the utmost necessity to curb future coastal State interference with oil tanker movements."

66 Examples include Article 22(3)(a) ("recommendations of the competent international organisation" in the designation of sea lanes and traffic separation schemes for e.g. tankers); Article 60(5) (breadth of safety zones taking into account applicable international standards); Article 41(4) (sea lanes and traffic separation schemes in straits) and in similar terms Article 53(9) (archipelagic sea lanes); and Article 211(6)(a) (special mandatory measures for vessel-source marine pollution in designated areas of the EEZ). On the approval role of the IMO, see further Harrison (n 3), pp. 179–190.

Quite apart from the reality of regional and international marine environmental regulation taking place outside the LOSC, a pragmatic consideration also militated in favour of the "taking account of," "no less effective than" approach contained in the specific pollution source articles of Part XII. This is the necessity for regular review, updating and amendment of marine pollution rules and standards to keep pace with changes in scientific and other knowledge of the marine environment. This is accomplished under MARPOL 73/78 by the use of annexes which are subject to the tacit acceptance amendment procedure.[67] The 1992 OSPAR Convention, with its annexes and appendices, is a further excellent example of flexible methods of treaty change and adaptation being deployed.[68]

The LOSC and Other Conventions and International Agreements

Another way in which external rules are referenced in the LOSC is in provisions addressed to its relationship with other conventions and international agreements.[69] As Harrison rightly observes, "[t]he Convention itself expressly foresees that States Parties will continue to regulate their relations through subsequent treaties."[70] The negotiation and conclusion of the LOSC did not take place in a vacuum, but rather against the backdrop of existing,[71] and continuing, concerns to regulate the environmental consequences of energy activities at sea. This is expressly recognised in Article 237 LOSC, which provides that Part XII is without prejudice to the specific obligations previously assumed under "special conventions and agreements" relating to the protection and

67 See (n 26).

68 For further discussion of the legal implications of such flexible amendment procedures under OSPAR, see L. de La Fayette, 'The OSPAR Convention Comes into Force: Continuity and Progress' (1999) 14(2) *IJMCL* 247–297.

69 Article 237 (marine environment) and Article 311 (general).

70 Harrison (n 3), at p. 85.

71 Such as the 1954 International Convention for the Prevention of Pollution of the Sea by Oil (OILPOL), London, 12 May 1954, in force 26 July 1958, 327 *UNTS* 3; the 1969 International Convention on Civil Liability for Oil Pollution Damage, Brussels, 29 November 1969, in force 19 June 1975, 973 *UNTS* 319; the 1969 International Convention Relating to Intervention on the High Seas in Cases of Oil Pollution Damage, Brussels, 29 November 1969, in force 6 May 1975, 970 *UNTS* 212; the 1971 Convention on the Establishment of an International Fund for Compensation for Oil Pollution Damage, Brussels, 18 December 1971, in force 16 October 1978, 11 *ILM* 284; and the 1972 London Convention on the Prevention of Marine Pollution by the Dumping of Wastes and other Matter, (n 61).

preservation of the marine environment, nor to subsequent agreements which are concluded in furtherance of the general principles of the LOSC. It further provides an obligation of consistency or "integrity," that is to say, that the obligations assumed under these special agreements must be carried out in a manner consistent with the general principles and objectives of the LOSC. In similar terms, Article 311 addresses the general relationship of the LOSC with other conventions and international agreements, with special protection for the common heritage of mankind principle in Article 136.

This saving of existing and future regulatory activity is not surprising, particularly if it is recalled that a major theme of the 1972 Stockholm Conference on the Human Environment[72] was the protection of the marine environment from pollution in particular, and that this sparked regional and global regulation pre- and post-Stockholm, just as UNCLOS III was getting underway. The 1972 Oslo[73] and London[74] Conventions addressed to prevention of dumping at sea at the regional and global levels, and MARPOL 73/78 on vessel-source marine pollution, illustrate the point. This was of course in the era of high-profile oil tanker spills and the generation of rules to address liability,[75] as well as standards for shipping. The former have developed outside of the LOSC, a reflection of the limited consideration within it both of liability and responsibility issues, and more generally of the significant role played by non-State actors[76] in the offshore energy sector.

---

72 The first United Nations Conference on the Human Environment, convened by UNGA Resolution 2398 (XXIII) 1968. It produced "the Stockholm Declaration" of environmental principles and an Action Plan. For analysis see L.B. Sohn, 'The Stockholm Declaration on the Human Environment' (1973) 14 *Harvard International Law Journal* 423–515.

73 The 1972 Oslo Convention for the Prevention of Marine Pollution by Dumping from Ships and Aircraft, Oslo, 15 February 1972, in force 7 April 1974, 932 *UNTS* 3. The Oslo and Paris (1974 Paris Convention for the Prevention of Marine Pollution by Land-Based Sources, Paris, 4 June 1974, in force 6 May 1978, 13 *ILM* 352 (1974)) Conventions were replaced by the 1992 Convention for the Protection of the Marine Environment of the North-East Atlantic (OSPAR, Article 31), (n 35).

74 The 1972 London Convention on the Prevention of Marine Pollution by Dumping of Wastes and Other Matter, (n 61).

75 See (n 71).

76 Indeed, Talus defines "international energy law" by reference primarily to the internationalization of energy markets and operations carried out principally by non-state actors: K. Talus, 'Internationalization of energy law' in Talus (n 58) 3–17, at p. 5. See also in this volume, the contributions by A. Bonfanti and F. Romanin Jacur, 'Energy from the Sea and the Protection of the Marine Environment: Treaty-Based Regimes and Ocean Corporate Social Responsibility'; and S. Trevisanut, 'The Role of Private Actors in the Offshore Energy: Shifting Models of Participation'.

The Function of GAIRS

One of the functions of GAIRS is therefore to harmonise the LOSC with existing instruments and replace the (generally unsatisfactory) *lex generalis* with explicit treaty rules (*lex specialis*) on the treaty relationship.[77] International trade and commerce is also facilitated by harmonisation of international standards (e.g., Articles 21(2) and 211(1) LOSC) and prevention of the undesirable proliferation of national standards. Of course such a restriction upon unilateral coastal State laws and regulations requires that international standards are adequate and appropriate, and that there is a degree of confidence in the fora for norm promulgation.[78]

A further function is to ensure the continued vitality of the LOSC without the need to go through the cumbersome and politically difficult process of treaty amendment. As Harrison notes, GAIRS "creates a degree of dynamism, as the standards may change over time, without having to amend the Law of the Sea Convention."[79] And not only the vitality, but also the integrity of the LOSC is safeguarded by ensuring the consistency of external norms with the LOSC as the "constitution for the oceans"[80] and the development of a "universal law of the sea."[81] Gap-filling is a related function given that certain technical developments could not have been foreseen, such as the extent of offshore renewables development and the need for related transmission infrastructure, the use of depleted offshore reservoirs for storage of CO_2 (carbon capture and

77 See further Boyle (n 29).

78 For example, Tan notes that contemporary discourse in the IMO takes place between flag State/commercial shipping interests resisting increasing regulation on the one hand, and coastal/environmental interests seeking greater control over polluting vessels on the other: Tan (n 20), at p. 102.

79 Harrison (n 3), at p. 171, citing L. Sohn, 'Implications of the Law of the Sea Convention regarding the protection of the marine environment' in R.B. Krueger and S.A. Reisenfeld (eds), *The Developing Order of the Oceans* (Law of the Sea Institute, Honolulu, 1985), at p. 109. Indeed, as Douay notes, the direct incorporation of technical rules and standards into the LOSC was discarded from the outset of the negotiations: C. Douay, 'Le droit de la mer et la préservation du milieu marin' in D. Bardonnet and M. Virally (eds), *Le nouveau droit de la mer* (Editions A. Pédone, Paris, 1983) 231–267, at p. 248.

80 Tommy T.B. Koh of Singapore (President of UNCLOS III), 'A constitution for the oceans', available at http://www.un.org/depts/los/convention_agreements/texts/koh_english.pdf; accessed 18 August 2014.

81 Harrison (n 3), at p. 279. However, as GAIRS themselves demonstrate, there may be considerable variation from the general framework of the LOSC—see for example the regional rules on decommissioning noted above—within the broad limits of compatibility required by Article 311 (relation to other conventions and international agreements).

storage (CCS)), and the exploitation of methane hydrates.[82] Nor does the LOSC fully take account of procedural requirements linked to participatory rights of citizens, such as EIA and access to justice. It does, however, require "that the risks or effects of pollution of the marine environment be observed, measured, evaluated and analysed by recognized scientific methods, as well as requiring the publication of reports of the results obtained" but is reliant on the articulation by other global fora of "practical guidance for the implementation of environmental impact assessments at the global level."[83] One example of internal guidance is the adoption by the Legal and Technical Commission of the International Seabed Authority of recommendations for the guidance of contractors for the assessment of the possible environmental impact assessments arising from exploration for marine minerals in the Area.[84] Externally there is the general application to offshore energy activities of the regional 1991 Espoo Convention on Environmental Impact Assessment in a Transboundary Context.[85] For example, it played an important harmonizing role with respect to the five national legal systems applicable to parts of the Nord Stream gas pipeline project in the Baltic, a marine region of particular environmental sensitivity and thus where consideration of the environmental impact of the construction, operation and decommissioning of the pipeline was a major element of the project.[86]

82 See further C. Redgwell and L. Rajamani, 'Energy Underground: What's International Law Got to Do with It?' in D.N. Zillman, A. McHarg, L. Barrera-Hernandez and A. Bradbrook (eds), *The Law of Energy Underground: Understanding New Developments in Subsurface Production, Transmission, and Storage* (Oxford University Press, Oxford, 2014) 101–123.

83 Report of the Secretary-General, *Oceans and the Law of the Sea*, UN Doc A/68/71 (2013), at para. 70.

84 ISA Legal and Technical Commission, *Recommendations for the guidance of contractors for the assessment of the possible environmental impacts arising from exploration for marine minerals in the Area*, Doc ISBA/19/LTC/8, 1 March 2013. Available at http://www.isa.org.jm; accessed 18 August 2014.

85 Espoo, 25 February 1991, in force 10 September 1997, 1989 *UNTS* 309.

86 See further discussion in Redgwell (n 60); and T. Koivurova and I. Polonen, 'Transboundary Environmental Assessment in the Case of the Baltic Sea Gas Pipeline' (2010) 25 *IJMCL* 151–181.

Conclusion

The LOSC was never intended to be a "one stop shop" for the regulation of all offshore energy activities, but rather to set forth fundamental rules and principles of enduring application functioning alongside more specific global and regional rules and standards. The role of other instruments has been one of facilitating, strengthening and updating the LOSC in the light of legal and technical developments since its conclusion. Nonetheless some significant gaps may be identified, in particular with respect to energy activities which have more fully emerged since the conclusion of the LOSC. One is the growth of transboundary cooperation with respect to the transmission of electricity generated offshore via interconnectors, adding to the considerable cooperation already in place with respect to the more conventional transboundary petroleum pipelines.[87] As noted above, there is no general treaty on submarine (power) cables, so it falls to the general provisions of the LOSC—and bespoke arrangements—for regulation.

Major blow-outs in the Timor Sea (Montara, 2009) and Gulf of Mexico (Deep Water Horizon, 2011) have focused renewed attention on the international regulatory gap with respect to pollution from offshore installations, but with little impact on international regulation.[88] This may be contrasted with vessel-source petroleum pollution which has been heavily regulated owing to the high visibility, and often high impact locally and transnationally, of oil tanker spills in particular. The regulation of offshore installations, on the other hand, continues (with the exception of the Offshore Protocol to the regional Barcelona Convention)[89] to be a notable gap in the international regulation of offshore energy activities, and in the scope of the LOSC itself.[90] Indeed, a 2008 UN Secretariat study prophetically called for further regional

87 See O. Woolley, P.J. Schaumberg and G. St. Michel, 'Establishing an Offshore Electricity Grid: A Legal Analysis of Grid Developments in the North Sea and in US Waters' in Roggenkamp *et al.* (eds) (n 60), at pp. 183–190 (gaps in LOSC legal framework); see also (n 58).

88 While most of the attention has been focused on liability and compensation for oil pollution damage from ships, the IMO is currently considering issues related to liability and compensation for transboundary pollution damage resulting from offshore oil exploration and exploitation activities. See further http://www.imo.org; accessed 18 August 2014.

89 See (n 31).

90 The absence of an international agreement addressed to the operational aspects of continental shelf activity is part of the 'unfinished business' of the LOSC: B. Flemming, 'Completing the Unfinished Business of UNCLOS III' in Nordquist *et al.* (eds) (n 53),

measures to address pollution from offshore installations, and the involvement of the oil and gas industry in BEP guidelines with respect to pollution from accidents on offshore installations.[91] Perhaps paradoxically, detailed global regulations[92] are now in place to regulate deep seabed mining, including its environmental impacts,[93] despite its nascent form. As new areas for petroleum exploration are opening up in fragile ecosystems such as the Arctic, these regulatory gaps may become all the more pressing.[94] Energy efficiency and international regulation of renewable energy are also attracting increasing international attention, as a reflection of the growing quest to decarbonize in pursuit of a sustainable energy future.[95] Last but not least,

---

pp. 355–58; and J.N. Moore, 'Comments on the Unfinished Business of UNCLOS III' in *ibid.*, pp. 359–368.

91 Oceans and the law of the sea, *Available assistance to and measures that may be taken by developing States, in particular the least developing States and small island developing States, as well as coastal African States, to realize the benefits of sustainable and effective development of marine resources and uses of the oceans within the limits of national jurisdiction*, UN Doc A/63/342, 3 September 2008, paras. D (a) and (b). Available at http://www.un.org; accessed 18 August 2014.

92 Regulations on Prospecting and Exploration for Polymetallic Nodules in the Area, ISBA/6/A/18, 4 October 2000; Regulations on Prospecting and Exploration for Polymetallic Sulphides in the Area, ISBA/16/A/12/Rev.1, 7 May 2010; and Regulations on Prospecting and Exploration for Cobalt-rich Ferromanganese Crusts in the Area, ISBA/18/A/11, 22 October 2012. See also (n 84).

93 Article 145 of the LOSC requires the ISA to adopt rules and regulations for the protection of the environment and the adequacy of these regulations for this purpose was considered by the Seabed Disputes Chamber of the ITLOS in an Advisory Opinion on the *Responsibilities and Obligations of States Sponsoring Persons and Entities with Respect to Activities in the Area.* Available at http://www.itlos.org; accessed 18 August 2014. For detailed comment see D. French, 'From the Depths: Rich Pickings of Principles of Sustainable Development and General International Law on the Ocean Floor—the Seabed Disputes Chamber's 2011 Advisory Opinion' (2011) 26 *IJMCL* 525–568.

94 Increasing attention is paid to offshore oil and gas activities by the Arctic Council. In 2013 the Arctic States adopted under the Council's auspices the Agreement on Cooperation on Marine Oil Pollution Preparedness and Response in the Arctic, and in March 2014 promulgated the 'Arctic Oil and Gas Guidelines on Systems Safety Management and Safety Culture', available at http://www.arctic-council.org; accessed 18 August 2014. The IMO is also developing a 'Mandatory Code for Ships Operating in Polar Waters', expected to be agreed by the end of 2014: see further http://www.imo.org; accessed 18 August 2014.

95 On gaps in international regulation, particularly of marine renewables development beyond national jurisdiction, with the LOSC performing a general framework role, see M.A. Castelos, 'Marine Renewable Energies: Opportunities, Law, and Management' (2014) 45(2) *ODIL* 221–237.

beyond the substantive regulation of new energy sources and activities, procedural tools such as BAT, BEP and EIA, so familiar in the context of large energy infrastructure activities, have developed largely externally to the LOSC, although key in its effective implementation to ensure, *inter alia*, the protection and preservation of the marine environment.

CHAPTER 3

Energy from the Sea and the Protection of the Marine Environment: Treaty-Based Regimes and Ocean Corporate Social Responsibility

Angelica Bonfanti and Francesca Romanin Jacur
Senior Research Fellows, Faculty of Law, University of Milan, Milan, Italy

Abstract

This chapter addresses treaty-based regimes and the so-called Ocean Corporate Social Responsibility (OCSR) that are relevant to marine environmental protection and energy activities. In this context, special attention is paid to the interactions among the legal regimes in which the environmental and safety rules and standards are adopted and to the effects of the regulatory technique of "legislation by reference". After examining the relevant obligations of States within the framework of the UN Convention on the Law of the Sea and the International Maritime Organization, the authors analyse OCSR, especially its preventive, damage mitigation and compensatory functions and its potential synergies with the treaty-based regimes.

Keywords

energy – marine environment – corporate social responsibility – law of the sea

* This chapter is the result of joint efforts and discussions by the authors, who wrote the Introduction and the Conclusion together. Angelica Bonfanti is the author of the section entitled "The Protection of the Marine Environment from Ocean Energy-related Activities through OCSR" and its sub-sections; and of the sub-sections entitled "Mitigating Damage through OCSR" and "Mitigating Damage and Compensating Losses through Contractual Schemes". Francesca Romanin Jacur has written the section entitled "The Protection of the Marine Environment from Ocean Energy-related Activities under the LOSC and IMO" and its sub-sections; and the sub-section "Compensating Losses through Civil Liability Treaty-based Regimes."

 | DOI 10.1163/9789004303522_005

Introduction

A great variety of energy-related activities is carried out at sea. First, one may think of the exploitation of traditional energy sources (such as oil, gas and minerals) and second, of the renewable energy sources (such as wind, solar, tidal and wave). The growing demand for energy sources, on the one hand, and the advanced technologies in energy extraction,[1] on the other, are elements that significantly affect the relationship between energy exploitation and the protection of the marine environment. Renewable energy from the sea[2] can as well entail potential adverse environmental effects.[3]

Besides the type of energy source, several activities that are part of the energy chain may have significant impacts on the marine environment. These include energy production (extracting oil, gas or other raw materials from or below the seabed), transformation (refinement of the extracted raw materials, production of energy from waves and tides), and transportation at sea by vessels (nuclear energy ships or oil cargoes).

Many of these activities are generally conducted by private operators. Important players in the ocean energy scene are: the owners of the infrastructure or vessels carrying out the energy activities, their charterers, the companies in charge of their technical management, the classification societies who certify the technical and safety standards of oil platforms and the seaworthiness of vessels, and the shipyards in charge of building and repairing the energy

---

1 S. Schackelford, 'Was Selden Right?: The Expansion of Closed Seas and its Consequences' (2011) 47 *Stanford Journal of International Law* 1–50, at p. 14.

2 M. Esteban and D. Leary, 'Current Developments and Future Prospects of Offshore Wind and Ocean Energy' (2012) 90(1) *Journal of Applied Energy* 128–136; T.J. Griset, 'Harnessing the Ocean's Power: Opportunities in Renewable Ocean Energy Resources' (2010) 16(2) *Ocean and Costal Law Journal* 395–434; D. Leary and M. Esteban, 'Recent Developments in Offshore Renewable Energy in Asia-Pacific Region' (2011) 42(1) *Ocean Development and International Law* 95–119.

3 According to the US Department of Energy potential negative impacts can consist of "alteration of currents and waves; alteration of substrates and sediment transport and deposition; alteration of habitats for benthic organisms; noise during construction and operation; emission of electromagnetic fields; toxicity of paints, lubricants, and rotors and other moving parts [...] effects on biological resources could include alteration of the behaviour of animals, damage and mortality to individual plants, and potentially larger, longer-term changes to plant and animals population and communities". US Department of Energy, Report to the Congress: Potential Environmental Effects of Marine and Hydrokinetic Energy Technologies, 2008, quoted in D. Leary and M. Esteban, 'Climate Change and Renewable Energy from the Ocean and Tides: Calming the Sea of Regulatory Uncertainty' (2009) 4(4) *The International Journal of Marine and Coastal Law* (*IJMCL*) 617–651, at p. 645.

facilities and ships. Thus, in addition to the law applicable to and adopted by States, the rules adopted by these non-state actors should be considered.

This chapter addresses the treaty-based regimes and the so-called Ocean Corporate Social Responsibility (OCSR) concepts that are relevant to marine environmental protection from energy-related activities. In this context, special attention is paid to the interactions among the legal regimes in which the environmental and safety rules and standards are adopted, and to the effects of the regulatory technique known as "legislation by reference".

The first part examines some of the relevant obligations of States adopted within the framework of the United Nations Convention on the Law of the Sea (LOSC)[4] and of the International Maritime Organization (IMO). The second examines OCSR, especially its preventive function, its legal status and its relationship with the LOSC-based obligations. The third part analyses the legal tools available to compensate losses arising from environmental disasters. In this context, in addition to the civil liability treaty-based regimes, OCSR initiatives and out-of-court settlements are considered. From the examination of these instruments and practices the authors conclude that interactions and potential synergies exist across the different legal regimes.

The Protection of the Marine Environment from Ocean Energy-Related Activities under the LOSC and IMO

Energy activities at sea are required to comply with the obligations to protect the marine environment as provided for by the LOSC, by regional treaties,[5] and by other multilateral agreements which mainly address marine pollution in general, but which also apply to energy-related operations at sea. This section examines LOSC provisions and focuses on the regulatory technique used by the LOSC to further elaborate and implement its environmental obligations through repeated references to more specific treaties, mainly adopted under the IMO regime.

The General Framework of the LOSC

The general legal framework for the protection of the marine environment is provided by Part XII of the LOSC. Section I places the general obligations upon

4 United Nations Convention on the Law of the Sea (Montego Bay, 10 December 1982, in force 16 November 1994) 1833 *UNTS* 396.

5 Many regional arrangements and binding Conventions have been adopted in the context of the Regional Seas Programme coordinated by the United Nations Environment Programme (UNEP). (http://www.unep.org/regionalseas).

States to prevent, reduce and control marine environmental pollution from all sources.[6] The LOSC adopts a comprehensive approach to the definition of pollution, expressly including any substance or energy which may directly or indirectly be introduced into the sea.[7] Likewise, with regard to its spatial scope, State obligations to protect the marine environment extend beyond the zones falling within their jurisdiction and include the high seas and the deep seabed beyond national jurisdiction (the Area).

The LOSC strongly encourages States to further develop their environmental protection commitments through global and regional cooperation. In this vein, LOSC Art. 197 requires States to

> ... cooperate [...] directly or *through competent international organizations* in formulating and elaborating *international rules, standards and recommended practices and procedures* [. . .] consistent with this Convention for the protection and preservation of the marine environment [...].[8]

This provision lays the basis for the interaction between the LOSC, as the overarching Convention, and treaties entrusted with the adoption of specific rules. This regime interaction is not merely left to the generic duty of States to cooperate but is strengthened by several references to rules and standards that States have adopted—or may adopt in the future—in the framework of these specialized treaties.

Particularly relevant to environmental protection are the "normative links" found in Section 5 of Part XII. This section envisages obligations upon States to adopt national legislation and international rules, "acting especially through competent international organizations" to prevent, reduce and control the pollution of the marine environment by different sources: land-based activities, seabed activities, activities in the Area, dumping and vessels. According to these provisions, the national laws should "take into account",[9] "be no less effective",[10] "at least have the same effect as"[11] or "conform to and give effect

---

6 LOSC, Art. 194(3) lists, *inter alia*, land-based facilities, vessels and installations used for the exploitation of natural resources in the subsoil.

7 LOSC, Art. 1(1)(4).

8 LOSC, Art. 197, emphasis added.

9 LOSC, Art. 207(1) and Art. 212(1).

10 LOSC, Art. 208(3) and Art. 210(6).

11 LOSC, Art. 211(2).

to"[12] "internationally agreed rules, standards and recommended practices and procedures".

The obligations to adopt international and national regulations are strengthened by Section 6 which—mirroring the provisions envisaged in Section 5—requires States to enforce these laws and regulations, and to "take other measures necessary to implement applicable international rules and standards established through competent international organizations" to prevent, reduce and control pollution from all sources.[13]

Besides Part XII, other LOSC provisions are relevant to energy-related activities at sea. Thus, for example, with regard to energy-related activities carried out in its territorial sea, the coastal State may adopt laws relating to innocent passage with respect to "the preservation of the environment of the coastal State and the prevention, reduction and control of pollution thereof,"[14] and may confine the passage of ships to designated sea lanes.[15]

Coastal States have become particularly sensitive with regard to whether nuclear-powered ships or ships carrying nuclear waste should enjoy full rights of passage through their territorial seas. In this context the risk of severe pollution to the marine environment may be characterized as a maritime security threat and therefore constitute a legitimate ground to deny the right of innocent passage.[16] In this regard LOSC Art. 23 provides that these ships "shall, when exercising the right of innocent passage through the territorial sea, carry documents and observe special precautionary measures established for such ships by international agreements." Particularly relevant to this *renvoi* are the MARPOL Convention[17] and the SOLAS Convention.[18]

Another energy sector in which the LOSC may play an increasingly important role is seabed mining. Although seabed mining in areas beyond national jurisdiction has not yet substantively developed, this might be happening soon,

12 LOSC, Art. 211(5).

13 LOSC, Arts. 213 and 214.

14 LOSC, Art. 21(1)(f).

15 LOSC, Art. 22(2).

16 This issue was already extensively debated at UNCLOS III because coastal states considered these ships as a threat to their marine environment. N. Klein, *Maritime Security and the Law of the Sea* (Oxford University Press, Oxford, 2011) at p. 318. On vessel-source marine pollution see E.J. Molenaar, *Coastal State Jurisdiction over Vessel-Source Pollution* (Kluwer Law International, The Hague, 1998).

17 International Convention for the Prevention of Pollution from Ships (London, 2 November 1973, amended by the 1978 Protocol (London, 1 June 1978) 1340 *UNTS* 184 (hereinafter MARPOL Convention).

18 International Convention for the Safety of Life at Sea (SOLAS) (London, 1 November 1974, in force 25 May 1980) 1980 *UKTS* 46.

in view of the technological advancements in extraction techniques. According to the LOSC, States Parties and international organizations have the responsibility to ensure that seabed activities in the Area performed by them directly or by persons acting under their sponsorship comply with the relevant LOSC provisions.[19] Further delineating the scope of a State's liability, the LOSC provides that the State will not be held liable for damage if it has adopted appropriate regulatory measures to ensure compliance by persons under its jurisdiction and nonetheless the sponsored entity fails to respect its obligations.[20]

The Development of Specific Rules under the Auspices of the IMO

The IMO is commonly recognized as one of the "competent international organizations" to which many LOSC provisions delegate law-making on various technical matters, *inter alia*, those related to marine environmental protection.[21] The IMO supports the negotiation and provides Secretariat functions for several treaties dealing with oil pollution from ships, civil liability and compensation for damages deriving from oil pollution from vessels and emergency responses in case of incidents. In addition, the IMO regularly adopts non-binding codes, recommendations and guidelines. Although non-legally binding, these latter regulatory instruments serve as interpretive tools, supplement and provide guidance for the effective implementation of binding provisions. These technical standards are formally addressed to States who are responsible for their implementation into national legislation. However, in practice, these standards mainly regulate activities of private operators at sea and ultimately require specific behaviours and compliance from those operators.

19 LOSC, Art. 139(1). Pursuant to the *Regulations on prospecting and exploration for polymetallic sulphides in the Area*, which set standard clauses for exploration contracts: "The Contractor shall take necessary measures to prevent, reduce and control pollution and other hazards to the marine environment arising from its activities in the Area as far as reasonably possible applying a precautionary approach and best environmental practices." International Seabed Authority, *Decision of the Assembly of the International Seabed Authority relating to the regulations on prospecting and exploration for polymetallic sulphides in the Area*, ISBA/16/A/12/Rev.1 (15 November 2010) Annex, Section 5.1. As noted by the Seabed Dispute Chamber of the International Tribunal for the Law of the Sea (ITLOS) in its Advisory Opinion, through this reference the precautionary approach becomes a contractual obligation. (Seabed Dispute Chamber, ITLOS, *Responsibilities and Obligations of States Sponsoring Persons and Entities with Respect to Activities in the Area*, Advisory Opinion, ITLOS Case no. 17, 1 February 2011, para. 133).

20 LOSC, Annex III, Art. 4(4).

21 Study by the Secretariat of IMO, *Implications of the United Nations Convention on the Law of the Sea for the International Maritime Organization*, IMO Doc. LEG/MISC/1 of 28 July 1987.

Among them, for instance, are the *1989 IMO Guidelines and Standards for removal of offshore installations.*[22] These Guidelines are mainly concerned with the case-by-case evaluation of decisions to remove offshore facilities, as well as standard setting and the detailed requirements to be met when carrying out the operation.[23] Another relevant instrument is the IMO *Code for the construction and equipment of mobile offshore drilling units*,[24] which formally provides States with "design criteria, construction standards and other safety measures for mobile offshore drilling units so as to minimize the risk to such units, to the personnel and to the environment".

The MARPOL Convention is the most important treaty within the IMO regime addressing pollution from the operation or accidents of vessels at sea, with 150 States Parties representing 99% of the world's ship tonnage. MARPOL covers pollution deriving from the intentional and unintentional discharge of harmful substances, notably oil.[25] In order to prevent accidents and oil spills, MARPOL has adopted detailed provisions on the design and operation of vessels, as well as on emissions standards.

In the context of the IMO's recent engagement in enhancing sustainable maritime transportation, particularly noteworthy is the *Amendment to MARPOL Annex VI*.[26] These provisions "intend to improve energy efficiency for ships through a set of technical performance standards, which would result in reduction of emissions of any substances that originate from fuel oil and its combustion process [...]."[27] Especially significant is the express recognition that they apply also to "every fixed and floating drilling rig and other platforms".[28] This amendment introduces a series of surveys to be performed periodically on ships and platforms of a certain tonnage, and requires the outcomes of these surveys to be endorsed in appropriate certificates. These certificates are a precondition that must be met before the ship sails to ports or

22 IMO, *Guidelines and standards for the removal of offshore installations and structures on the continental shelf and in the exclusive economic zone*, Res. A.672(16), 19 October 1989. Hereinafter "*1989 IMO Guidelines and Standards for removal of offshore installations*".

23 E.D. Brown, *Sea-Bed Energy and Minerals: The International Legal Regime* (Martinus Nijhoff Publisher, Dordrecht, 1992), at pp. 385–386.

24 IMO, *Code for the Construction and Equipment of Mobile Offshore Drilling Units*, consolidated edition, 2001. Hereinafter "*IMO Code*".

25 MARPOL (n 18) Art. 2(3).

26 *Amendment to MARPOL Annex VI on Regulation for the Prevention of Air Pollution from Ships by Inclusion of New Regulations on Energy Efficiency for Ships* (hereinafter "*Amendment to MARPOL Annex VI*"), Res. MEPC. 203(62), Doc. MEPC 62/24/Add/1, adopted on 15 July 2011, in force 1 January 2013.

27 *Ibid.*, Preamble.

28 *Ibid.*, Annex, Chapter 2, Regulation 5(4).

offshore terminals under the jurisdiction of other Parties.[29] The *Amendment to MARPOL Annex VI* is complemented by a series of IMO Resolutions (hereinafter "the *IMO Energy Efficiency Resolutions*"),[30] which provide additional information and requirements for its implementation. As further examined below, these Resolutions, albeit formally addressed to States, in practice indicate standards to be complied with by ship operators.

The Circulation of Standards across Regimes between the LOSC and MARPOL

Environmental and safety standards relating to ocean energy-related activities circulate and influence legal regimes in different ways. A first way can be characterized as a formal *renvoi* and occurs when standards adopted within one regime are incorporated in the more general provisions of another. This occurs when the LOSC refers to more detailed rules and standards adopted by the competent international organizations.[31] A second rather informal way is that of cross-fertilization, which occurs when legal and technical developments within one regime influence the content or interpretation of similar rules in other regimes, or act as a stimulus for their adoption.[32]

By virtue of this regulatory technique, referred to as "legislation by reference" or "incorporation by reference",[33] the "texture" of the LOSC opens to include legal and technical developments occurring within other regulatory

29 *Ibid.*, Regulation 6(12).

30 IMO, *2012 Guidelines on the method of calculation of the attained energy efficiency design index (EEDI) for new ships*, Resolution MEPC.212(63), MEPC 63/23, 2 March 2012; IMO, *Guidelines for the Development of a Ship Energy Efficiency Management Plan (SEEMP)*, Resolution MEPC 212(63), 2 March 2012; IMO, *2012 Guidelines on survey and certification of the energy efficiency design index (EEDI)*, Resolution MEPC.214(63), 2 March 2012; IMO, *Guidelines for calculation of reference lines for use with the energy efficiency design index (EEDI)*, MEPC 63/23/Add.1, Res. MEPC.215(63), 2 March 2012.

31 S. Trevisanut, 'La Convention des Nations Unies sur le droit de la mer et le droit de l'environnement: développement intrasystémique et renvoi intersystemique', in H. Ruiz Fabri and L. Gradoni (eds), *La circulation des concepts juridiques: le droit international de l'environnemnt entre mondialisation et fragmentation* (Société de législation comparée, Paris, 2009) 397–426.

32 J. Morrison and N. Roht-Arriaza, 'Private and Quasi-Private Standard Setting', in D. Bodansky, J. Brunnée and E. Hey (eds), *The Oxford Handbook of International Environmental Law* (Oxford University Press, Oxford, 2007) 499–527, at p. 521.

33 C. Chinkin and A. Boyle, *The Making of International Law* (Oxford University Press, Oxford, 2007) at p. 247.

regimes that have "lighter" decision-making processes.[34] Rules and standards circulate across regimes and allow the LOSC to adapt to changing circumstances, such as new environmental challenges, technological progress and the related legal side-effects, without needing to engage in formal amendment of the LOSC itself.[35]

These rules and standards thereby become the legal parameters that States must transpose into their national legislation and that thereby apply to energy operators in conducting their activities. As States generally prescribe and enforce national legislation in accordance with these international rules and standards, their circulation contributes to the harmonization of national laws and regulations.

In order to be eligible for incorporation into the LOSC, rules and standards must meet the requirement of being "generally accepted". The LOSC does not provide any guidance on the meaning of this concept and therefore its interpretation is left to subsequent State practice or to judicial interpretation in the case of a dispute on the matter.[36] As MARPOL enjoys almost global participation, rules and standards adopted within this regime commonly meet the test of being "generally accepted standards," in the terms of several LOSC's provisions.[37] However, it is necessary to ascertain whether and to what extent annexes adopted within the MARPOL regime have been ratified by the Parties.

As an example of the practical implications of the "incorporation by reference," consider the amendments to MARPOL requiring double hulls on oil tankers.[38] To ensure marine environmental protection and safety, certain States recognized a limited right of passage within their EEZ to ships that did not comply with MARPOL's double-hull requirements. In response, some shipping bodies claimed that such limitations were in violation of the LOSC,

34 Pursuant to the tacit amendment procedures under many IMO Conventions, amendments to annexes enter into force automatically after a certain period of time for all States Parties, except those that declare their intention to opt out. F. Romanin Jacur, *The Dynamics of Multilateral Environmental Agreements* (Editoriale Scientifica, Napoli, 2013) at p. 85.

35 On this point, see D. Freestone and A.G. Oude Elferink, 'Flexibility and Innovation in the Law of the Sea—Will the LOS Convention Amendment Procedures Ever Be Used?', in A.G. Oude Elferink (ed), *Stability and Change in the Law of the Sea: The Role of the LOS Convention* (Martinus Nijhoff, Leiden, 2005) 169–221.

36 Molenaar (n 17), at p. 151.

37 See, for instance, LOSC, Arts. 211, 217 and 220.

38 See MARPOL, Annex I, Regulation 13F and Regulation 13G.

because they allegedly limited their freedom of navigation.[39] Relevant to this controversy is LOSC Art. 211 which provides that:

> Coastal States [...] may in respect of their exclusive economic zones adopt laws and regulations for the prevention, reduction and control of pollution from vessels *conforming to and giving effect to generally accepted international rules and standards established through the competent international organization* [...].[40]

In light of this provision, read *iuncto* with MARPOL rules, the coastal States' measures may be deemed to be consistent with the LOSC because—by being raised in Art. 211—they integrate and implement this LOSC provision.

This system of legislation by reference from the LOSC to MARPOL has far-reaching outcomes in terms of the scope of the rules and standards originally adopted within the MARPOL framework. Indeed, the LOSC functions as a "sounding board" for these treaty-based rules. A first effect is that, through their incorporation into the LOSC, they become applicable also to States Parties to the LOSC that are not Parties to MARPOL and who did not consent to be bound by them.[41] Through this same technique, they become applicable also to States Parties to MARPOL who may have objected to their adoption: even though these States are not legally bound under the MARPOL regime, they will eventually find themselves bound by MARPOL standards to the extent that they have been transposed into the LOSC legal regime.

The legal nature of these standards and rules and their "trips" across different regimes merit some reflection. When the rules and standards are set by an annex to the treaty, no doubt exists that (after the entry into force of the annex) they are legally binding. These provisions maintain the same legal value when they are incorporated by the LOSC. Standards established by non-binding instruments, such as MARPOL Resolutions, are a different case: could originally non-binding standards become legally binding by their incorporation into the

---

39 T. Scovazzi, 'The Evolution of International Law of the Sea: New Issues, New Challenges' (2000) 286 *Recueil des Cours* 39–243, at p. 228 notes that "the needs of navigation (...) have to be balanced with other interests (...) such as the protection of the marine environment (...)".

40 LOSC, Art. 211(5), emphasis added. In this same vein LOSC Art. 219 entitles a State to adopt administrative measures to prevent the vessel from sailing, if the latter is in violation of applicable international rules and standards relating to seaworthiness and therefore constitutes a threat to the marine environment.

41 Molenaar (n 17), at p. 157.

LOSC regime? Although scholars maintain different views on this matter,[42] we are of the opinion that when these rules meet the requirement of being "generally accepted" and are transposed into the LOSC provisions, they acquire the legal nature of the incorporating treaty provision and they become binding upon the LOSC Parties.[43]

The Protection of the Marine Environment from Ocean Energy-Related Activities through OCSR

Alongside States' international obligations described above, international law addresses business operators with recommendations and standards of conduct to be complied with when conducting their activities. The main business operators investing in marine energy are multinational corporations operating in the oil and gas and renewable energy fields, as well as their service suppliers and contractors. As the question of their accountability is strongly connected with the idea of Corporate Social Responsibility (CSR), this section develops some reflections on this concept and on its application to the field of marine environmental protection, through OCSR.

CSR and OCSR: Definitions and Legal Framework

There is no consensus definition of CSR. For the World Bank, CSR is

> [t]he commitment of business to contribute to sustainable economic development working with employees, their families, the local community, and society at large to improve their quality of life, in ways that are both good for business and good for development.[44]

---

42 *Ibid.*, at pp. 142, 157; P. Birnie, 'The Status of Environmental "Soft Law": Trends and Examples with Special Focus on IMO Norms', in H. Ringbom (ed), *Competing Norms in the Law of Marine Environmental Protection* (Kluwer Law International, The Hague, 1997) 31–57, at p. 46.

43 In this sense, see D.R. Rothwell and T. Stephens, *The International Law of the Sea* (Hart Publishing, Oxford, 2010) at p. 344; T. Treves, 'Navigation', in R.J. Dupuy and D. Vignes (eds), *A Handbook on the New Law of the Sea* (Martinus Nujhoff Publishers, Dordrecht, 1991) 835–976, at p. 876.

44 World Bank Group, Corporate Social Responsibility Practice, Strengthening Implementation of Corporate Social Responsibility in Global Supply Chains, October 2003, p. 1, available at http://siteresources.worldbank.org/INTPSD/Resources/CSR/Strengthening_Implementatio.pdf/; accessed 12 September 2014.

CSR pursues two objectives: filling in the details of international legal principles, either conventional or customary, that provide for the protection of common concerns, such as the environment, and focusing the private companies' attention on the needs of the society in which they operate.[45]

CSR has been acquiring relevance at the international law level since the 1970s when some international organizations started working on normative instruments, with the purpose of recommending to business operators specific standards of conduct when conducting their economic activities. Relevant instruments in the field of environmental protection are the *OECD (Organization for Economic Co-operation and Development) Guidelines for Multinational Enterprises*[46] and the *United Nations Global Compact*.[47]

These instruments are generally drafted as international soft-law instruments, i.e., the body of norms that "are neither law nor mere political or moral statements, but lie somewhere in the middle".[48] Being "intentionally non-binding arrangements"[49] with some kind of expectation that they will be legally relevant, respected or, at least, given some indirect effect,[50] they form part of the broader normative context within which reasonable or proper State and business behaviour is formed.

As far as OCSR is specifically concerned, the authors submit that its legal framework is composed of different categories of standards. As regards their content, OCSR embodies non-binding general principles of responsible conduct and technical guidelines. With regard to their addressees, two categories

45 E. Morgera, *Corporate Accountability in International Environmental Law* (Oxford University Press, Oxford, 2009) at pp. 11–12, 18. See also: A. Bonfanti, 'Applying Corporate Social Responsibility to Foreign Investments: Failures and Prospects', in T. Treves, S. Trevisanut and F. Seatzu (eds), *Foreign Investment, International Law and Common Concerns* (Routledge, London, 2014) 230–246.

46 OECD, *OECD Guidelines for Multinational Enterprises. Recommendations for Responsible Business Conduct in a Global Context*, 25 May 2011, no. I.3, hereinafter '*OECD Guidelines for Multinational Enterprises*'.

47 The UN Global Compact is available at https://www.unglobalcompact.org/; accessed 11 September 2014.

48 M.G. Desta, 'Soft Law in International Law: an Overview', in A.K. Bjorklund and A. Reinisch (eds), *International Investment Law and Soft Law* (Elgar, Cheltenam, 2012) 39–50, at p. 40. See also: C.M. Chinkin, 'The Challenge of Soft Law: Development and Change in International Law' (1989) 38 *International and Comparative Law Quarterly* 850–866, at p. 850.

49 W.M. Reisman, 'Soft Law and Law Jobs' (2011) 2(1) *Journal of International Dispute Settlement* 25–30, at p. 25.

50 T. Meyer, 'Soft Law as Delegation' (2009) 32(3) *Fordham International Law Review* 888–942, at pp. 889–890.

of OCSR instruments exist: those establishing standards of conduct directly addressing business operators, and those formally addressing States with recommendations to be complied with by private operators. We can also categorize based on source; thus we can identify guidelines promulgated by international organizations and States, and codes adopted by business professional associations. Finally, OCSR can play different roles: it can either contribute to preventing pollution and environmental disasters, or serve as a tool in mitigating damage and compensating losses, once a disaster has occurred.

OCSR as a Preventive Tool

Several OCSR instruments address marine business operators with standards aimed at preventing pollution and environmental disasters. Among them are the *OECD Guidelines for Multinational Corporations* and the *UN Global Compact*. They are non-binding recommendations adopted at an intergovernmental level that establish general principles of responsible conduct. The former calls upon multinational corporations "within the framework of laws, regulations and administrative practices in the countries in which they operate, and in consideration of relevant international agreements, principles, objectives, and standards" to "take due account of the need to protect the environment, public health and safety, and generally to conduct their activities in a manner contributing to the wider goal of sustainable development".[51] Likewise, the *UN Global Compact* supports a precautionary approach to environmental challenges, through the systematic application of risk assessment, risk management and risk communication and the implementation of decision-making processes involving scientific and technological evaluation, economic cost-benefit analysis and political considerations.[52]

Among the intergovernmental technical regulations that, although not expressly providing for CSR, develop environmental protection and prevention standards to be followed by marine business operators, the above-mentioned *IMO Energy Efficiency Resolutions* can be included. They provide that the Ship Energy Efficiency Management Plan should be

51 *OECD Guidelines for Multinational Enterprises*, Chapter VI. On the *OECD Guidelines*, see E. Morgera, 'An Environmental Outlook on the OECD Guidelines for Multinational Enterprises: Comparative Advantage, Legitimacy, and Outstanding Questions in the Lead Up to the 2006 Review' (2005–2006) 18 *Georgetown International Environmental Law Review* 751–777, at p. 751; D.J. Johnston, 'Promoting Corporate Responsibility: the OECD Guidelines for Multinational Enterprises' in R. Mullerat (ed), *Corporate Social Responsibility: The Corporate Governance of the 21st Century* (Kluwer, Alphen aan den Rijn, 2011) 275–283, at pp. 275–283.

52 UN Global Compact (n 48), Principles Nos. 7, 8, 9.

> linked to a broader corporate energy management policy for the company that owns, operates and controls the ship" and assume that "many companies [...] already have an environmental management plan (...) in place under ISO 14001.[53]

Thus, the standards of conduct on environmental protection under the *IMO Resolutions* are combined with other environmental standards established at international level.[54]

Several initiatives emphasizing the preventive function of OCSR were launched in the aftermath of the *Montara*[55] and *Deepwater Horizon* oil spills.[56] At the national level, the UK regulators formed the *UK Oil Spill Prevention and Response Advisory Group* (OSPRAG), with the task of reviewing the sector's offshore drilling practices in the UK continental shelf.[57] Likewise, the G20 launched the *Global Marine Environmental Protection* (*GMEP*) *Initiative*,[58] with the mandate to share the best practices to protect the environment and prevent accidents related to offshore oil and gas exploitation and marine transportation among its participants, including the OECD, the Organization of the Petroleum Exporting Countries (OPEC), the IMO, the International Organization for Standardization (ISO), and many other institutions. The *GMEP Initiative* has been working on a considerable series of guidelines and best practices.[59]

Whereas these standards have been adopted at an intergovernmental level, others are the result of the standardization process performed by the relevant professional associations. This is the case of the International Regulators' Forum (IRF),[60] an international association of eleven regulators of health and safety in the offshore upstream oil and gas industry. The IRF has instituted a new forum aimed at discussing national experiences with respect to offshore safety, and understanding the causes and considering the measures by industry

53 IMO, Resolution MEPC 212(63), Art. 3(3).

54 *Ibid.*

55 The *Montara* accident occurred on 21 August 2009 and consisted of an oil and gas leak, with a subsequent slick, in the Timor Sea, off the northern coast of Western Australia.

56 The *Deepwater Horizon* accident occurred on 20 April 2010: a drilling rig, owned by Transocean and leased by British Petroleum to explore the Macondo oil field, exploded, caught fire and sank in the Gulf of Mexico.

57 Available at http://www.oilandgasuk.co.uk/knowledgecentre/OSPRAG.cfm; accessed 25 July 2014.

58 Available at http://www.g20gmep.org/; accessed 25 July 2014.

59 Available at http://www.g20gmep.org/best-practice-areas/; accessed 25 August 2014.

60 Available at www.irfoffshoresafety.com; accessed 25 July 2014.

and regulators to prevent future major accidents. In addition, many standards of conduct have been specifically tailored to renewable marine energy by specialized professional organizations, such as the International Electrotechnical Commission (IEC)[61] and collected by the UN International Renewable Energy Agency.[62]

All the above-listed standards and guidelines address their recommendations directly to companies. By contrast, the *IMO Code* formally addresses States, and provides criteria and safety standards to be applied by offshore drilling units. The same approach is followed by the *1989 IMO Guidelines and Standards for Removal of Offshore Installations* and by the *1982 UNEP Environmental Law Guidelines and Principles.*[63] The latter establish general directives to be adhered to by States in their national laws and set out recommendations on the authorization of offshore operations, environmental assessment and monitoring systems, information and consultation processes, safety measures, liability and compensation. Finally, the *2007 International Finance Corporation (IFC) Environmental, health, and safety guidelines for offshore oil and gas development* (hereinafter "*IFC EHS Guidelines*") provide for technical reference documents with general and industry-specific examples of good international industry practices to be respected when one or more Member States of the World Bank are involved in a project.[64] Even if formally addressed to States, the above-mentioned codes and standards are to be complied with by private companies seeking to construct, run, remove and invest in mobile offshore drilling units.

---

61 IEC, *International standards on electrical power quality requirements for wave, tidal and other water current energy systems and other water current converters and the Guidelines for the early stage development of wave energy converters: Best practices and recommended procedures for the testing of pre-prototype scale devices.* Information available at: http://www.tc114.us/standards-development/project-teams/pt-62600-103/; accessed 25 July 2014.

62 UN International Renewable Energy Agency, *Inventory of standards relevant to renewable energy used for the study "international standardisation in the field of renewable energy"*, March 2013, available at: http://www.irena.org/DocumentDownloads/Publications/Inventory_renewable_energy_standards.pdf; accessed 25 July 2014.

63 UNEP, *Environmental Law Guidelines and Principles: Offshore Mining and Drilling*, 31 May 1982, GC Dec10/14/VI. See: Z. Gao (ed), *Environmental Regulation of Oil and Gas* (Kluwer, London, 1998) at pp. 113–115.

64 IFC, *Environmental, health, and safety guidelines for offshore oil and gas development*, 2007, available at http://www.ifc.org/wps/wcm/connect/65f8ae00488558a380d4d26a6515bb18/Final%2B-%2BOffshore%2BOil%2Band%2BGas%2BDevelopment.pdf?MOD=AJPERES&id=1323153218959; accessed 25 July 2014.

The Circulation of Standards across Regimes: From the LOSC to OCSR

In light of the preceding remarks, the relationship existing between the treaty-based obligations of the LOSC and the standards recommended by the OCSR instruments is now considered.

As observed above, the LOSC provides for several norms establishing that States shall cooperate directly or "through competent international organizations" in formulating "international rules, standards and recommended practices and procedures" consistent with the LOSC for the protection and preservation of the marine environment.[65] Does this phrase include OCSR standards of conduct?

Bearing in mind that the OCSR legal framework is composed of general principles and technical standards, it can be assumed that the latter are certainly invoked by the LOSC. For instance, it can be concluded that the *IMO Energy Efficiency Resolutions*, the *1989 IMO Guidelines and Standards for removal of offshore installations* and the *IMO Code* amount to "international standards and recommended practices and procedures" under the Convention. Thus, through "legislation by reference", they can harden into binding law as a consequence of their transposition into the LOSC.

By contrast, it can be concluded that the LOSC did not aim to formally invoke non-binding instruments establishing OCSR general principles, such as the *OECD Guidelines* and the *UN Global Compact*. This is because the adopting bodies lacked specific competence in the field of marine environmental protection and thus could not be considered as "competent international organizations" within the meaning of the relevant LOSC provisions. Nonetheless, by elaborating the international legal principles on environmental protection with further details, standards of responsible conduct *de facto* cross-fertilize and strengthen the LOSC's legal framework and contribute to the development of international law in the field of energy-related activities at sea. In this light, they can be certainly referenced as interpretative tools of the LOSC.[66] Furthermore, if supported by general practice and acceptance, for instance through their uniform incorporation within the relevant contracts[67] and the

65 See *supra*.

66 On the role of soft law as an interpretive tool, see C. Chinkin, 'Normative Development in the International Legal System', in D. Shelton (ed), *Commitment and Compliance: The Role of Non-Binding Norms in International Legal System* (Oxford University Press, Oxford, 2000) 21–42, at pp. 30–31.

67 A study developed by the International Institute on Sustainable Development (IISD) of 41 upstream oil and gas contracts demonstrates that often the parties include a reference to the international industry standards. IISD, 'Foreign investment contracts in the oil and gas sector: a survey of environmentally relevant clauses', 7 October 2011, available at

internal corporate codes of conduct, the standards of responsible conduct could be regarded as a source of law by arbitrators and courts.[68]

Addressing Environmental Disasters: OCSR and Civil Liability Issues

The last issue this chapter examines is how OCSR and treaty-based regimes address environmental disasters. This part is divided into three sections: it first analyses the role of OCSR in mitigating environmental damage, then examines civil liability regimes and finally considers the role of OCSR in compensating losses.

Mitigating Damage through OCSR

As observed above, OCSR mainly pursues a preventive function. However, as demonstrated below, OCSR also plays a role in mitigating damage and compensating losses arising from environmental disasters. This conclusion is supported by some factual evidence regarding the *Montara* and *Deepwater Horizon* oil spills. Following the accidents, the Association of Oil and Gas Producers (OGP)[69] instituted the *Global Industry Response Group* (GIRG), charged with the task of identifying the key questions to prevent accidents in the future and to exchange related information and lessons. The *International Recommendations on well incident prevention, intervention and response*, adopted by the OGP Wells Expert Committee, call on and encourage operators and contractors to respect the internationally and nationally agreed standards and to develop new technical operational practices. A newly created consortium of the nine largest oil companies,[70] known as Subsea Well Response Project (SWRP) is currently reviewing, selecting and designing the measures considered to be adequate to react to environmental disasters at sea, i.e., the specific operational procedures for capping wells and containing hydrocarbons.[71] In addition, the Joint Industry Project (JIP) is improving the coordination among the key stakeholders, with the aim of ensuring effective responses to

---

http://www.iisd.org/itn/2011/10/07/foreign-investment-contracts-in-the-oil-gas-sector-a-survey-of-environmentally-relevant-clauses/; accessed 11 September 2014.

68 P. Sanders, 'Codes of Conduct and Sources of Law' in P. Fouchard, P. Kahn and A. Lyon-Caen (eds), *Le droits des relations économiques internationales. Etudes offertes à Berthold Goldman* (Litec, Paris, 1982) 281–298, at pp. 295–298.

69 Available at www.ogp.org.uk; accessed 25 August 2014.

70 BT Group, BP, Chevron, ConocoPhillips, ExxonMobil, Petrobras, Shell, Statoil and Total.

71 Information available at http://subseawellresponse.com/; accessed 25 August 2014.

well accidents through the development of recommended practices. Finally, OGP is focusing on standardization, in the framework of the international standard ISO/TC67 on materials, equipment and offshore structures for petroleum, petrochemical and natural gas industries.[72]

The International Petroleum Industry Environmental Conservation Association (IPIECA) has also paid specific attention to damage mitigation[73] and has published nineteen documents of good practices on preparedness and response (*Oil Spill Response Series*), a global overview of the relevant issues, such as the biological impacts of oil pollution, contingency planning and the use of dispersants.

Compensating Losses through Civil Liability Treaty-Based Regimes

Marine pollution and other damage caused by oil spills at sea could plainly fall under State responsibility or liability under public international law. However, since grave accidents causing huge environmental disasters have occurred, an alternative approach to address these problems has developed: the management and compensation of damage deriving from oil spills is mainly provided by treaty-based civil liability regimes in an attempt to provide more adequate responses to the victims.[74]

These regimes establish a strict but limited liability for the owners and the operators of the vessels, coupled with mandatory insurance. Today, these regimes provide for a three-tier compensation mechanism. The first layer is the International Convention on Civil Liability for Oil Pollution Damage (hereinafter 1992 CLC Convention).[75] The 1992 CLC Convention provides for a strict but limited liability of the ship-owner for pollution resulting from the discharge of oil carried as a cargo on a vessel.[76] The CLC Convention covers oil spills

72 ISO/TC 67 Management Committee, Proposed ISO/TC 67 programme for drilling, well construction and well operations standards, resulting from the Montara and Macondo accidents, ISO/TC 67 N 1119, 1 March 2011.

73 Available at www.ipieca.org; accessed 25 August 2014.

74 For an overview of the evolution of oil pollution civil liability regimes, see A. Daniel, 'Civil Liability Regimes as a Complement to Multilateral Environmental Agreements: Sound International Policy or False Comfort?' (2005) 12(3) *Review of European Community and International Environmental Law* 225–241; L. Rodriguez-Lucas, 'Compensation for Damage to the Environment *Per Se* under International Civil Liability Regimes', in S. Maljean-Dubois and L. Rajamani (eds), *The Implementation of International Environmental Law* (Martinus Nijhoff, Leiden, 2011) 419–467, at p. 422.

75 International Convention on Civil Liability for Oil Pollution Damage (Brussels, 29 November 1969) as amended by the 1992 Protocol (London, 27 November 1992, in force 30 May 1996) 1956 *UNTS* 255.

76 1992 CLC Convention, Art. III(1).

occurring in the areas under the jurisdiction of the State. Pursuant to this civil liability regime, the ship-owner must be covered by insurance and cannot be exonerated from liability except in rare and exceptional circumstances.[77] As a counterbalance to the strict liability regime, the ship-owner's liability is limited and proportional to the size of the ship.[78] In addition to the ship-owner's liability, Art. III(4) of the 1992 CLC Convention provides that a compensation claim can be brought against other subjects involved in the oil transportation when "the damage resulted from their personal act or omission, committed with the intent to cause such damage, or recklessly and with knowledge that such damage would probably result." The interpretation of this provision was one of the central issues in the legal saga before the French judges regarding the compensation proceedings for damage resulting from the *Erika* oil spill.[79]

Particular consideration should be given to the role of OCSR intergovernmental standards and internal corporate codes of conduct in judicial civil liability proceedings. An outstanding issue to consider in this regard is whether non-compliance by an operator with the OCSR standards of conduct could be considered as "negligence" and thereby trigger liability under the treaty-based civil liability regime. This issue emerged in the *Erika* case, where the French Court of Appeal exonerated Total, the oil company chartering the ship at the time of the incident, from liability under Art. III(4) of the 1992 CLC Convention. The reasoning of the Court focused precisely on the non-legally binding nature of Total's internal rules and reached the conclusion that, as such, there was no legal obligation upon the company to carry out the inspections.[80] However, this judgment was later reversed by the *Cour de Cassation*, which held that Total's omission to perform the controls was indeed reckless in the meaning of Art. III(4), albeit without giving a specific reason for this *revirement*.

To complement the civil liability regime of the 1992 CLC Convention, States Parties to the IMO concluded the International Convention on the Establishment of an International Fund for Compensation for Oil Pollution Damage (hereinafter 1992 IOPC Convention).[81] This second layer of compensation relies on the fund established by the 1992 IOPC Convention which is

77 *Ibid.*, Art. III(2).

78 *Ibid.*, Art. V(1).

79 For a thorough analysis of the case see V. Rebeyrol, 'The Erika Case: an Incitement to Rewrite the CLC' (2013) 1 *European Energy and Environmental Law Review* 33–43.

80 *Ibid.*, at p. 37.

81 International Convention on the Establishment of an International Fund for Compensation for Oil Pollution Damage (Brussels, 18 December 1971) as amended by the 1992 Protocol (27 November 1992, in force 30 May 1996) 11 *ILM* 284 (1972).

periodically replenished by cargo owners. The third layer is the 2003 Supplementary Fund Protocol.[82]

According to the 1992 CLC and IOPC Conventions: "[...] compensation for impairment of the environment other than loss of profit from such impairment shall be limited to costs of reasonable measures of reinstatement actually undertaken or to be undertaken [...]."[83] Although this solution avoids the complex issue of evaluating pure environmental damage,[84] it does not indicate how the "reasonableness" of the reinstatement measure should be assessed. Useful guidance on this issue is found in the 1992 IOPC Convention Claims Manual,[85] which states the conditions to be met for a claim for compensation to be admissible, i.e., when the measures of reinstatement are judged reasonable. These rules were drafted by a Working Group and then adopted by the Meeting of the Parties. Even though originally the criteria cannot be considered as legally binding, if repeatedly and consistently applied in the compensation claims, they could reflect the subsequent practice of States Parties and as such may "upgrade" to higher standards of legality.[86]

These civil liability regimes, notably with the extension of those liable to make contribution through the 1992 IOPC Convention, internalize the costs of pollution and thereby represent a far-reaching implementation of the polluter-pays principle. These regimes should also induce more virtuous behaviour by the operators involved and thereby prevent future accidents. In fact, the contributors to the fund are the oil companies who ship the oil cargo—or to whom it is shipped. Furthermore, as the level of contribution to the fund is indexed to the total quantity of oil imported per year, these regimes establish a liability nexus which aligns the interests of the shipping and oil industry to prevent oil pollution incidents. These regimes provide an effective response to environmental accidents because they facilitate claims for compensation

82 Protocol to the 1992 IOPC Convention (London, 16 May 2003, in force 3 March 2005) IMO Doc. LEG/CONF.14/20.

83 See 1992 CLC Convention, Article 1(6); and by reference, 1992 IOPC Convention, Article 1(2) and the 2003 Supplementary Protocol, Article 1(6). This same approach is adopted also by the HNS Convention (35 *ILM* 1415 (1996)), Art. 1(6)(c) and the Bunker Convention, (40 *ILM* 1493 (2001)) Art. 1(9)(a).

84 Rodríguez-Lucas (n 75), at p. 437.

85 1992 IOPC Convention Claims Manual, October 2013 Edition (available at www.iopcfunds.org; accessed 25 July 2014).

86 On the legal nature of these legal instruments, see Romanin Jacur (n 35), at p. 195. From the perspective of regime interaction, it is worth noting that due to the close connection among these IMO Conventions, these compensation criteria are also likely to be considered as relevant indicators by the 1996 HNS Convention and by the 2001 Bunker Convention. See Rodríguez-Lucas (n 75), at p. 460.

by the victims. However, improvements are still needed to make them more effective, especially when major disasters occur which often trigger long and complex judicial proceedings before national courts.[87]

Mitigating Damage and Compensating Losses through Contractual Schemes

Respect for voluntary standards can also play a role in mitigating damage and compensating losses arising from environmental disasters. Private voluntary civil liability agreements and contractual schemes of compensation have been agreed, in order to define the terms and conditions to be followed when environmental disasters occur. Among them are the *1974 Offshore Pollution Liability Agreement* (OPOL)[88] and, before their termination in 1997, the *1969 Tanker Owners Voluntary Agreement concerning Liability for Oil Pollution* (TOVALOP)[89] and the *1971 Contract Regarding an Interim Supplement to Tanker Liability for Oil Pollution* (CRISTAL).[90] Even though they cannot literally be considered as instruments requiring responsible conduct from business operators, nonetheless they pursue the objective of setting standards aimed at reducing damage and granting victims the right to be compensated. As far as their legal status is concerned, they are contracts. It is worth recalling that OCSR standards are also often embodied into contractual agreements, with the effect of transforming them into contractual obligations.[91]

As regards OPOL, its parties are operators of offshore oil and gas facilities from which a risk may exist of an escape or discharge of oil causing pollution damage. It applied initially to offshore facilities within the jurisdiction of the United Kingdom; it was subsequently extended to offshore facilities within the jurisdictions of Denmark, Germany, France, Ireland, the Netherlands, Norway, the Isle of Man, the Faroe Islands and Greenland; now it can be extended so as to apply within the jurisdiction of any other State, except for offshore facilities located in the Baltic and Mediterranean Seas. OPOL applies

87 J. Juste-Ruiz, 'Freedom of Navigation and Responsibility for Damage to the Marine Environment', in M.C. Ribeiro (ed), *30 Anos da Assinatura da Convenção das Nações Unidas sobre o Direito do Mar: Protecção do Ambiente e o Futuro do direito do Mar* (Coimbra Editora, Coimbra, 2014) 85–111, at p. 99.

88 The text of the agreement and the relevant information are available at http://www.opol.org.uk/; accessed 25 August 2014.

89 Reproduced in 8 *ILM* 497 (1969).

90 Reproduced in 10 *ILM* 137 (1971). On these instruments see S. Bloodworth, 'Death on the High Seas: The Demise of TOVALOP and CRISTAL' (1998) 132 *Florida State University Journal of Land Use & Environmental Law* 443–458.

91 See (n 68).

to offshore facilities in waters within the jurisdiction of a State designated in OPOL, while the location of the pollution damage or of the remedial measures are not governing factors. Two classes of claimants are admitted under OPOL: governments which claim in respect of remedial measures to prevent, mitigate, eliminate, remove or neutralize pollution damage; and anyone, including governments, claiming compensation for pollution. Pollution damage is defined as direct loss or damage caused by contamination. Claims are made directly against the operator and must be filed within one year of the date of the incident. Parties accept strict liability and agree on a maximum liability amounting to US $250,000,000 per incident, made up of US $125,000,000 to cover pollution damage claims and US $125,000,000 for remedial measures. In the event of any dispute arising between a claimant and a party, provision is made for arbitration in London in accordance with the rules of the International Chamber of Commerce (ICC).[92]

Conclusion

Effective regulation of marine pollution requires constant updating to take into account new challenges and evolving technologies. The LOSC responded to this regulatory need by incorporating the technical rules and standards elaborated in the framework of specific regimes, which, on the one hand, have "lighter" decision-making processes and, on the other hand, are supported by adequate technical and scientific knowledge.

Likewise, private standards and rules present similar positive characteristics in that they are adopted through more agile decision-making procedures compared to multilateral negotiations and by players directly involved and well equipped to recognize the problematic issues, and to identify adequate solutions relating to the marine energy sector.

Looking at the interaction of treaty-based regimes with OCSR, a regulatory approach emerges which relies on multiple "incorporation by reference" mechanisms: first, the LOSC delegates technical law-making to IMO; second, IMO Resolutions may refer to—and thereby to some extent incorporate—OCSR instruments. It follows that through this multi-layered "incorporation by reference", OCSR standards may become legal parameters relevant under the LOSC.

92 All of the material in this paragraph is based on information available at http://www.opol.org.uk/; accessed 25 August 2014.

A telling example of this regulatory mechanism is provided by the above-mentioned IMO *Energy Efficiency Resolutions*. Considering that these Resolutions incorporate OCSR instruments, such as the Environment Management Plan of ship operators, should they be invoked by the LOSC provisions, they would bring OCSR rules and standards into the LOSC regime as part of their content. Echoing the pragmatic approach of the LOSC negotiators, this circulation of standards may be seen as a positive outcome, because it builds a regulatory regime based on public and private standards and law-making processes that complement and support each other.[93]

Furthermore, in addition to the above-described formal incorporation of rules and standards, another notable normative evolution is the cross-fertilization between the treaty-based regimes and OCSR instruments, which leads to strengthening and interpreting the treaty obligations of the former through the standards of responsible conduct established by the latter. Such an evolution is supported by the development of a coherent practice of incorporation of the relevant standards within the internal corporate codes of conduct and the contracts entered into by the marine energy operators. In this way, normative synergies can emerge and lead to a more effective response to pollution from energy-related activities at sea.

---

93 E. Hey, 'Reviewing Implementation of the LOS Convention and Emerging International *Public* Law', in Oude Elferink (n 36) 75–88, at p. 81, notes that "the LOS Convention empowers States and international institutions (...) to regulate ocean uses in the interest of the international community" and that this lawmaking system is characterized for being "a multifaceted and multi-localized process of normative development in which delegated public powers are exercised by a variety of actors (...)."

CHAPTER 4

The Role of Private Actors in Offshore Energy: Shifting Models of Participation

Seline Trevisanut
Assistant Professor of International Law, Netherlands Institute for the Law of the Sea / Utrecht Centre for Water, Oceans and Sustainability Law, Utrecht University School of Law, Utrecht, The Netherlands

Abstract

The role of private actors in the offshore energy industry has expanded with regard to both the law-making processes and the implementation of the relevant legal framework. This chapter critically examines the role private actors are playing in the offshore energy sector in order to delineate some trends in the ways in which private actors act and interact at the international level. It focuses in particular on instances where there is a delegation of regulatory powers or the implementation duties from the international and supranational level to the private actors. The chapter ultimately strives to identify which model(s) of participation by private actors the offshore energy sector is developing.

Keywords

offshore energy sector – private actors – multilateral environmental agreements – EU law

Introduction

The offshore energy sector has greatly expanded in the last 20 years. The reasons are manifold. Technological development has enabled resources to be exploited in deeper waters and in locations further away from the coast. Concerns for the environmental consequences of oil exploitation have led to increased attention to the exploitation of offshore natural gas and the development of offshore renewable energy sources. The offshore energy sector

 | DOI 10.1163/9789004303522_006

is a highly technical, economically important and environmentally sensitive sector.[1] It is also an economically risky sector in the sense that

> [c]ontracts between energy companies and host governments are unique transactions. The duration of energy contracts and risk exposure is long-term, capital investment is intensive, and the project risk (geological, commercial, and political) is particularly acute.[2]

This statement is particularly salient concerning offshore energy production where the investor bears considerable costs before production commences, whereas the host State wants guarantees concerning the implementation of the investment, which is of fundamental importance for its economy and its energy security.[3] Moreover, the private actor, namely the investor or operator, will have a deeper knowledge of the risks and needs of this economic sector than governments. Thus with the expansion of the offshore sector we are also witnessing an increase in and a strengthening of the role of private actors at the international level.

Private actors are more and more involved in the law-making processes and in the mechanisms of implementation and enforcement of international rules. On the one hand, civil society, in particular local communities, can actively affect the decision-making processes thanks to their participation rights, which are guaranteed, *inter alia*, by the Aarhus Convention on Access to Information, Public Participation in Decision-making and Access to Justice in Environmental Matters,[4] and the Espoo Convention on Environ-

1 Portman rightly noted that "[o]ffshore energy projects (...) tend to be high profile because they employ new technologies, impact sensitive areas, use resources held in public trust, and engender conflicts with other uses such as tourism, shipping, and fishing"; M. Portman, "Involving the public in the impact assessment of offshore renewable energy facilities" (2009) 33 *Marine Policy* 332–338, at p. 332.

2 M. Flores, 'A Practical Approach to Allocating Environmental Liability and Stabilizing Foreign Investment in the Energy Sectors of Developing Countries' (2001) 12 *Colorado Journal of Environmental Law and Policy* 141–163, at p. 147.

3 P.B. Stephan, 'Energy Development and Distribution—What Can the Law Do?', in M. Nordquist, J.N. Moore, and A.S. Skaridov (eds), *International Energy Policy, the Arctic and the Law of the Sea* (Martinus Nijhoff, Leiden, 2005) 201–212, at p. 202. See also S. Trevisanut, 'Foreign Investments in the Offshore Energy Industry: Investment Protection *v.* Energy Security *v.* Protection of the Marine Environment' in T. Treves, F. Seatzu, S. Trevisanut (eds), *Foreign Investment, International Law and Common Concerns* (Routledge, London, 2004) 247–264.

4 Convention on Access to Information, Public Participation in Decision-Making and Access to Justice in Environmental matters of the United Nations Economic Commission for Europe (Aarhus, 25 June 1998, in force 30 October 2001), 2161 *UNTS* 450.

mental Impact Assessment in a Transboundary Context.[5] On the other hand, private actors economically involved in the activities (i.e., investors and insurance companies) bear obligations under specific international instruments, such as the Barcelona Convention Offshore Protocol,[6] and Annex VI of the Helsinki Convention on the Protection Marine Environment of the Baltic Sea Area.[7]

This chapter critically examines the role private actors are playing in the offshore energy sector in order to delineate some trends in the ways in which private actors act and interact at the international level. It focuses in particular on instances where there is a delegation of regulatory powers or implementation duties from the international or State level to the private actors. Such instances occur in all phases of the life of energy projects, from planning to the construction, operation, and removal of the structures. The present analysis is based in particular on two sets of documents: the work of the National Commission on the British Petroleum (BP) Deepwater Horizon Oil Spill and Offshore Drilling;[8] and the EU Directive 2013/30 on safety of offshore oil and gas operations,[9] which is examined in its normative context, including the above-mentioned Barcelona Convention Offshore Protocol and Annex VI

5 Espoo, 25 February 1991, in force 10 September 1997, 1989 *UNTS* 310.

6 Protocol for the Protection of the Mediterranean Sea against Pollution Resulting from Exploration and Exploitation of the Continental Shelf and the Seabed and its Subsoil to the Convention for the Protection of the Mediterranean Sea Against Pollution (Barcelona Convention) (Madrid, 14 October 1994, in force 24 March 2011), UNEP(OCA)/MED IG.4/4.

7 Helsinki, 24 September 1992, in force 17 January 2000, 1507 *UNTS* 167. The Helsinki Convention has been amended many times since 1992. Any reference in the present text refers to the last version as in force in 2008, and as available on the website on the Baltic Marine Environment Protection Commission—Helsinki Commission (HELCOM) at http://www.helcom.fi; accessed 11 September 2014. Annex VI of the Helsinki Convention concerns the prevention of pollution from offshore activities and its text is available at http://www.helcom.fi/about-us/convention/annexes/annex-vi; accessed 11 September 2014.

8 The reports elaborated by the National Commission in the BP Deepwater Horizon Oil Spill and Offshore Drilling are available at http://cybercemetery.unt.edu/archive/oilspill/20121210172821/http://www.oilspillcommission.gov/; accessed 11 September 2014. U.S. President Barack Obama established this Commission through Executive Order 13543 on 21 May 2010 (available at http://www.whitehouse.gov/the-press-office/executive-order-national-commission-bp-deepwater-horizon-oil-spill-and-offshore-dri; accessed 11 September 2014). The Commission examined the facts and circumstances concerning the root causes of the Deepwater Horizon explosion and developed options to guard against, and mitigate the impact of, any oil spills associated with offshore drilling in the future.

9 OJ L 178/66, 28 June 2013.

of the Helsinki Convention, and the OSPAR Decision 98/3 on the Disposal of Disused Offshore Installations.[10]

These documents show some common patterns: the proclaimed need for a more active role for the industry in guaranteeing the safety of offshore platforms, in particular by better monitoring the construction and operation of the installations; the suggestion of having 'international' management of the sector through the creation of an association/organization, which would bring together representatives of all stakeholders (States, industry, local communities, workers, etc.); and the development of corporate social responsibility instruments.[11]

The analysis here is threefold. First, the chapter identifies the private actors in the offshore energy sector. In order to do so, it focuses on the private actors encompassed in the existing regulation, who are directly targeted by the analysed legal instrument. Next, the three main roles of private actors are analysed: as recipients of rights; as recipients of obligations; and as participants in rule-making and standard-setting. The final part discusses the model of participation that the existing legal framework has created or aims at shaping. The present chapter argues that, from a "model of surveillance",[12] the increasing role of private actors has entailed a shift towards a "model of transparency", namely a model in which "non-state actors contribute primarily to the definition of the issues that should be dealt with at the international level, even if the last word in terms of policy orientations might often belong to States or to international organisations".[13] In the offshore energy sector, in particular in the oil and gas industry, private actors may sometimes actually have the last word.

---

10 Commission of the Convention for the Protection of the Marine Environment of the North-East Atlantic (OSPAR Convention (Paris, 22 September 1992, in force 25 March 1998) 2354 *UNTS* 67), OSPAR 98/14/1-E, 22–23 July 1998, Annex 33.

11 Issues of corporate social responsibility are not addressed in the present chapter but are analysed in this special issue by Bonfanti and Romanin Jacur, see A. Bonfanti and F. Romanin Jacur, 'Energy from the Sea and the Protection of the Marine Environment: Treaty-Based Regimes and Ocean Corporate Social Responsibility' (2014) 29(4) *International Journal of Marine and Coastal Law* 622–644, this issue.

12 M.M. Mbengue, 'Non-state actors in international environmental law, A Rousseauist approach', in J. d'Aspremont (ed), *Participants in the Legal System, Multiple Perspectives on Non-State Actors in International Law* (Routledge, London, 2011) 372–389, at p. 379: "[in a model of surveillance] non-state actors participate in the 'sustainable development contract' by adhering or subscribing to rules and principles of treaty law or of customary international law, that is rules and principles generated by states and international organizations."

13 *Ibid.*, at p. 380.

Identifying the Private Actors in the Offshore Energy Sector

Many categories of private actors appear in different texts and instruments. The following terms are commonly used: licensees; operators; owners; contractors; industry; promoters; professional associations; certification authorities; insurance companies; etc. The Directive 2013/30/EU specifically affirms: "Best global practice requires *licensees, operators and owners* to take primary responsibility for controlling the risks they create by their operations, including operations conducted by contractors on their behalf and therefore to establish within a corporate major accident prevention policy the mechanisms and highest level of corporate ownership to implement that policy consistently" (Preamble, para. 36, emphasis added).

In Article 2(5), the Directive defines the operator as the "entity appointed by the licensee or licensing authority to conduct offshore oil and gas operations, including planning and executing a well operation or managing and controlling the functions of a production installation". This definition, on the one hand, expands the definition of the same term in the Barcelona Offshore Protocol by including a list of activities which pertain to the operator. On the other hand, it limits its scope of application to the 'formal' operator and does not encompass "[a]ny person who *does not hold* an authorization within the meaning of this protocol but is *de facto in control of such activities*".[14] Thus the contracting parties to the Barcelona Offshore Protocol must implement their obligations in relation to any activity under their jurisdiction, even when performed by an operator who is not formally authorized, but EU Mediterranean States[15] can only apply the safety regime created by the Directive 2013/30/EU to authorized operators; *de facto* operators are only subject to the Protocol's regime. The term operator also appears in Annex VI of the Helsinki Convention[16] and OSPAR Decision 98/3 on the Disposal of Disused Offshore Installations[17] but neither text provides a definition.

14 Art. 1(g)(ii) Barcelona Offshore Protocol, emphasis added.

15 The EU ratified the Barcelona Offshore Protocol in 2013. Consequently, it applies to all EU Mediterranean States, which are also EU Members, within the limits of EU competences. At the time of writing, the only EU Mediterranean State which has ratified the protocol is Cyprus; information available at http://www.unepmap.org/index.php?module=content2&catid=001001004; accessed 11 September 2014.

16 Regulation 6 Annex VI of the Helsinki Convention.

17 OSPAR 98/14/1-E, 22–23 July 1998, Annex 33, at p. 8, para. 6.

Directive 2013/30/EU also defines the licensee, namely the "holder or joint holders of a licence,"[18] the contractor, i.e., an "entity contracted by the operator or owner to perform specific tasks on behalf of the operator or owner",[19] and the owner, i.e., "an entity legally entitled to control the operation of a non-production installation."[20] Moreover, the same directive translates into legal terms the concept of "industry", which consists of "entities that are directly involved in offshore oil and gas operations covered by the directive or whose activities are closely related to those operations."[21] This definition is novel and suggests a wide understanding of industry, which encompasses not only the oil and gas companies, but also any material or service provider whose activities are "closely related" to the oil and gas operations.

The Directive also defines "public," that is "one or more entities and, in accordance with national legislation or practice, their associations, organizations or groups."[22] The Directive reproduces the definition in Article 2(4) of the Aarhus Convention. The Espoo Convention, on the other hand, provides a more general and vague definition of public, as "one or more natural or legal entities". Both the Aarhus Convention and the Directive 2013/30/EU refer also to the concept of "public concerned".[23] Pursuant to the Aarhus Convention, the "public concerned" means "the public affected or likely to be affected by, or having an interest in, the environmental decision-making; for the purposes of this definition, non-governmental organizations promoting environmental protection and meeting any requirements under national law shall be deemed to have an interest."[24] The Directive uses a similar definition with specific reference to the "decision to allow exploration operations" and includes "relevant non-governmental organisations such as those promoting environmental protection, and other relevant organisations."[25]

None of these texts refer to indigenous people and their participation or consultation rights under international law.[26] Indigenous peoples, in particular

18 Art. 2(11). A licence is "an authorization for offshore oil and gas operations pursuant to directive 94/22/EC" (Art. 2(9)).

19 Art. 2(12).

20 Art. 2(27).

21 Art. 2(35).

22 Art. 2(18).

23 Respectively, Arts. 6(2) and 5(2)(b).

24 Art. 2(5) Aarhus Convention; for a comment, see C. Pitea, *Diritto internazionale e democrazia ambientale* (ESI, Naples, 2013), at pp. 216 ff.

25 Art. 5(2)(b) Directive 2013/30/EU.

26 See, for instance, the ILO Convention n 169 concerning indigenous and tribal peoples in independent countries (adopted 27 June 1989, 28 *ILM* 1382), which provides for the prior

in the Arctic area, have an increasing interest in participating in the decision-making processes concerning energy projects. The ILO Convention n 169 concerning indigenous and tribal peoples in independent countries applies to:

> tribal peoples (...) whose social, cultural and economic conditions distinguish them from other sections of the national community, and whose status is regulated wholly or partially by their own customs or traditions or by special laws or regulations

and to "peoples in independent countries who are regarded as indigenous".[27]

Moreover, "[s]elf-identification as indigenous or tribal shall be regarded as a fundamental criterion for determining the groups to which the provisions of this Convention apply."[28]

A last category of private actors is the 'promoter'. This term appears in the 2008 OSPAR Guidance on Environmental Considerations for Offshore Wind Farm Development.[29] The 2008 OSPAR Guidance does not give any definition, but from its content it appears that the term "promoter" is used as a synonym of 'applicant,' i.e., the entity who wants to develop an offshore wind farm project in the OSPAR maritime area. The term "applicant" is particularly useful in order to identify in legal terms the private actor in the period between the application for a licence and the granting of that license by a competent national authority. The 2008 OSPAR Guidance emphasizes in particular the role of the promoter in the environmental impact assessment (EIA) procedures prior to the licensing of the project. This is a very important role of the private actor, which unfortunately has not been incorporated by Directive 2013/30/EU in the field of oil and gas operations.

The Main Roles of Private Actors in the Offshore Energy Sector

Private Actors as Recipients of Rights

International law guarantees rights of participation and consultation to private actors in decision-making processes regarding offshore energy projects. This

---

consultation on State decisions affecting indigenous peoples. See also the United Nations Declaration on the Rights of Indigenous Peoples, UNGA Res. 61/295, UN doc. A/RES/47/1, 13 September 2007.

27 Art. 1(1)(a)–(b) ILO Convention n 169.

28 Art. 1(2) ILO Convention n 169.

29 Reference number: 2008-3, available at www.ospar.org; accessed 11 September 2014.

section provides a brief and non-exhaustive survey of the two main instruments that regulate how private actors can participate, namely the 1991 Espoo[30] and the 1998 Aarhus Conventions.[31]

The private actors concerned in both instruments are the "public," as defined above. Public participation can take different forms: public hearings, surveys, advisory committees, calls for comments on the proposed projects, workshops, etc. Under the Espoo Convention, parties have a duty to require an environmental impact assessment (EIA) in order to "prevent, reduce and control significant adverse transboundary environmental impact from proposed activities."[32] States parties must also establish procedures which permit public participation. Pursuant to the Espoo Convention Guidance, adopted by the meeting of the parties in 2004,[33] the domestic EIA procedure should include the necessary provisions so that:

> (a) the public is informed on any proposals relating to an activity with potential adverse environmental impacts in cases subject to an EIA procedure in order to obtain a permit for a given activity; (b) the public in the areas likely to be affected is entitled to express comments and opinions on the proposed activity when all options are open before the final decision on this activity is made; (c) reasonable time-frames are provided allowing sufficient time for each of the different stages of public participation in the EIA procedure; (d) in making the final decision on the proposed activity, due account is taken of the results of the public participation in the EIA procedure.[34]

The 2003 Protocol on Strategic Environmental Assessment (SEA)[35] to the Espoo Convention allows the public to be involved in the decision-making process earlier than in general EIA procedure. A SEA involves

30 Espoo Convention (n 5).

31 Aarhus Convention (n 4).

32 Art. 2(1) Espoo Convention.

33 Meeting of the Parties to the Convention on Environmental Impact Assessment in a Transboundary Context, Guidance on Public Participation in Environmental Impact Assessment in a Transboundary Context, Decision III/8, Report of the Third Meeting, ECE/MP.EIA/6, 13 September 2004, Annex VIII.

34 *Ibid.*, para. 14. For a comment, *inter alia* see J. Ebbesson, 'A Modest Contribution to Environmental Democracy and Justice in Transboundary Contexts: The Combined Impact of the Espoo Convention and the Aarhus Convention' (2011) 20 *Review of European Community and International Environmental Law* (RECIEL) 248–257.

35 Kiev, 21 May 2003, in force 10 July 2010, ECE/MP.EIA/2003/2, 21 May 2003, available at http://www.unece.org/env/eia/sea_protocol.html; accessed 11 September 2014.

> the evaluation of the likely environmental, including health, effects, which comprises the determination of the scope of an environmental report and its preparation, the carrying out of public participation and consultations, and the taking into account of the environmental report and the results of the public participation and consultations in *a plan or programme*.[36]

So through SEAs the public participates in government policies and program decisions, and not only in relation to a specific project. Art. 8 of the SEA Protocol regulates public participation and provides that contracting parties "*shall ensure* early, timely and *effective* opportunities for public participation" and "using electronic media or other appropriate means, shall ensure the timely public availability of the draft plan or programme and the environmental report."[37] Finally, States parties "shall ensure that the public (…) has the opportunity to express its opinion on the draft plan or programme and the environmental report within a reasonable time frame."[38] SEAs thus require more than a mere effort to engage with the public. They require an actual engagement which assures the participation of the public in the outcome of the procedure.[39]

There are many similarities between the Espoo Convention system and the Aarhus Convention concerning the modalities through which the public should have access to the relevant procedures and documents.[40] One main difference is however, that the Aarhus Convention not only applies in transboundary contexts but also regulates public participation in a purely domestic setting. Moreover, the Aarhus Convention creates a presumption of access.[41] National authorities must justify any refusal or delay in the disclosure of the documents.[42] The Compliance Committee of the Aarhus Convention has enhanced the level of protection of public rights by affirming that "the Parties may implement the Convention in different ways, e.g., by fully transforming the provisions through national legislation or by, to some extent relying on notions of direct effect"[43]

---

36 Art. 2(6) SEA Protocol, emphasis added.

37 Art. 8(1)–(2) SEA Protocol, emphasis added.

38 Art. 8(4) SEA Protocol.

39 M. Doelle, N. Bankes and L. Porta, 'Using Strategic Environmental Assessments to Guide Oil and Gas Exploration Decisions: Applying Lessons Learned from Atlantic Canada to the Beaufort Sea' (2013) 22 *RECIEL* 103–116, at p. 109.

40 For an in depth analysis of the Aarhus Convention, see Pitea (n 24), in particular at pp. 225 ff.

41 Ebbesson (n 34), at p. 249.

42 Art. 4 Aarhus Convention.

43 Case ACCC/C/2007/22 (France), Findings and Recommendations (3 July 2009), UN doc. ECE/MP.PP/C.1/2009/4/Add.1 (8 February 2011), para. 49.

and that "the direct applicability of international agreements in some jurisdictions may imply the alteration of established court practice."[44] Consequently, the Aarhus Compliance Committee has suggested that the Convention might have priority over domestic law and that the public can directly invoke the rights created by the Convention in front of domestic courts.[45]

A last point concerns the participation rights of indigenous peoples. Without entering into too much detail, the United Nations Declaration on the Rights of Indigenous Peoples[46] affirms that "indigenous peoples have the right to participate in decision-making in matters which would affect their rights"[47] and

> [s]tates shall consult and cooperate in good faith with the indigenous peoples concerned through their own representative institutions in order to obtain their free, prior and informed consent before adopting and implementing legislative or administrative measures that may affect them.[48]

Moreover, ILO Convention n 169 especially safeguards the "rights of the peoples concerned to the natural resources pertaining to their lands."[49] Contracting parties

> shall establish or maintain procedures through which they shall consult these peoples, with a view to ascertaining whether and to what degree

44 Case ACCC/C/2005/11 (Belgium), Findings and Recommendations (16 June 2006), UN doc. ECE/MP.PP/C.1/2006/4/Add.2 (26 July 2006), para. 43. On the direct applicability of international norms and the self-executing nature of some international law norms, see *inter alia* T. Buergenthal, 'Self-Executing and Non-Self-Executing Treaties in National and International Law' (1993-IV) 235 *Recueil des cours* 303–400; A. Nollkaemper, 'The Duality of Direct Effect of International Law'(2014) 25 *European Journal of International Law* (*EJIL*) 105–125; J.J. Paust, 'Self-Executing Treaties' (1988) 82 *American Journal of International Law* (*AJIL*) 760–783; C.M. Vàzquez, 'The Four Doctrines of Self-Executing Treaties' (1995) 89 *AJIL* 695–723; J. Verhoeven, 'La notion d' "applicabilité directe" du droit international' (1980) 15 *Revue belge de droit international* 243–264.

45 Case ACCC/C/2005/11 (n 44). The Aarhus Committee reached the same conclusion also in relation to EU law; see Case ACCC/C/2006/17 (European Community), Findings and Recommendations (April 2008), UN doc. ECE/MP.PP/2008/5/Add.10 (2 May 2008), para. 58. The Aarhus Convention is often analysed in the context of human rights law and in reference to the concept of environmental democracy; see Ebbesson (n 34); Pitea (n 24).

46 UN Declaration on the Rights of Indigenous Peoples (n 26).

47 Art. 18 UN Declaration on the Rights of Indigenous Peoples.

48 Art. 20 UN Declaration on the Rights of Indigenous Peoples.

49 Art. 15(1) ILO Convention n 169.

> their interests would be prejudiced, before undertaking or permitting any programmes for the exploration or exploitation of [mineral or sub-surface resources or rights to other resources pertaining to lands]. The peoples concerned shall wherever possible participate in the benefits of such activities, and shall receive fair compensation for any damage which they may sustain as a result of such activities.[50]

The Convention defines "land" as "territories, which covers the total environment of the areas which the peoples concerned occupy or otherwise use."[51] It could be argued that this also includes the maritime areas used by the indigenous peoples and in which an energy project is planned.

Private Actors as Recipients of Obligations

Some multilateral environmental agreements (MEAS) provide for the involvement of private actors. Brunnée and Hey identify three ways in which an MEA can engage with the private sector, in an endeavour of "naming and shaming":

> 1) MEA may require State parties to ensure that private actors present evidence of their compliance with the regulations in place; 2) MEA requires information about the non-compliant actor to be made public or shared with other States; 3) MEA requires that either the State of export or a private actor communicate information about a traded product to the State of import.[52]

An example of a "naming and shaming" mechanism is the International Convention for the Prevention of Pollution from Ships (MARPOL Convention):[53] ships subject to certification under the MARPOL regulations must have certificates on board for inspections by port State authorities.[54] State parties must also report incidents involving harmful substances and maritime casualties[55]

---

50 Art. 15(2) ILO Convention n 169.

51 Art. 13(2) ILO Convention n 169.

52 J. Brunnée and E. Hey, 'Transparency and International Environmental Law' in A. Bianchi and A. Peters (eds) *Transparency in International Law* (Cambridge University Press, Cambridge, 2013) 23–48, at p. 43.

53 London, 2 November 1973, amended by the 1978 Protocol (London, 1 June 1978), 1340 *UNTS* 184.

54 Art. 5(1) MARPOL.

55 Arts 8, 11–12 MARPOL.

to the flag States and to the IMO.[56] The names of the inspected ships not complying with the MARPOL regulations or involved in incidents are then available in the IMO reports.

A comparable mechanism does not yet exist at the international level concerning the offshore energy industry. At the regional level, Directive 2013/30/EU imposes an obligation to report in case of major hazards (Art. 11.1.e) for a production installation (Art. 12) and for a non-production installation (Art. 13) operating within EU maritime areas. Annex VI of the Helsinki Convention also clearly provides an obligation of reporting in its Regulation 6:

> Each Contracting Party shall require that the *operator* or *any other person* having charge of the offshore unit shall report in accordance with the provisions of Regulation 5.1 [on reporting procedure] of Annex VII [on response to pollution incident] of this Convention.[57]

Moreover, Directive 2013/30/EU asks Member States to

> require companies registered in their territory and conducting, themselves or through subsidiaries, offshore oil and gas operations *outside the Union*, as license holders or operators, to report to them, *on request*, the circumstances of any major accident in which they have been involved (Art. 20, emphasis added).

Furthermore, it provides for the exchange of information among the competent national authorities, *inter alia*, through the EU Offshore Oil and Gas Authorities Group (EUOAG).[58] The EUOAG releases offshore safety statistics[59] concerning, for instance, incidents causing injuries for offshore workers or well incidents. However, no data are available concerning which company is

---

56 IMO, Casualty-Related Matters, Reports on Marine Casualties and Incidents: Harmonized Reporting Procedures—Reports Required under SOLAS Regulation I/21 and MARPOL, Articles 8 and 12, MSC-MEPC.3/Circ.3, 18 December 2008. See also IMO, Casualty-Related Matters, Reports on Marine Casualties and Incidents: Revised Harmonized Reporting Procedures Reports Required under SOLAS Regulation I/21 and MARPOL, Articles 8 and 12, MSC-MEPC.3/Circ.4, 28 August 2013.

57 Annex VI of the Helsinki Convention (n 7), emphasis added.

58 The EUOAG was established in 2012 with Commission Decision C 18/17 (OJ C 18/8, 21 December 2012) and it is formed by Member States' authorities covering both safety and environmental protection aspects. For more information see EUOAG website euoag.jrc.ec.europa.eu; accessed 11 September 2014.

59 Available at http://euoag.jrc.ec.europa.eu/node/40; accessed 11 September 2014. The most recent report relates to the period 2011/2012.

responsible for the most incidents, or in which geographical area those incidents concentrate.[60]

Aside from the obligation of reporting, private actors have a central role in the implementation of safety standards adopted at the international or supranational level. As already mentioned, private actors are the main object of Directive 2013/30/EU. Article 19 on the prevention policy clearly affirms that operators have "*primary responsibility* for, *inter alia*, the control of risks of a major accident that are a result of its operations and for continuously improving control of those risks as to ensure a high level of protection at all time."[61] Moreover, the Barcelona Offshore Protocol directly addresses the operator in relation to the obligation of monitoring[62] and to the removal of the installations.[63] In the latter provision it is clearly stated that "[p]rior to such removal, the operator *under its responsibility shall* take all necessary measures to prevent the spillage or leakage from the site of activities."[64] Pursuant to the IMO Removal Guidelines, the coastal State should identify the "*party responsible*", i.e. "*any juridical or physical person*", "for monitoring the condition of remaining material", and "should also ensure that the *responsible party* conducts periodic monitoring, as necessary, to ensure continued compliance with these guidelines and standards."[65] In relation to the treatment of disused installations, Annex VI of the Helsinki Convention states that: "The Contracting Parties shall ensure that abandoned, disused offshore units and accidentally wrecked offshore units are entirely removed and brought ashore *under the responsibility of the owner* (...)."[66]

Rule-Making and Standard-Setting

The regulation of the offshore energy sector, specifically the oil and gas industry, is fragmented at the international level. As already mentioned in the

60 The lack of such data is censurable in the light of a sustainable use of the oceans, but it is also understandable. Such data would disclose which Member States do not effectively control their coasts and oil and gas companies do not behave completely by the rules.

61 Art. 19 Directive 2013/30/EU, emphasis added.

62 Art. 19 Barcelona Offshore Protocol (n 6): "The operator shall be required to measure, or to have measured by a qualified entity, expert in the matter, the effects of the activities on the environment (...) and to report in them periodically or upon request by the competent authority for the purpose of an evaluation (...)."

63 Art. 20 Barcelona Offshore Protocol.

64 Art. 20.1 *in fine*, Barcelona Offshore Protocol, emphasis added.

65 IMO, Guidelines and standards for the removal of offshore installations and structures on the continental shelf and in the exclusive economic zone (hereinafter "IMO Removal Guidelines"), Res. A.672(16), 19 October 1989; para. 3.10, emphasis added.

66 Regulation 8 Annex VI of the Helsinki Convention, emphasis added.

introduction, there is no dedicated global intergovernmental instrument, which regulates these activities comprehensively. Soft-law instruments[67] have mainly been adopted in order to set some common standards in the field of safety and pollution prevention, control and reduction.[68] These soft law instruments rely, on the one hand, on the voluntary compliance of States, which are supposed to adopt consistent legislation at the domestic level and, on the other hand, on the self-regulation of private actors involved in the targeted activities.

The latter element is particularly problematic because international law does not have "teeth" to directly act against private actors and private actors might disguise reality.[69] For instance, before the *Deepwater Horizon* incident, BP had a very good reputation for its environmental standards; it was considered a safe company. Self-regulation by private actors may lead to self-promotion. Notwithstanding this, the BP National Commission encourages "self-regulation and co-regulation following the example of other economic sectors, such as fisheries, chemical industry, nuclear power industry."[70]

67 See in particular the instruments developed by the IMO, which has taken the lead in recent years concerning the elaboration of standards and best practice related to the offshore industry, e.g. IMO, Guidelines for safety zones and the safety of navigation around offshore installations and structures, SN.1/Circ.295, 7 December 2010.

68 Art. 208(5) of the United Nations Convention on the Law of the Sea (LOSC) (Montego Bay, 10 December 1982, in force 16 November 1994) 1833 *UNTS* 396) provides: "States, acting especially through competent international organizations or diplomatic conference, shall establish global and regional rules, standards and recommended practices and procedures to prevent, reduce and control pollution of the marine environment referred to in paragraph 1 [namely, the pollution arising from or in connection with seabed activities subject to their jurisdiction and from artificial islands, installations and structures under their jurisdiction, pursuant to articles 60 and 80]. Such rules, standards and recommended practices and procedures shall be re-examined from time to time as necessary." 2 According to Roach, there is a hierarchy of the actions States are required (*shall establish*) to adopt on the basis of this provision: legally binding rules and non-legally binding standards and recommended practices. So far, States, also within the IMO, have preferred to elaborate non-legally binding instruments and have not yet reached an agreement upon the adoption of a legally binding instrument regulating seabed activities (J.A. Roach 'International Standards for Offshore Drilling' in M.H. Nordquist, J.N. Moore, A. Chircop and R. Long (eds), *The Regulation of Continental Shelf Development, Rethinking International Standards* (Martinus Nijhoff, Leiden, 2013) 105–121, at p. 107).

69 "[E]ntity self-generated standards empower them to manage the data-driven construction of their reality"; L. Catá Backer, 'Transparency and Business in International Law: Governance between Norm and Technique' in Bianchi and Peters (n 52) 477–501, at p. 499.

70 BP National Commission 'Industry's Role in Supporting Health, Safety and Environmental Standards: Options and Models for the Offshore Oil and Gas Sector' (Staff Working

It justifies this approach by affirming that governments cannot compete with private-sector salaries for the most talented experts.[71] However, self-regulation should not become "a substitute of government but serves as an important supplement to government oversight."[72]

The crucial point, both at the national and the international level, is then to find a balance between the necessary involvement of the private actors and the regulatory power of States. It is then a bit surprising to read among the final recommendations of the BP National Commission that: "Congress should enact legislation creating a mechanism for offshore oil and gas operators to provide ongoing and regular funding of the agencies regulating offshore oil and gas development".[73] In the author's opinion, such a funding mechanism might undermine the independence of the regulatory agencies towards the industry.

Private actors include not only individual companies, but also their professional associations. In the United States, for instance, the American Petroleum Institute (API) has played a dominant role in developing safety standards. But API also regularly resisted "agency rulemakings that government regulators believe would make those operations safer", and has favoured "rulemaking that promotes industry autonomy from government oversight".[74] At the EU level, the pressure exercised by some representatives of the industry, such as Oil and Gas UK,[75] contributed to the decision to change the proposed instrument from a regulation to a directive.[76]

Paper No. 9) (2011), at p. 2, available at http://cybercemetery.unt.edu/archive/oilspill/20121210172821/http://www.oilspillcommission.gov/; accessed 11 September 2014.

71 *Ibid.*

72 BP National Commission, *Final Report*, Chapter 8 'Safety and Industry' (2011), at p. 234.

73 *Ibid.*, Chapter 9 'Develop options for guarding against, and mitigating the impact of, oil spills associated with offshore drilling', at p. 290, , available online at http://cybercemetery.unt.edu/archive/oilspill/20121210172821/http://www.oilspillcommission.gov/; accessed 11 September 2014.

74 *Ibid.*, Chapter 8 'Safety and Industry', at p. 225.

75 "We [Oil and Gas UK] believe the EC would best achieve its goal through a properly worded Directive, instead of Regulation. (...) A properly worded Directive would encourage Member States which do not currently achieve the recognised high standards present in the North Sea, to do so in a way which blends with their established legislation. This would protect the existing strong safety regime in the UK, minimise disruption to operators and regulators and eliminate the additional risk that the Regulation presents;" Oil and Gas UK, *Proposed Regulation on Offshore Safety*, available at http://www.oilandgasuk.co.uk/ProposedEURegulation.cfm; accessed 11 September 2014.

76 For a comment, see L. Schiano di Pepe, 'Offshore Oil and Gas Operations in the Mediterranean Sea: Regulatory Gaps, Recent Developments and Future Perspective' in

Professional associations are also involved in safety issues and liability coverage. The Offshore Pollution Liability Association (OPOL),[77] for instance, is a private agreement between certain European States[78] and the major participants in their offshore industries. Most participating States now require applicants for offshore exploration, exploitation and pipe-laying licenses to be a party to OPOL. Industry is also an important source of high quality and comprehensive data to ensure science-based standard setting.[79] The International Regulators' Forum (IRF) is a group of offshore health and safety regulators for the oil and gas industry, created in order to promote information sharing and collaboration through joint programmes. The participants in the IRF Global Offshore Safety are: Australia (National Offshore Petroleum Safety Authority); Brazil (National Agency of Oil, Gas and Biofuels); Canada (Canada Newfoundland and Labrador Offshore Petroleum Board & Canada-Nova Scotia Offshore Petroleum Board); Netherlands (State Supervision of Mines); New Zealand (Department of Labour); Norway (The Petroleum Safety Authority); United Kingdom (Health and Safety Executive); United States (Bureau of Ocean Energy Management Regulation and Enforcement). IRF is a very important network for the exchange of information and the collection of data. However, it consists of very different administrations, with different mandates and priorities, at different regulatory levels and with different expertise. Consequently, the type and the quality of data might diverge. There is no guarantee of coherence at the domestic level concerning the standard-setting activity that such a network generates.

J. Juste Ruiz and V. Bou Franch (eds), *Derecho del mar y sostenibilidad ambiental en el Mediterráneo* (Tirant Lo Blanch, Valencia, 2014) 363–387, at p. 379.

77 Under the Offshore Pollution Liability Agreement (concluded on 4 September 1974), operating companies agree to accept strict liability for pollution damage and the cost of remedial measures, with only certain exceptions, up to a maximum of US $250,000,000 per incident. The operating companies which are parties to OPOL also undertake to establish and maintain their financial responsibility to meet claims arising under OPOL by producing evidence of insurance, self-insurance or other satisfactory means. They also jointly agree that in the event of a default by one of the parties, each will contribute proportionally to meet claims. For more information, see www.opol.org.uk; accessed 11 September 2014.

78 The European States in which OPOL applies are: United Kingdom and Northern Ireland (including Isle of Man), Denmark (including Faroe Islands and Greenland), Germany, France, Ireland, Netherlands, Norway.

79 BP National Commission, 'Collecting high quality, objective, comprehensive data' (Staff Working Paper No. 18), 2011.

The Shifting Model of Participation of Private Actors in the Offshore Energy Industry

Since the *Montara*[80] and *Deepwater Horizon*[81] incidents, much debate ensued on the need for an international instrument to regulate the offshore energy sector in order to prevent other incidents of such magnitude and to provide for adequate compensation mechanisms. Discussions are on-going and no direction is yet foreseeable concerning the institutional setting in which (the) new instrument(s) would be drafted,[82] and the type of instrument it would be.[83]

---

80 On 21 August 2009, a well of the Montara platform, located in the Australian waters of the Timor Sea, blew out and caused a leak of an estimated rate 400 barrels (approximately 64 tonnes) of crude oil a day. The uncontrolled release continued until 3 November 2009. The blowout caused transboundary pollution damage in the Indonesian exclusive economic zone (see "Oil leaking 'five times faster' than thought" in *ABC News* (22 October 2009) available at www.abc.net.au/news; accessed 11 September 2014; Australian Maritime Safety Authority "Response to the Montara Wellhead Platform Incident, Report of the Incident Analysis team" (March 2010) at 7, available at www.amsa.gov.au; accessed 11 September 2014).

81 See (n 8).

82 As mentioned above, the IMO has taken the lead in the elaboration of instruments concerning the offshore industry. However, its mandate, as amended, includes "the general adoption of the highest practicable standards in matters concerning the maritime safety (…) and prevention and control of marine pollution from *ships*" (Convention on the Intergovernmental Maritime Consultative Organization (Geneva, 6 March 1948, in force 17 March 1958) 289 *UNTS* 3; emphasis added). The IMO Legal Committee has however pointed out: "while pollution directly arising from exploration/exploitation is however not of direct concern of IMO, the Organization may contribute to the establishment of international regulations"; see 'Implications of the United Nations Convention on the Law of the Sea for the International Maritime Organization', IMO Doc. LEG/Misc.7 Annex, 19 January 2012, at p. 18. The IMO Legal Committee in particular supports the development of guidance for States in their effort to conclude arrangements at the bilateral and regional level on liability and compensation issues connected to transboundary pollution damage resulting from offshore oil exploration and exploitation; see IMO doc. LEG 99/14, 24 April 2012, at para. 13.16. Not all contracting parties support this extension of the IMO mandate; for a comment, see Roach (n 68).

83 Some suggest the necessity of, for example, an energy protocol to the LOSC, see M. Tsamenyi and M. Herriman, 'Ocean Energy and the Law of the Sea: The Need for a Protocol' (1998) 29 *Ocean Development and International Law* (*ODIL*) 3–19. Others support the adoption of an *ad hoc* Convention regulating only the offshore oil and gas sector; see T.C.C. Childs 'Update in *Lex Petrolea*: The continuing development of customary law relating to international oil and gas exploration and production' (2011) 4 *Journal of World*

One point is however clear: the key actors in the offshore energy industry have to be closely involved, both in the drafting of the instrument and in subsequent implementation and compliance monitoring.[84] Such an approach is incorporated in Principle 10 of the Rio Declaration on Environment and Development, which affirms that: "environmental issues are best handled with the participation of all concerned citizens."[85]

The need to involve the industry is evident in Directive 2013/30/EU and is strongly supported by the BP National Commission on the *Deepwater Horizon* incident. This approach reflects the wider ongoing debate concerning the role of private actors within international environmental law. As rightly pointed out by Brunnée and Hey: "it is not states that are most directly impacted by or directly cause degradation and resources scarcity, but *individuals and groups in society*, such as farmers or industries."[86] Consequently, it is no longer convincing to maintain the legal fiction that states are the only relevant actors and the only source of international authority.[87] The OSPAR Decision 98/3, for instance, provides for the participation of the operator of the installation, whose removal is under scrutiny, within a consultation procedure that involves all OSPAR Contracting Parties and all observers to the OSPAR Commission.[88]

Energy Law and Business 214–259; S. Rares 'An International Convention on offshore hydrocarbon leaks?' (2011) 12 *Lloyd's Maritime and Commercial Law Quarterly* 361–371. Finally, some others audaciously suggest the negotiation of a brand new law of the sea convention; see F. Galea 'A Legal Regime for the Exploration and Exploitation of Offshore Renewable Energy' (2011) 25 *Ocean Yearbook* 101–129.

84 R. Shaw, 'Regulation of Offshore Activity—Pollution Liability and other Aspects, An Introduction', (2011–2012) Beijing I *CMI Yearbook* 302–310, at p. 309. Shaw in particular argues that: "Active participation by the insurers involved would be a pre-requisite to any project to develop an international convention on offshore activity, as much as that of the offshore operators themselves"; *ibid.*, at p. 310.

85 United Nations Conference on Environment and Development, Declaration on Environment and Development, Rio 1992, available on line: http://www.unep.org/Documents.Multilingual/Default.asp?documentid=78&articleid=1163; accessed 11 September 2014.

86 Brunnée and Hey (n 52), at p. 26.

87 Telesetky considers it "dangerous" to maintain this legal fiction; A. Telesetky 'Co-Regulation and the Role of Transnational Corporations as Subjects in Implementing International Environmental Law' in A. Byrnes *et al.* (eds), *International Law in the New Age of Globalization* (Brill, Leiden, 2013) 287–319, at p. 287. Also Ebbesson remarks that: "By requiring the parties to ensure opportunities and rights for members of the public to participate in decision making concerning the environment (...), the Espoo Convention with the SEA Protocol and the Aarhus Convention go beyond such a State-centred structure of international law"; Ebbesson (n 34), at p. 255.

88 OSPAR decision 98/3 (n 17), at p. 8.

The role of private actors, i.e., international oil companies, and their willingness to respect safety standards depend also on the type of contract they concluded with the coastal State.[89] Balleisen and Eisner conclude that five factors are particularly important to the effectiveness of regulatory frameworks that combine government oversight with industry self-policing:

> (1) the depth of concern for their reputation among regulated businesses; (2) the relevance of flexibility in regulatory detail; (3) the existence of sufficient bureaucratic capacity and autonomy on the part of nongovernmental regulators; (4) the degree of transparency in regulatory process; and (5) the seriousness of accountability.[90]

Consequently, mechanisms of "naming and shaming"[91] could help to enhance participation in law-making processes and, subsequently, in compliance. But before involving the private actors, competent authorities at any level of governance need to create the relevant institutional and regulatory framework in order to prioritize the achievement of specific goals, such as the protection of the environment and of workers' safety, which do not necessarily correspond to the interests promoted by the private actors. In this context, it is then particularly problematic that the institutional actors involved, namely States and international organizations, have not yet efficiently implemented Article 208.5 LOSC, which provides that "States, acting especially through competent international organizations or diplomatic conference, *shall* establish *global* and regional rules, standards and recommended practices and procedures to prevent, reduce and control pollution of the marine environment" (emphasis added).[92]

The LOSC and many of the environmental treaties above mentioned suggest that the private actors are involved in the decision-making process and the implementation of the international legal framework pursuant to what

89 P. Park, *International Law for Energy and the Environment*, 2nd ed. (CRC Press, Boca Raton, 2013) at pp. 75 ff.

90 E.J. Balleisen and M. Eisner 'The Promise and Pitfalls of Co-Regulation: How Governments Can Draw on Private Governance for Public Purpose' in D. Moss and J. Cisternino (eds), *New Perspectives on Regulation* (The Tobin Project, Cambridge, MA, 2009) 127–149, at p. 131; see also BP National Commission SW Paper No. 9 (n 66), at pp. 12–13.

91 Note that the MARPOL system has not proven to be as efficient as expected; see IMO, Flag State Implementation, Failure to submit maritime casualty reports, MSC 92/12/4, 8 April 2014. It represents however an interesting example for future similar 'naming and shaming' mechanisms.

92 See (n 68).

Mbengue defines a "model of surveillance": "non-state actors participate in the 'sustainable development contract'[93] by adhering or subscribing to rules and principles of treaty law or of customary international law, that is rules and principles generated by States and international organizations."[94] See, for instance, OSPAR Decision 98/3,[95] the above-mentioned IMO Removal Guidelines,[96] or the Barcelona Offshore Protocol.[97] The principles and standards contained in these instruments have been developed in an intergovernmental framework and contain a series of obligations whose implementation is delegated to the private actors concerned, who are deemed to subscribe to the said principles and standards. This is also the model regulating public participation in decision-making under the Aarhus and Espoo Conventions.

The UN Global Compact[98] buttresses the same model and "offers, *inter alia*, to non-state actors—and in particular to the business sector—a framework for the implementation of and compliance with principles and rules of international environmental law."[99] The UN Global Compact is a strategic policy initiative that affirms ten principles which are considered "universally accepted" in the areas of human rights, labour, environment and anti-corruption. Principles 7–9 refer to the environment and State that "Businesses should support a precautionary approach to environmental challenges" (principle 7), "undertake initiatives to promote greater environmental responsibility, and" (principle 8) "encourage the development and diffusion of environmentally friendly technologies" (principle 9).

The model of surveillance does not seem to work properly in practice, if we look at the offshore energy sector at the global level. At the regional level, many are the examples mentioned earlier where specific treaties and related institutions set in precise enough terms the limits of private actors' agency. Relevant again here are the Barcelona Offshore Protocol[100] and the Annex VI of the Helsinki Convention.[101] But, also at the regional level, private actors are

93 "The sustainable development contract (...) focuses on the necessity of balancing or integrating social concerns, economic considerations and environmental preoccupations in any process of development. As such, the sustainable development contract appeals to a broader range of non-state actors"; Mbengue (n 12), at p. 375.

94 *Ibid.*, at p. 379.

95 OSPAR Decision 98/3 (n 17).

96 IMO Removal Guidelines (n 65).

97 Barcelona Offshore Protocol (n 6).

98 See the dedicate website: https://www.unglobalcompact.org; accessed 11 September 2014.

99 Mbengue (n 12), at p. 379.

100 Barcelona Offshore Protocol (n 6).

101 Annex VI of the Helsinki Convention (n 7).

also more clearly determining the outcomes of the law-making processes and implementation mechanisms.[102] It can then be argued that there is now a shift towards a "model of transparency" in the offshore energy sector, at least at the regional level. Following Mbengue, such a model of participation entails that "non-state actors contribute primarily to the definition of the issues that should be dealt with at the international level, even if the last word in terms of policy orientations might often belong to states or to international organisations."[103] This model well describes the above-mentioned example of rule-making and standard-setting in which the private actors, namely the industry, play an important role in the making of principles and standards which regulate the sector.

Conclusions

Environmental law has strongly affected the offshore energy sector. Even if it remains a business-led sector, the public participation mechanisms provided by some of the MEAs analysed above favour taking account of and protecting multiple interests. They also act as yard-sticks for the self-regulation or co-regulation phenomenon, which strongly characterises the offshore energy sector and which is still supported by the main stakeholders.[104] The growth of self-regulation is not only a risk for the protection of the environment and the safeguard of other non-economic interests, but it can also threaten the coherence of the legal framework; it can lead "to the same risk of fragmentation within specific areas of international law."[105]

---

102 See the above-mentioned change of legislative support for what is now EU Directive 2013/30/EU; Schiano di Pepe (n 73).

103 Mbengue (n 12), at p. 380.

104 BP National Commission, SW Paper No. 9 (n 70).

105 Mbengue (n 12), at p. 385.

CHAPTER 5

Recent Framework Agreements for the Recognition and Development of Transboundary Hydrocarbon Resources

Nigel Bankes
Professor of Law, The University of Calgary, 2500 University Drive NW, Calgary, Alberta T2N 1N4 Canada; Adjunct Professor, University of Tromsø and the KG Jebsen Centre, Tromsø, Norway
ndbankes@uclagary.ca

Abstract

Hydrocarbon accumulations straddle international boundaries and maritime zones. Historically states dealt with this reality by negotiating unity-of-deposit clauses in maritime delimitation agreements, followed by specific agreements upon the discovery of a straddling deposit. A more recent trend is to negotiate framework agreements which are designed to put in place a set of procedures for dealing with the discovery and exploitation of transboundary hydrocarbon resources. This chapter examines selected aspects of five recent framework agreements.

Keywords

transboundary hydrocarbons – unitization

Introduction

It has long been understood that hydrocarbon accumulations straddle international boundaries and maritime zones.[1] State treaty practice responded to this geological reality in two stages. The first stage saw the inclusion of a so-called unity-of-deposit clause in continental shelf delimitation agreements. Such

1 G.H. Blake and R.E. Swarbrick, 'Hydrocarbons and International Boundaries: A Global Overview' in Gerald Blake, Martin Pratt, Clive Schofield and Janet Allison Brown (eds), *Boundaries and Energy: Problems and Prospects* (Kluwer Law International, London, 1998) 3–27.

 | DOI 10.1163/9789004303522_007

clauses contemplated that in the event that the parties identified a geological structure that straddled the delimitation line and which was exploitable from either side, then the parties will seek to reach agreement on the manner of exploitation of the deposit and its apportionment. Article 3 of the 1965 agreement between Norway and the United Kingdom is representative:[2]

> If any single geological petroleum structure or petroleum field, or any single geological structure or field of any other mineral deposit, including sand or gravel, extends across the dividing line and the part of such structure or field which is situated on one side of the dividing line is exploitable, wholly or in part, from the other side of the dividing line, the Contracting Parties shall, in consultation with the licensees, if any, seek to reach agreement as to the manner in which the structure or field shall be most effectively exploited and the manner in which the proceeds deriving therefrom shall be apportioned.

This is the simplest version of the clause. It contains no reference to third-party assistance in reaching an agreement, but it does contemplate that the parties will involve their licensees. Some recent agreements still follow this model.[3]

In the second stage, states negotiated individual treaties to deal with specific straddling deposits as they were discovered and developed. The first such agreement was the Frigg Field Reservoir Agreement (1976)[4] in the North Sea between Norway and the United Kingdom. This was followed by other agreements between those two countries with respect to the Statfjord Field Reservoirs (1979),[5] and Murchison (1979).[6] The pattern was extended to the Netherlands with the adoption of the Markham Agreement between the United Kingdom and the Netherlands in 1992.[7]

2 London, 10 March 1965, 551 *UNTS* 213.

3 See for example Article 4 of the Treaty between the Government of Australia and the Government of New Zealand Establishing Certain Economic Zone Boundaries and Continental Shelf Boundaries, Adelaide, 25 July 2004 (2004), 55 *LOSB* 40.

4 Agreement relating to the exploitation of the Frigg Field Reservoirs and the transmission of gas therefrom to the United Kingdom (London, 10 May 1976) 1098 *UNTS* 3.

5 Agreement relating to the exploitation of the Statfjord Field Reservoirs and the offtake of petroleum therefrom (Oslo, 16 October 1979) 1254 *UNTS* 379.

6 Agreement relating to the exploitation of the Murchison Field Reservoir and the offtake of petroleum therefrom (Oslo, 16 October 1979) 1249 *UNTS* 173.

7 Agreement relating to the exploitation of the Markham Field Reservoirs and the offtake of petroleum therefrom (The Hague, 26 May 1992) 1731 *UNTS* 30235.

More recently however, several states have negotiated framework agreements dealing with transboundary hydrocarbon deposits. These agreements go far beyond the unity-of-deposit clause found in the early shelf delimitation agreements, but fall short of effecting a unitization and apportionment of particular deposits. These agreements are the subject of this paper. These agreements represent a significant step forward over the simple unity-of-deposit clauses of delimitation agreements insofar as they establish in advance useful ground rules and procedures which should help facilitate development and avoid disputes over the development of transboundary hydrocarbon resources. This should provide some certainty for industry and affords licensees comfort that they will be able to proceed to production in a timely way in the event that they invest in expensive drilling activities and make a discovery in an area close to a boundary.

Framework Agreements for Transboundary Hydrocarbon Resources

As the name implies, such agreements establish relevant principles that the parties will apply to future discoveries of transboundary deposits. Crucially, they also establish various institutional and dispute-resolution mechanisms to help the parties develop concrete arrangements for particular hydrocarbon deposits.

The first of these agreements was the Framework Agreement between the United Kingdom and Norway concerning Cross-Boundary Petroleum Co-operation (2005).[8] It has since been followed by four other such agreements, (1) Agreement between Canada and the French Republic Relating to the Exploration and Exploitation of Transboundary Hydrocarbon Fields (2005),[9] (2) Framework Treaty relating to the unitization of hydrocarbon reservoirs that extend across the delimitation line between the Republic of Trinidad and Tobago and the Bolivarian Republic of Venezuela,[10] (3) Treaty between Norway and the Russian Federation concerning Maritime Delimitation

8 Oslo, 4 April 2005, Cm 6792.

9 Signed 17 May 2005. Not yet in force and unpublished (copy on file with author). The Agreement enters into force (Article 21) following notification that all necessary internal requirements have been fulfilled.

10 Caracas, 20 March 2007, *UNTS* registration # 50196. The parties have also negotiated one reservoir-specific agreement since the framework agreement, Unitization Agreement for the Exploitation and Development of hydrocarbon reservoirs of the Loran-Manatee

and Cooperation in the Barents Sea and Arctic Ocean (2010) and its attached Annex II dealing with Transboundary Hydrocarbon Deposits,[11] and (4) Agreement between the United States and the United Mexican States Concerning Transboundary Hydrocarbon Reservoirs in the Gulf of Mexico (2012).[12] The UK and Norway have supplemented their Framework Agreement with a set of joint Guidelines for Development of Trans-boundary Oil and Gas Fields (UK\Norway Guidelines).[13]

While each of these agreements adopts a framework approach and starts from a common point (i.e., an agreed delimitation), there is one significant difference between the situation in the North Sea (UK\Norway) and the other marine areas. In particular, while the other four agreements generally deal with marine areas where there were at the time no existing transboundary unitization agreements and little or no history of drilling in those boundary areas,[14] the UK\Norway Agreement covers a mature basin where there is already considerable experience with transboundary unitization and cooperation in the use of infrastructure, as well as a number of reservoir-specific treaties as noted above.

The motivation for these different framework agreements is therefore likely to be different. The four later agreements self-evidently aim at avoiding conflict by establishing a set of rules to govern exploration and production that take place in the area of maritime boundaries. But in the case of the UK\Norway Agreement, the parties were incentivized to negotiate the agreement in order to facilitate the development of marginal fields located close to the maritime

---

field that extends across the delimitation line (Caracas, 16 August 2010) *UNTS* registration # 50197.

11 Murmansk, 15 September 2010. The treaty was concluded in Norwegian and Russian. An English translation is available here: http://www.regjeringen.no/upload/ud/vedlegg/folkerett/avtale_engelsk.pdf; accessed 15 September 2014.

12 Los Cabos, 20 February, 2012 available here: http://www.state.gov/p/wha/rls/2012/185259.htm; accessed 15 September 2014. For background see C.L. Hagerty and J.C. Uzel, 'Proposed U.S.-Mexico Transboundary Hydrocarbons Agreement: Background and Issues for Congress', 29 August 2013, Congressional Research Service Report, 7-5700; Jorge E. Vargas, 'The 2012 U.S.—Mexico Agreement on Transboundary Hydrocarbon Reservoirs in the Gulf of Mexico: A Blueprint for Progress or a Recipe for Conflict?' (2012) 14 *San Diego Int'l L.J.* 3–76.

13 Available on the website of the UK Department of Energy and Climate Change, at https://www.gov.uk/government/uploads/system/uploads/attachment_data/file/15574/nor-guide.pdf; accessed 15 September 2014.

14 There is a long history of oil and gas production in the Gulf of Mexico, but not in the area close to the delimitation line.

boundary. This point is clearly made in the report of a bilateral industry\government working group, *Unlocking Value through Closer Relationships*,[15] which informed the negotiation of the treaty.[16] The report emphasised the need to provide industry with clear guidance and rules to facilitate development of discoveries within a corridor (the "co-operation corridor") 60 km either side of the median line. This might allow formerly stranded resources (i.e., discovered but uneconomic reserves) to be tied in to existing infrastructure on either side of the median line.[17] Thus the UK and Norwegian authorities sought to address not just straddling deposits, but also more generally how to most efficiently exploit resources located close to the median line and to ensure that the boundary should not pose an obstacle.

This chapter examines some elements of these recent agreements in an effort to identify the extent to which they provide evidence of a common approach to resolving the challenges and opportunities associated with the development of transboundary hydrocarbon deposits and other deposits located close to maritime boundaries. The chapter does not deal with the discrete topic of joint development zones[18] (although it is perhaps worthy of note that none of these agreements adopts a joint development approach). Neither

---

15 Report of the UK-Norway North Sea Cooperation Workgroup, *Unlocking Value Through Closer Relationships*, London and Oslo, August 2002, available at http://www.regjeringen.no/upload/kilde/oed/rap/2002/0005/ddd/pdfv/159318-report_uk-norway_workgroup_-final.pdf; accessed 15 September 2014. For further comment see Peter Cameron, 'The Rules of Engagement: Developing Cross-Border Petroleum Deposits in the North Sea and the Caribbean' (2006) 55 *ICLQ* 559–586 at pp. 571–574.

16 The report is expressly referenced in the preamble (para. 6) to the UK\Norway Framework Agreement.

17 Thus *Unlocking Value* (n 15) at p. 10 notes that on the UK side of the median line there were some 32 potential developments with a further 75 discoveries not currently commercial; and on the Norwegian side some 31 potential developments with 7 other discoveries not currently commercial.

18 There is an extensive literature on joint development zones. Some of the more important contributions include: David Ong, 'Joint Development of Common Offshore Oil and Gas Deposits: 'mere' state practice or customary international law?' (1999) 93 *AJIL* 771–304, esp. at pp. 787–795; Masahiro Miyoshi, 'The Basic Concept of Joint Development of Hydrocarbon Resources on the Continental Shelf: with special reference to the discussion of the East-West Centre workshops on the South-East Asian Seas' (1988) 3 *International Journal of Estuarine and Coastal Law* 1–18; and International Law Association, International Committee on the Exclusive Economic Zone, Joint Development of Non-Living Resources in the Exclusive Economic Zone, Report of the Sixty-third Conference (Warsaw) at pp. 509–569 (hereafter ILA, Joint Development Report).

does the chapter directly address the question of whether or not there is a rule of customary law that requires states to unitize shared deposits.[19]

These agreements typically address a number of different topics including: scope or coverage of the agreement, purpose and objectives, identification of transboundary accumulations and duties to exchange information, authorization for production of transboundary accumulations and the role of unitization, determination and redetermination of reserves and their allocation, technical issues (measurement, etc.), fiscal issues (royalties and taxation), infrastructure issues, environmental issues, institutions and dispute resolution, decommissioning, duration and termination. I cannot deal with all of these issues here and thus have elected to deal with four central issues: (1) the identification of transboundary accumulations, (2) authorization for production, (3) the role of unitization, and (4) institutions and dispute resolution.

Identification of Transboundary Accumulations and Duties to Exchange Information

Most of the substantive provisions of these agreements are only triggered in the event that there is a hydrocarbon deposit that straddles a delimitation line.[20] This may not always be obvious when the first well is drilled on a geological structure since, even if such a well identifies an accumulation of hydrocarbons with commercial potential, it may not reveal the geographical extent of that accumulation. It is therefore important to understand the procedure by which the parties to the treaty identify when an accumulation extends across the delimitation line.

Given the importance of the issue, it is perhaps surprising that some of the agreements do not have more to say than they do on the subject. For example, the UK\Norway Agreement hardly goes beyond the unity-of-deposit clause

---

19 Those arguing that such a rule is emerging include William T. Onorato, 'Apportionment of an International Common Petroleum Deposit' (1977) 26 *ICLQ* 324–337; those expressing skepticism include Miyoshi, *ibid.*, at pp. 8–10 and Cameron (n 15) suggesting that the background rules of international law provide states with rules of engagement rather than rules of cooperation. Other authors conceded that unitization may be common and indeed the most advisable option for preserving "the unity" of a straddling deposit, but are still reluctant to concede that there is a duty to conclude a unitization agreement. See Rainer Lagoni, 'Oil and Gas Deposits Across National Frontiers' (1979) 73 *AJIL* 215–243, esp. at pp. 218–221; and Ong, *ibid.*, esp. at pp. 778–780, 792.

20 This general statement needs to be qualified in the context of UK\Norway Agreement, given its broader scope.

of the initial 1965 delimitation agreement.[21] Article 3.1(1) of the Framework Agreement simply provides that:[22]

> Where the two Governments, after consultation with their respective Licensees, agree that a Petroleum reservoir is a Trans-Boundary Reservoir which should be exploited, it shall be exploited as a single unit in accordance with the terms of this Agreement, unless otherwise agreed by the two Governments.

The UK\Norway Guidelines take this a little further and perhaps in a different direction insofar as the Guidelines contemplate that it is the licensees that may take the initiative by informing the authorities of their home country when they wish to start development of a petroleum structure that is considered, by virtue of geological/geophysical mapping, "to extend across the delimitation line."[23] The Trinidad and Tobago\Venezuela Agreement is similarly premised on the unity-of-deposit clause of an earlier treaty[24] and has nothing to say about procedures that might be adopted to assist the Parties in deciding whether any particular accumulation is or might be a transboundary accumulation. Rather, the premise is simply that there are such accumulations.[25]

The Norway\Russia Agreement invests more deeply in this issue, providing that if there is a discovery on the shelf of one Party (A), the other Party (B) may "initiate discussions on the extent of the hydrocarbon deposit and the possibility for exploitation of the deposit as a unit" if B is "of the opinion that the said deposit extends to its continental shelf." Party B is obliged to support its

---

21 Text to (n 2) and referenced in the preamble to the Framework Agreement (n 8).

22 UK\Norway Agreement, Article 3.1(1). Cameron (n 15) makes the point (at pp. 571–572 and 574–575) that Article 4 of the 1965 Agreement (n 2) is only triggered if the trans-boundary field is also "exploitable, wholly or in part, from the other side of the dividing line", whereas the trigger in the 2005 Agreement is simply the shared understanding that there is a trans-boundary reservoir that *should* be exploited and as a single unit.

23 UK\Norway Guidelines (n 13) s.1.1.

24 See preamble para. 1 of the Trinidad and Tobago\Venezuela Agreement which refers to Article VII (Unity of Deposits) of the Treaty on Delimitation of Marine and Submarine Areas, Caracas, 18 April 1990, 1654 *UNTS* 293 and goes on recite that "the Parties after holding the appropriate technical considerations, have determined that there exist hydrocarbon reservoirs that extend across the Delimitation line, which are exploitable, wholly or in part, from either side of the line."

25 In the subsequent Loran\Manatee Agreement (n 10) Article 2, the parties confirmed the identification of six transboundary reservoirs and excluded an additional identified reservoir from the unitization on the basis that the available data suggested that the gas accumulations were located solely in Venezuela.

opinion "with evidence from geophysical data and/or geological data, including any existing drilling data." In addition, both Parties are to "make their best efforts to ensure that all relevant information is made available for the purposes of these discussions." If the Parties conclude, based on these discussions, either that the deposit may be worked from either side of the line, or that exploitation by one Party would "affect the possibility" of exploitation by the other, then they shall move to the negotiation and conclusion of a unitization agreement in accordance with Annex II to deal with the exploitation of the deposit as a unit, including apportionment.[26]

The Canada\France Agreement provides an even more procedurally intense regime. Article 2 requires each Party (Party A) to provide the other (Party B) prescribed information, results and data from any well drilled within 10 nautical miles (nm) of the maritime boundary within 60 days of receiving that information from its licensee. In addition, where all the available information allows Party A to conclude that a hydrocarbon accumulation does or does not exist, Party A shall so notify the other (B) and such a notice "shall specify, *inter alia*, whether there is reason to believe that the accumulation is or is not of a transboundary nature."[27] There are two exceptions to this rule. The first is that if, after one year after a second well has been drilled on the same geological prospect, Party A has yet to provide the notice referred to, Party B may request that the matter be referred to a technical working group (discussed further below in the section on institutions and dispute resolution) at which time Party A "shall show [Party B] the information that it has derived from the drilling and explain why the information is insufficient" to provide the notice.[28] The second exception is that the notice shall be given "in any event" no later than one year after three wells have been drilled on the same geological prospect.[29]

Where the notice concludes that the well or wells have discovered an accumulation of hydrocarbons, but Party A does not believe that there is evidence of a transboundary accumulation, then "it shall support this conclusion with evidence from technical information." Party B may in any event refer the matter to the technical working group or, if it disagrees with the conclusion set out in the notice, may refer the matter to a single expert whose decision shall be final and binding on both parties.[30]

---

26 All quotations from Norway\Russia Agreement, Article 5(2).

27 Canada\France Agreement, Article 3(1).

28 Canada\France Agreement, Article 2(1)(b).

29 Canada\France Agreement, Article 3(1).

30 Canada\France Agreement, Article 3(2), discussed further *infra*.

Once the expert has determined, or the Parties agree, that there is a transboundary accumulation of hydrocarbons, Party A is obliged to provide additional prescribed information as it becomes available from its licensee.[31] Finally, where the licensee in these circumstances has informed Party A that it intends to start production, Party A shall inform Party B "forthwith" and request that the two reach agreement on the terms of an Exploitation Agreement.[32] If the Parties are unable to reach agreement, either Party may refer the finalization of the Agreement to arbitration. An "Exploitation Agreement" is an agreement between the Parties themselves which must provide for the continuing exchange of information and must address all of the matters referred to in Articles 5–18 of the Agreement.[33]

In the case of the US and Mexico, an earlier agreement between the two states concerning the delimitation of the continental shelf beyond the 200 nm EEZ devoted two articles to the possibility that transboundary reservoirs might be discovered in the area covered by the treaty.[34] The US\Mexico framework agreement builds on this with its Article 4 entitled "Activity Near the Delimitation Line." This Article contemplates that the Parties will consult annually with respect to exploration and exploitation activities carried out within three statute miles of the delimitation line and exchange all relevant and available geological information. Each Party also agrees to notify the other of any submission of an application or approval to carry out seismic activity, an exploration plan, drill a well, or a plan for the development of production within the same area, and give the other notice where it is "aware of the likely existence of a Transboundary Reservoir" and the discovery of any hydrocarbon occurrence "near the Delimitation Line."[35]

In sum, the agreements do not do as thorough a job as one might anticipate of creating a procedural framework within which the Parties and their licensees might seek to reach agreement on whether or not any particular accumulation of hydrocarbons is a transboundary deposit. The Canada\France Agreement provides the most detailed and sophisticated treatment of this issue.

31 Canada France Agreement, Articles 2(1)(c) and 3(3) and Annex II.

32 Canada\France Agreement, Articles 3(4) and 4.

33 Canada\France Agreement, Article 4(2).

34 Treaty between the US and Mexico on the Delimitation of the Continental Shelf in the Western Gulf of Mexico beyond 200 Nautical Miles (Washington, 9 June 2000) 2143 *UNTS* 417. An even earlier treaty delimiting the EEZ and Fisheries Zones out to 200 nm is, like most US maritime delimitation agreements, completely silent on the topic of transboundary reservoirs: Treaty on Maritime Boundaries between the United Mexican States and the United States of America (Caribbean Sea and Pacific Ocean) (Mexico City, 4 May 1978) 2143 *UNTS* 405.

35 US\Mexico Agreement, Article 4(2) paras. (a) & (d).

Authorization for Production of Transboundary Accumulations

There is a considerable debate in the literature as to whether or not it is lawful for one state to authorize production from a straddling reservoir (or perhaps even a reservoir that may be a straddling reservoir) without the agreement of the other state(s). In some of the literature this is framed in terms of whether international law adopts the idea of the rule of capture in relation to migratory resources in general, and specifically in relation to hydrocarbons, or whether the prevailing norm is that of equitable apportionment.[36] This is likely to be an oversimplification of the debate, but if the rule of capture is the dominant rule, a state (A) that authorizes capture commits no wrong if it authorizes production from a straddling deposit from its side of the boundary without prior agreement with the other state (B), even where production from A's side of the line causes resources to migrate (drain) across the boundary line from under B's territory.[37]

Most commentators reject the applicability of the rule of capture at the international level,[38] but many also doubt whether one state can

---

36 J. Morris, 'The North Sea Continental Shelf: Oil and Gas Legal Problems' (1967) 2 *International Lawyer* 191–214, at pp. 205–210 (arguing that the jurisdictions adjoining the North Sea—specifically referring to England, Scotland and Norway—might each adopt the rule of capture internally; Morris does not deal with the question of whether the rule might apply as between the states, *contra* is Miyoshi (n 18) who asserts that (at p. 6, n 28) that Morris "affirms applicability of the 'rule of capture' ... in international law").

37 In both the United States and Canada it is clear that the rule of capture serves as a "no liability rule," meaning that owner A commits no wrong if production from under A's lands causes hydrocarbons to migrate from under B's lands to A's land. In the parlance of international law we would say that the authorization of production by state A does not breach a primary rule of international law and does not engage the responsibility of state A in relation to state B. For further discussion see D. Roughton, 'Rights (and Wrongs) of Capture: International Law and the Implications of the Guyana/Suriname Arbitration' (2008) 26 *JENRL* 374–401, esp. at pp. 382–384.

38 Miyoshi (n 18) at p. 6: "the lawyers at the third workshop were broadly agreed that there is no international 'rule of capture'"; Vargas (n 12) at pp. 60–61; Lagoni (n 19) at p. 220; ILA Joint Development Report (n 18) at para. 26 "... neither the rule of capture nor any prior appropriation rule can be regarded as a rule or a general principle of general international law." Ong (n 18) at pp. 778–779, 798–799 distinguishing between exploration and exploitation and referring to the provisional measures decision in *Aegean Sea Continental Shelf*, 1976 ICJ Rep 3, is of a similar view. Cameron (n 15) at p. 569 is more equivocal. On the one hand he suggests that a state may well contemplate unilateral action if met with intransigence, while on the other hand he asserts that "Variously described as 'prior appropriation' or the operation of a 'rule of capture', this option is usually assumed to be unacceptable."

stymie development by refusing to reach agreement, on, say, the terms of apportionment.[39]

Most of these framework agreements make it clear that there can be no production from a straddling deposit absent agreement. For example, Article 5(3) of the Norway\Russia Agreement provides that: "Exploitation of any hydrocarbon deposit which extends to the continental shelf of the other Party may only begin as provided for in the Unitisation Agreement." The UK\Norway Framework Agreement similarly provides (unless otherwise agreed) that neither government shall permit production to commence until the Governments have jointly approved the Licensees' Agreement, the appointment of the unit operator and the development plan.[40]

The Canada\France Agreement achieves the same result by providing that "Commercial production in the transboundary field shall not commence until an Exploitation Agreement has been concluded"[41] and furthermore that production shall not commence until the unit operator has submitted and each of the Parties has approved both a development plan and a benefits plan for the field.[42] There is no express prohibition on production absent agreement in the Trinidad and Tobago\Venezuela Agreement, but it is evident that the entire treaty is premised on the idea that production from a transboundary deposit should only occur in accordance with appropriate unit agreements and development plans.[43] However, the Treaty does contemplate that where the

39 Miyoshi (n 18) at pp. 13–14 (with reference back to the much more dogmatic position on the rule of capture); and Ong (n 18) at pp. 800–801. The tension is also evident in the Arbitral Award in *Guyana v Suriname*, Permanent Court of Arbitration, 17 September 2007, http://www.pca-cpa.org/showpage.asp?pag_id=1147; accessed 15 September 2014, at para. 460, and in the context of Articles 74(3) and 83(3) of UNCLOS, the tribunal notes that the obligation to promote interim regimes and practical measures constitutes an implicit acknowledgment of the importance of avoiding the suspension of economic development in a disputed maritime area, as long as such activities do not affect the reaching of a final agreement. Such arrangements promote the realisation of one of the objectives of the Convention, the equitable and efficient utilisation of the resources of the seas and oceans." The tribunal suggested that the duty to make every effort not to jeopardize reaching a final agreement would (at paras. 466–470) preclude unilateral exploitation activities, but not seismic exploration activities.

40 Norway\UK Agreement, Article 3.10 and UK\Norway Guidelines, 4.1 "Production Permit" (specifies when national production authorization will be required from each government).

41 Canada\France Agreement, Article 4(1).

42 Canada\France Agreement, Article 9(1).

43 Venezuela\Trinidad and Tobago Agreement, Article 3.6. The subsequent Loran-Manatee Agreement, *supra* (n 10), recites in its Preamble that the parties desire to make provision

Parties are unable to agree upon the allocation of reserves, "unitized exploitation may proceed on a provisional basis without prejudice to the position of either Party."[44]

The position under the US\Mexico Agreement is much more complex. While the Agreement clearly seeks to encourage the development of transboundary reservoirs through unitization agreements[45] (which agreements must be approved by both parties), the Agreement does *not* require that production from transboundary reservoir must occur under the terms of a unit agreement, or that such production from either side of the boundary can only occur with the agreement of both States. This is evident from the complex language of Article 7 of the Agreement.[46] Complex as that provision is, there are two key conclusions. The first is that the Agreement contemplates that both the licensees and the executive agencies should endeavour to reach agreement on all matters. Second, if the parties cannot agree, each Party can authorize its licensee to proceed—subject only to the obligation of the parties to exchange production data on a monthly basis.[47]

In sum, most of the agreements inferentially reject the applicability of the rule of capture to transboundary hydrocarbon resources. The US\Mexico Agreement is clearly exceptional in this regard and is perhaps unlikely to be followed in other agreements.

The Role of Unitization

In domestic law a unitization agreement is an agreement between all of the working interest owners (licensees)[48] within a reservoir or pool to operate the reservoir as if the reservoir were owned by a single party.[49] The parties agree to share the capital and operating costs of the unit and any production in

---

for the exploitation of the discovered transboundary reservoirs as a single unit before production commences and in accordance with the Framework Treaty.

44 *Ibid.*, Article 3.2.3. There was a similar provision in the field-specific agreements between Norway and the UK. See the Frigg Agreement (n 4), Article 2(3), Statfjord Agreement (n 5), Article 2(3), Murchison Agreement (n 6), Article 2(3).

45 US\Mexico Agreement, Article 6(1).

46 Article 7 is entitled "Management of a Transboundary Reservoir Prior to the Formation of a Transboundary Unit."

47 US\Mexico, Article 7(6).

48 In some cases royalty owners will also be necessary parties insofar as their rights will be affected by a unitization.

49 See also J. Weaver and D. Asmus, 'Unitizing Oil and Gas Fields Around the World: A Comparative Analysis of National Laws and Private Contracts' (2006) 28 *Houston Journal of International Law* 3-197. Weaver and Asmus define unitization (at p. 7) as "the

accordance with the proportion of reserves allocated to each title unit or tract within the reservoir or pool (the tract participation factor). Unitization serves to eliminate the waste (e.g., competitive drilling) and inefficiency that might result where each working interest owner exploits its tract or license block as it sees fit. In addition to a unitization agreement which deals with these "property" matters, there may also be a unit operating agreement which deals with procedural matters (e.g., how the working interest owners make operational decisions, e.g., the drilling of a new well) and accounting matters.[50]

In some jurisdictions the government regulatory authorities (e.g., the UK or Norway) will require unitization before production commences wherever an accumulation of hydrocarbons extends outside the boundaries of a licence block.[51] In other jurisdictions (e.g., most U.S. states), parties may commence production and may subsequently negotiate a unitization agreement, or, if that is not possible, seek the regulator's assistance in effecting the terms of a compulsory unitization.[52] In a few jurisdictions (e.g., Texas), there is no form of compulsory unitization. The most difficult issue in any unitization is the challenge of reaching agreement on the apportionment of reserves or the tract participation factor.

With the exception of the US\Mexico Agreement, these agreements all either assume or require that a transboundary unitization agreement will be a condition precedent to production from a transboundary field. The Venezuela\Trinidad and Tobago Treaty includes the idea of unitization in its title and in

joint, coordinated operation of a petroleum reservoir by all of the owners of rights in the separate tracts overlying the reservoir."

50 Weaver and Asmus, *ibid.*, at pp. 18 and 68 (suggesting that the practice of two agreements is more common in Canada and the US than in other jurisdictions). Several of the Framework Agreements also refer to both unitization agreements and unit operating agreements. See, e.g., the Venezuela\Trinidad and Tobago Agreement, which offers a definition of each agreement. The unitization agreement is an agreement to be executed by the Ministers; the unit operating agreement is an agreement to be executed by the licensees. See also the US\Mexico Agreement referring to a unitization agreement in Article 6 and a unit operating agreement in Article 10.

51 For Norway see F. Arnesen, Ulf Hammer, Per Håkon Høisveen, Knut Kaasen and Dagfinn Nygaard, 'Energy Law in Norway' in M. Roggenkamp, C. Redgewell, I Del Guayo and A Rønne (eds), *Energy Law in Europe* (Oxford, University Press, Oxford, 2nd ed., 2007) 881–975, at pp. 92–903. For the UK see S. Dow, 'Energy Law in the United Kingdom', in Roggenkamp *et al.* (eds), *ibid.*, 1169–1261, at p. 1193.

52 For US states see, B. Kramer and P. Martin, *The Law of Pooling and Unitization* (New York, M. Bender, 3rd ed., 2003); and Weaver and Asmus (n 49) at pp. 18–22.

the statement of the treaty's purpose[53] and Article 3 prescribes that any cross-border hydrocarbon reservoir "shall be exploited and developed … as a single unit …". The treaty seems to contemplate that the unitization agreement will be effected by the Parties based on proposals from the Reservoir Technical Working Group which will, *inter alia*, seek to agree on the estimated volumes in place and the allocation of those volumes.[54] The Norway\Russia Treaty similarly contemplates that the unitization agreement shall be between the Parties, and not the working interest owners.[55] Annex II to the Treaty stipulates a number of matters that the unitization agreement must address. Outstanding disputes as to the terms of the unitization agreement may be referred to an *ad hoc* arbitral tribunal unless the failure to reach agreement pertains to the apportionment of the deposit, in which case the matter is to be referred to an independent expert.[56]

The other framework agreements, however, all assume that the unitization agreement will be negotiated between their respective licensees. Article 5 of the Canada\France Agreement achieves this result and the UK\Norway Framework Agreement similarly provides that a trans-boundary reservoir shall be exploited as "a single unit",[57] and to that end each Government "shall require its Licensees to enter into a Licensees' Agreement to regulate the Exploitation of a Trans-Boundary Reservoir in accordance with this Agreement."[58] The Licensees' Agreement shall include proposals to address issues related to ascertaining reserves and the apportionment of such reserves and crucially must also specify "the procedures" for the resolution of any dispute as between the Licensees.[59] The UK\Norway Guidelines provide additional details including (in an Annex) the table of contents of an example unitization and unit operating agreement.[60] The Guidelines underline the significant role of the licensees.

While the US\Mexico Agreement permits the possibility that production may commence even in the absence of a unitization agreement, it is clear that such a situation would be exceptional and that unitization is expected to be

53 Venezuela\Trinidad and Tobago Agreement, Article 2, scope and purpose.

54 *Ibid.*, Article 3.2.1.

55 Norway\Russia Agreement, Article 5(2) and Annex II, Article 1 and specifically the chapeau to the Article which provides that "The Unitization Agreement between the Parties … shall provide for the following …".

56 *Ibid.*, Annex II, Article 4(1). The dispute settlement provisions are examined in greater detail below.

57 UK\Norway Agreement, Article 3.1(1).

58 UK\Norway Agreement, Article 3.2(1).

59 UK\Norway Agreement, Article 3.3(2)(b).

60 UK\Norway Guidelines, s.1.2 and Appendix 2.

the norm. Article 6 contemplates that the executive agencies should develop "one or more model unitization agreements" for execution by their licensees and lists the matters that might be included in such an agreement.[61]

A crucial element in any unitization arrangement in domestic law or international law is the allocation of reserves to the different tracts or licensed areas. In domestic law it is important that each separate tract (i.e., each titled or licensed area) receives an allocation (often known as the tract participation factor). For the purposes of international law all that really matters is the gross allocation to each state. Allocation will be effected on the basis of an expert understanding of the reserves underlying each tract. This in turn requires adequate knowledge and understanding of the reservoir, which can only be obtained by drilling wells.

One of the significant features of all of the UK\Norway Agreements, i.e., both the Framework Agreement and the earlier field-specific agreements, is the idea that neither state should oppose the drilling of a well that may help identify the geography of the accumulation or assist in the allocation of reserves.[62] The Norway\Russia Agreement contains a similar provision.[63] There is no similar provision in any of the other agreements, which seems surprising, given the importance to all parties of being able to assess the extent of any transboundary accumulation.

Most of the agreements recognize that the licensees or the unit operator on behalf of the licensees will need to take the lead in estimating total reserves in place and proposing how they might be apportioned. This approach is evident, for example, in the Canada\France Agreement,[64] the US\Mexico Agreement,[65] and the UK\Norway Agreement.[66] The other two agreements, however, seem to envisage more direct state (Party) involvement in this exercise.[67] This division between the agreements parallels the relative allocation of responsibility under the agreements for the negotiation of the initial unitization agreement.

---

61 US\Mexico Agreement, Article 6(2).

62 UK\Norway Agreement, Article 3.8, "appraisal wells". For the earlier agreements see Frigg Agreement (n 4) Article 2(5), Murchison Agreement (n 6) Article 2(6), Statfjord Agreement (n 5), Article 2(6). There is no similar clause in the UK\Netherlands Markham Agreement (n 7).

63 Norway\Russia Agreement, Annex II, Article 1(7).

64 Canada\France Agreement, Article 8.

65 US\Mexico Agreement, Article 8.

66 UK\Norway Agreement, Article 3.2 & 3.3.

67 Norway\Russia, Article 5(2) and Annex II; Venezuela\Trinidad and Tobago Agreement, Article 3.2.

Each of the agreements contemplates that the licensees\and or the Parties might require some neutral expert assistance in reaching agreement on apportionment matters. Indeed, most of the agreements contemplate that an expert may be able to make a binding apportionment order for the Parties.[68] The exception is the Venezuela\Trinidad and Tobago Agreement, where the role of the expert is simply to facilitate the Parties in reaching an agreement.[69]

All of the agreements envisage that it may be necessary to restate the reserves and\or change the apportionment formula, although the UK\Norway Agreement considers that the licensees' agreement may provide alternatively for an apportionment that will apply "for all time to all activities" or for an apportionment that is subject to redetermination.[70] One of the issues that the Parties need to deal with if there is a redetermination is the question of whether the new apportionment only applies prospectively or whether it is to be backdated to the commencement of production. The Venezuela\Trinidad and Tobago treaty[71] and the Canada France Agreement make it clear that any redetermination is to have retrospective effect.[72] None of the other three agreements address the issue and therefore it would have to be dealt with as part of the redetermination exercise itself.[73]

In conclusion, and while not universally required (the US\Mexico Agreement is again exceptional), unitization agreements are clearly the preferred means by which states and their licensees might agree to produce transboundary hydrocarbon resources. The agreements do, however, differ to some extent on

68 UK\Norway, Article 3.4 and Annex D, para.5; Canada\France Agreement, Article 8 and Annex 3; Norway\Russia Agreement, Annex II, Article 4(1). In the case of the US\Mexico Agreement, allocation questions are first referred to the Joint Commission if the Executive Agencies cannot agree on a proposed allocation (Article 8(3)). It is only if the Joint Commission cannot resolve the matter that it is referred (Article 14(6)) to the binding expert determination procedure (Article 16(9)).

69 Venezuela\Trinidad and Tobago Agreement, Article 3.3.

70 UK\Norway Agreement, Article 3.3(2)(a). A similar idea is also present in the Venezuela\Trinidad and Tobago Agreement, Article 3.8.2 of which provides that the Parties may include a provision in a unitization agreement limiting the number and timing of redeterminations.

71 Venezuela\Trinidad and Tobago Agreement, Article 3.8.4. See also the subsequent Loran-Manatee Agreement (n 10), Article 4.4.

72 Canada\France Agreement, Article 8(8).

73 The failure to address this in the UK\Norway Agreement seems odd in light of their past treaty practice. All of the earlier field-specific agreements provided that the redetermination should have retrospective effect: Frigg Agreement (n 4), Article 3(3) Statfjord (n 5) Article 3(7), and Murchison (n 6) Article 3(7).

the division of responsibilities between the state and its licensees in developing the applicable unitization arrangements.

Institutions and Dispute Resolution

For the most part, the framework agreements display considerable sophistication in the design of the accompanying institutions and dispute-resolution mechanisms. These arrangements include standing commissions, expert determination, arbitration, and technical working groups, as well as references to negotiation, consultation and mediation. The only agreement that does not provide for any form of compulsory dispute settlement is the Venezuela\Trinidad and Tobago Agreement.

Standing Commissions

All of the agreements, except the Canada\France Agreement, provide for some form of standing commission, that is generally composed of senior officials rather than technical experts, to help ensure that the agreement operates smoothly and is implemented effectively. These Commissions (or their equivalents) have different spheres of operation. For example, in the case of the Norway\Russia Treaty, the Treaty itself does not establish the Commission, but instead contemplates that each of the unitization agreements that the Parties negotiate will establish such a Commission.[74] Thus there is no single Commission, but potentially multiple Commissions. Inevitably therefore the role of the Commission under this Treaty is not to facilitate the operation of the Treaty as such, but rather the individual unitization agreements. The Commission's role, once established, is to be a forum for[75]

> ... consultations between the Parties on issues pertaining to any planned or existing unitized hydrocarbon deposits, providing a means for ensuring continuous consultation and exchange of information between the two Parties on such issues and a means for resolving issues through consultations.

By contrast, the other agreements all envisage that the Commission will play a role with respect to the framework agreement\treaty itself. In the UK\Norway Agreement the standing commission is referred to as the "Framework Forum."[76] The role of the Forum is quite explicitly to facilitate co-operation

---

74 Norway\Russia Agreement, Annex II, the chapeau to Article 1 and para. 13.

75 *Ibid.*, para. 13.

76 UK\Norway Agreement, Article 1.15.

and to *avoid* engaging the dispute-resolution provisions of the Agreement.[77] While the Forum is principally a Forum for the two Governments, it is also contemplated that the Governments may agree to "other parties attending when appropriate."[78] The text does not expressly refer to licensees, but such entities would certainly fall within this phrase.

The Venezuela\Trinidad and Tobago Agreement establishes a "joint Ministerial Commission" "to govern the implementation and execution of this Treaty and other agreements related to this unitization process."[79] The Commission is established at the Ministerial level and is to operate by consensus.[80] The US\Mexico Agreement similarly mandates the creation of a Joint Commission "to assist the Executive Agencies in Administering the Agreement."[81] The Joint Commission is designated as "the competent body" to, in the first instance, "examine any dispute or other matter referred to it by either Executive Agency relating to the interpretation and implementation of this Agreement, or any unforeseen issues arising under this Agreement."

Expert Determination

All of the agreements, with the exception of the Venezuela\Trinidad and Tobago treaty, provide that where the Parties (either on their own or on the advice of the licensees separately or through the unit operator) are unable to reach agreement on certain technical matters relating to reserves and their apportionment, either may refer the matter to expert determination.[82] Under the UK\Norway framework Agreement, expert determination may be resorted to in respect of the following matters:[83]

(a) the geographical and geological characteristics of the Trans-Boundary Reservoir;
(b) the total amount of the reserves and the methodology used for the calculation; and

77 *Ibid.*
78 *Ibid.*
79 Venezuela\Trinidad and Tobago Agreement, Article 5.1.
80 *Ibid.*, Article 5.2.
81 US\Mexico Agreement, Article 14(1).
82 Under the Venezuela\Trinidad and Tobago Agreement, as noted previously, the Parties may jointly consult experts to assist them in determining an appropriate allocation: Article 3.3.
83 UK\Norway Framework Agreement, Articles 3.3(1) and 3.4 and Annex D.

(c) the apportionment of the reserves as between the Licensees of each Government.

The decision of the expert "shall be final and binding on the two Governments," except in the case of fraud or manifest error and the two governments shall take steps to ensure that the decision is implemented by the unit operator.[84] Similarly, the Parties to the Canada\France Agreement may use the expert determination procedure where the Parties cannot agree through their technical working group if an accumulation of hydrocarbons constitutes a transboundary accumulation,[85] or if they cannot agree upon "the position, extent and estimated total hydrocarbon reserves" or their apportionment,[86] or any subsequent reapportionment.[87] In each case, the expert's final decision "shall be final and binding on both Parties", and, in the case of reserves and apportionment decisions, "on the Mineral Title Holders."[88]

Either Party to the US\Mexico Agreement may resort to the expert procedure where the two governments cannot agree on either an estimate of recoverable hydrocarbons in the reservoir under original conditions on each side of the line or "the associated allocation of production."[89] "Determinations of the expert shall be final and binding on the Parties."[90] The Norway\Russia Treaty seems narrower than the other agreements insofar as it provides that the only matter that may be referred to the expert determination is the question of apportionment and apparently only with the agreement of both Parties.[91]

The expert determination procedure is less well developed in the Venezuela\Trinidad and Tobago Agreement and indeed is perhaps best described in that treaty as an expert facilitation mechanism. Thus Article 3.3 contemplates that "The Parties may jointly consult experts in the determination of the allocation of the reserves" for a cross-border reservoir. There is no suggestion that the expert(s) will have any authority to bind the Parties or their licensees.

---

84 *Ibid.*, Annex D, para. 5.

85 Canada\France Agreement, Article 3(2).

86 *Ibid.*, Article 8(1) & (3).

87 *Ibid.*, Article 8(7).

88 *Ibid.*, Articles 3(2) & 8(3) and Annex III, para. 14. Article 8(6) goes on to provide that any Unitization Agreement shall be interpreted as if the results of the expert's determination had been incorporated in that Agreement.

89 US\Mexico Agreement, Article 7(1)(b) and (3) and Article 16.

90 *Ibid.*, Article 16(9).

91 UK\Norway Agreement, Annex II, Article 4. As with the other agreements, the expert's determination is binding on the Parties (although the Parties, Article 4(2), may agree on a reapportionment).

The agreements offer slightly different approaches to the selection of an expert. While all agree on the need for expertise in the field and the absence of any conflict of interest, where agreement cannot be reached the Canada\France Agreement favours selection by lottery,[92] whereas the UK\Norway Agreement refers this to an independent third party.[93] The US\Mexico Agreement foresees that each Party shall choose "appointing experts," who shall in turn agree upon the appointment of an expert and set the expert's terms of engagement.[94] The Norway\Russia Agreement lacks a detailed procedural annex describing the expert procedure and thus does not address how an expert is to be selected and appointed if the parties cannot agree.[95]

Arbitration

With the exception of the Venezuela\Trinidad and Tobago Agreement, all of the agreements contemplate some role for arbitration. The broadest provisions are those of the UK\Norway Agreement.[96] While this Agreement uses the term "Conciliation Board," the procedure contemplated is more correctly denominated as arbitration, since matters may be referred by one government unilaterally and decisions of the Board "shall be binding on the two Governments."[97] Ether Government may refer any matter related to "the interpretation or application of this Agreement, including any matter to be resolved under it" to the Board, except for matters that fall under the expert procedure.[98] Thus the Agreement contemplates a relatively permanent standing body, rather than an *ad hoc* tribunal put together for each individual dispute.

The scope of arbitration under the US\Mexico Agreement is almost as broad,[99] but there are three reasons for concluding that the Agreement does not provide for binding decisions, notwithstanding the use of the term

---

92 Canada\France Agreement, Annex III, paras. 3–4.

93 UK\Norway Agreement, Annex D para 3 refers the matter to the President of the Institut français du pétrole to choose between the two candidates nominated by each party and or to determine the mandate or terms of reference.

94 US\Mexico Agreement, Article 16(2). This Agreement anticipates that the Joint Commission will elaborate more detailed arrangements for the expert determination.

95 Norway\Russia Agreement, Annex II, Article 4, which simply provides that the Parties "shall appoint an independent expert to decide on such apportionment". The Venezuela\Trinidad and Tobago Agreement is silent on the appointment of experts, but inferentially they must be jointly appointed: Article 3.3.

96 UK\Norway Agreement, Chapter 5, Article 5.

97 UK\Norway Agreement, Chapter 5, Article 5(1)(vii).

98 *Ibid.*, Chapter 5, Article 5(1).

99 US\Mexico Agreement, Article 17.

'arbitration'. First, the Agreement expressly uses the "final and binding" formulation in relation to the expert determination procedure, but not with respect to arbitration. Second, the award is said to take the form of a "final recommendation" (not decision),[100] and finally, if the Joint Commission fails to accept the recommendation, the matter is to be returned to the Parties.[101]

The scope of the arbitration option is more narrowly defined in each of the Norway\Russia and Canada\France Agreements. In the case of the Norway\Russia Treaty the only matter that may be referred to an *ad hoc* three-person arbitral body is the conclusion of a Unitization Agreement between the Parties, where this cannot be resolved by negotiation or any other means.[102] Similarly, in the Canada\France Agreement, the arbitration option is confined to the situations where the Parties are unable to conclude an Exploitation Agreement within the prescribed time,[103] or agree upon the terms of a Development Plan or a Benefits Plan.[104]

Technical Working Groups

The Canada\France Agreement is the only agreement to contemplate a specific role for a technical working group. Other agreements refer to working groups more in passing. For example, the US\Mexico Agreement contemplates that in establishing its functions, the Joint Commission "may establish working groups or expert groups".[105] Similarly, the Venezuela\Trinidad and Tobago Treaty provides that the Steering Committee of the Ministerial Commission "may establish working groups for each Cross-border Hydrocarbon Reservoir in order to implement the provisions of the Treaty."[106]

The Canada\France Agreement envisages a rather large role for its Technical Working Group (TWG). The TWG is to consist of two national sections, each with a chair and a secretary,[107] generally to "examine technical issues that arise from the implementation of this Agreement or from any Exploitation Agreement."[108] The Agreement also assigns some specific roles to the TWG. Thus, Article 2(1)(b) considers that the TWG may be asked to examine whether wells drilled on a

100 *Ibid.*, Article 14(7).
101 *Ibid.*
102 Norway\Russia Agreement, Annex II, Article 3.
103 Canada\France Agreement, Article 4(5).
104 *Ibid* Article 9(1).
105 US\Mexico Agreement, Article 14(3).
106 Venezuela\Trinidad & Tobago Agreement, Article 5.6.1.
107 Canada\France Agreement, Article 17(2).
108 *Ibid.*, Article 17(1).

geological prospect have revealed the existence of an accumulation of hydrocarbons and Article 3(2) contemplates that the TWG may be asked to review the information and supporting data on the question of whether or not such an accumulation represents a transboundary accumulation.[109] The TWG, however, has no decision-making competence. Its role is evidently to facilitate a common understanding of the geology with a view to helping the Parties reach consensus. If the TWG is unable to reach that goal, then the remedy for either Party is to trigger the expert determination procedure.[110] The TWG's facilitation role is expressed even more clearly in Article 17(3), which articulates two specific mandates for the TWG. The first is to provide the vehicle within which the Parties can "review and discuss all information related to the regional geological setting and geological basins" relevant to the Agreement.[111] The second is to meet to "review concerns or issues" relating to Development Plans or Benefits Plans or preliminary versions thereof. The TWG may, if either Party requests, examine any questions relating to the implementation of any such Plan and "may make recommendations regarding modifications to the Plan or Plans concerned." It may also identify "possible issues for recourse to arbitration."[112]

Negotiation, Consultation and Mediation

All of the agreements refer in some way or other to these forms of non-binding dispute settlement. They are most dominant in the Venezuela\Trinidad and Tobago Treaty, where Article 21 (headed "dispute resolution") provides that any dispute arising out of the interpretation or application of the Treaty should be resolved in the first instance through consultation or negotiation by the Steering Committee or by the Ministerial Commission,[113] failing which any continuing dispute "shall be settled amicably by direct consultation or negotiating between the Parties."[114] Negotiation is also the default means for resolving disputes under the Canada\France Agreement, unless the dispute is a dispute that is expressly subject to expert determination or binding arbitration.[115]

The theme of consultation pervades the UK\Norway Agreement. For example, one Government must consult the other prior to altering or modifying any

109 *Ibid.*, Articles 2(1)(b) and 3(2).

110 *Ibid.*

111 *Ibid.*, Article 17(3)(a).

112 *Ibid.*, Article 17(3)(b).

113 Venezuela\Trinidad and Tobago Agreement, Article 21.1.

114 *Ibid.*, Article 21.2. The subsequent Loran-Manatee Agreement (n 10) maintains this approach, see Article 9, Dispute Resolution.

115 Canada\France Agreement, Article 18(1).

authorization for a Cross-Boundary Project, where such an amendment might materially affect the interests of the other Government;[116] there shall be "full consultation" between the two Governments with a view to the adoption of common health, safety and environmental (HSE) standards or at least to ensure that such standards are compatible;[117] the Governments shall consult with respect to HSE standards for host facilities and any reservoir connected with such facilities;[118] the Governments shall consult with respect to environmental and safety matters;[119] etc.

In sum, most of the agreements have adopted sophisticated institutional and dispute settlement arrangements to help them manage the challenge of producing valuable resources from shared accumulations. One of the outstanding features of these arrangements is that the Parties have evidently designed different forms of dispute settlement for different types of issues. For example, the agreements generally prefer expert determinations for technical issues associated with assessing reserves and their apportionment; compulsory arbitration is reserved for other more generic issues; but all agreements, except the Venezuela\Trinidad and Tobago Agreement, do provide for some form of compulsory dispute settlement for at least some sub-set of issues.

Conclusions

The framework agreements discussed in this chapter confirm that state treaty practice has come a long way since the unity-of-deposit clauses of the continental shelf delimitation treaties of the 1960s. This is hardly surprising in the case of the UK and Norway, given the extensive experience that these two states and their operators have gained over the last half-century. This experience includes not only experience in exploiting cross boundary deposits, but also experience with cooperative arrangements for exploiting and tying in discoveries in the vicinity of the median line, even where such discoveries occur entirely on one side of the line. It is perhaps more surprising that other states are also choosing to negotiate complex framework agreements even before there has been much exploration in areas close to agreed boundaries. However, this is

116 UK\Norway Agreement, Article 1.4(3).

117 *Ibid.*, Article 1.5(2).

118 *Ibid.*, Article 1.5(3).

119 *Ibid.*, Article 1.5(4). For the US\Mexico Agreement, see Article 15 which contemplates the resolution of differences through consultation within the Joint Commission or potentially mediation by a third party.

clearly an encouraging development, since such agreements serve to establish useful ground rules and procedures which should help facilitate development and avoid disputes. This should provide some certainty for industry and afford licensees comfort that they will be able to proceed to production in a timely way in the event that they invest in expensive drilling activities and make a discovery in an area close to a boundary.

The analysis of these agreements generally reveals a common approach and content. But there are some notable exceptions. For example, not all of the agreements take the space to specify procedures for the designation of transboundary deposits, and while most of the agreements are premised on the idea that production from a transboundary reservoir will only occur in accordance with the terms of a unitization agreement (or its equivalent, or an interim arrangement), the US\Mexico Agreement is a clear outlier. Similarly, most of the agreements make some provision for binding third-party dispute resolution (expert determination or arbitration), although the scope of the matters that may be submitted to either form of dispute resolution does vary. Finally, while the agreements all recognize the need to involve the respective licensees, as well as the Parties themselves, some of the agreements (e.g., Norway\Russia and Venezuela\Trinidad and Tobago) seem to envisage a more significant role for the state Parties.

It is still the case that many maritime delimitation treaties do not address the issue of transboundary hydrocarbon resources or address the issue through a unity-of-deposit clause such as that found in the Norway\UK Agreement of 1965. The agreements discussed here offer a rich suite of provisions from which to choose should states wish to go beyond such simple arrangements and provide a clear framework for the development of transboundary resources.

CHAPTER 6

Harnessing Offshore Wind Energy: Legal Challenges and Policy Conundrums in the European Union

Ronán Long
Jean Monnet Chair European Union Law,
National University of Ireland, Galway, Ireland

Abstract

Contemporary trends in European offshore wind power are explored, including: the status of the industry and its future prospects for growth; EU treaty and legislative obligations; as well as regulatory and policy issues pertaining to energy and climate change objectives. Special mention is made of EU case law on national renewable energy support schemes, along with the European Directive on maritime spatial planning; focusing on the need for further EU law reform and Member State legislative action to promote the regionalisation of the sector and the establishment of a new Energy Union.

Keywords

offshore wind energy – Renewable Energy Directive – *Ålands Vindkraft* case – maritime spatial planning – new European Energy Union – climate change law – *lex ferenda*

Introduction

The genesis of the European Union (EU) integration process may be traced back to the conclusion of three treaties in the 1950s.[1] At the time, the collaborative arrangements did not extend to the establishment of a common energy

1 Treaty Establishing the European Coal and Steel Community, 18 April 1951, 261 *UNTS* 140, Expired by its terms 23 July 2002; Treaty Established the European Economic Community, 25 March 1957, 298 *UNTS* 3. Treaty Establishing the European Atomic Energy Community, 25 March 1957, 298 *UNTS* 259.

 | DOI 10.1163/9789004303522_008

market.[2] As a result, EU Member States have long since retained considerable discretion in pursuing national policies promoting particular sources of energy, namely: nuclear power in France, Belgium and Sweden, oil in the United Kingdom, gas in the Netherlands, and coal in Germany.[3]

Rather surprisingly, the development of a common policy on energy lacked a specific legal basis in EU primary law prior to the ratification of the Treaty on the Functioning of the European Union (TFEU), which amongst other matters aims to promote new and renewable forms of energy.[4] Although the EU treaties are silent on which sources of renewable energy ought to be developed in the Member States,[5] it is clearly apparent from the widespread development of wind farms in the North Sea and elsewhere that offshore wind power now forms an essential component of Europe's energy mix and has the potential to make a significant contribution to security of energy supply, as well as the reduction of greenhouse gas emissions (GGEs) in line with the EU's ambitious commitments to combat the causes of climate change.[6] Moreover, the development of offshore wind power can also help the EU achieve some of the broader public interest objectives under its internal market and environmental policies including enhanced cross-border trade in so-called "green electricity", while ensuring at the same time that the energy sectors in the Member States remain sustainable, secure and highly competitive as part of the world's largest low-carbon economy.[7]

Ironically, despite the laudatory nature of the aforementioned objectives, EU law does not encourage directly, or indeed compel, the 23 coastal Member States to maximise the offshore wind resource in sea areas under their sovereignty and jurisdiction.[8] As a result, the industry has evolved in a haphazard fashion at a pan-European level and this trend was further exacerbated by the absence until recently of common EU rules on maritime spatial planning

---

2 A. Talus, *EU Energy Law: A Critical Account* (Oxford: Oxford University Press, 2013) *passim*.

3 L. Krämer, *EU Environmental Law*, 7th Ed., (Sweet and Maxwell, London, 2011) at p. 381.

4 Art. 194(1)(c) TFEU.

5 Art. 192(2) TFEU.

6 Council Dec. 94/69/EC, OJ 1994 L 33, 07 February 1994; Council Dec. 2002/358/EC, OJ L 130, 15 May 2002; Commission Dec. 2006/944/EC, OJ L 358, 16. December 2006; amended by Commission Dec. 2010/778/EU, OJ L 332, 16 December 2010.

7 COM (2010) 639, 10 November 2010.

8 Belgium, Bulgaria, Croatia, Cyprus, Denmark, Estonia, France, Finland, Germany, Greece, Ireland, Italy, Latvia, Lithuania, Malta, the Netherlands, Poland, Portugal, Romania, Slovenia, Spain, Sweden, and the UK.

(MSP) aimed at mitigating the cross-boundary impacts of wind farm development on other legitimate uses of the marine environment.

This state of affairs may soon change, however, as major developments are afoot within the EU legal order as a result of a judgment of the Court of Justice of the European Union (CJEU) in a recent case concerning the legality of national support schemes promoting renewable energy in Sweden,[9] and in the form of a European Directive on maritime spatial planning,[10] along with the EU's current priority commitment to establish a new Energy Union as it faces one of the most testing periods in its history in relation to energy security and climate change.[11]

All of these developments also suggest that the time might be right for further law reform to ensure that the regulatory framework is focused more directly on promoting a regional seas solution to the future expansion of the offshore wind sector and in a manner that accords fully with the central thrust of the European Energy Security Strategy,[12] the Blue Growth Strategy,[13] and the EU's Integrated Maritime Policy,[14] all of which advance a centralist European economic perspective on the strategic growth of key industries in the Member States. In order to provide some context for a discussion of these issues from a legal perspective, it is first necessary to outline the current status of the industry and to identify some of the factors that are influencing its prospects for future growth.

Status of the Industry

The European coastal environment has one of the best wind energy resources in the world and the rapid growth of the offshore wind industry since the early

9 Case C-573/12, *Ålands Vindkraft AB v Energimyndigheten*, Judgment of the Court (Grand Chamber) 1 July 2014.

10 Dir. 2014/89/EU, OJ L257/135, 28 August 2014.

11 J-C. Juncker, 'A New Start for Europe: My Agenda for Jobs, Growth, Fairness and Democratic Change, Political Guidelines for the next European Commission', Strasbourg, 15 July 2014, at pp. 5–6. Available at: http://ec.europa.eu/about/juncker-commission/docs/pg_en.pdf; accessed 12 September 2014.

12 COM(2014) 330, 28 May 2014.

13 COM(2012) 494, 13 September 2012.

14 COM(2007) 575, 10 October 2007.

1990s is impressive.[15] Over the relatively short period of two decades, the sector had grown to 69 farms in 10 EU Member States and Norway by the end of 2013.[16]

Consequently, European coastal States are now considered world leaders in the deployment of offshore wind turbines. The most suitable sites for development are in the relatively shallow waters of the North Sea, the Baltic Sea and to a lesser extent along the Atlantic coastline, all of which are in close proximity to major centres of industry in north-western Europe.[17] Quite clearly, however, the growth of the industry is not uniform at a pan-European level and there is considerable disparity in national figures, as can be seen from the information shown on Table 1 below, with some Member States such as the UK leading the field with 23 offshore farms operational by the end of 2013, followed by Germany (13 farms) and Denmark (12 farms).[18]

The number of farms is a poor indicator of the status of the sector in real terms, as the size and scale of both the individual farms and the power of the turbines has also increased considerably over time, as typified by the construction of the world's largest offshore wind power installation, the so-called London Array, in the outer approaches to the Thames Estuary. This Array is capable of generating enough green electricity to power half a million homes and reduce GGEs by over 900,000 tonnes a year.[19] Furthermore, the growth of the offshore industry in several European countries including Finland (9 offshore turbines), Ireland (7), as well as Norway (1), Portugal (1), and Spain (1), has shown little progress.[20]

15 Updated from R. Long, 'Offshore wind energy and ecosystem-based management: Are the EU regulatory answers really blowing in the wind?', in M. Nordquist, J. Norton Moore, A. Chircop and R. Long (eds), *The Regulation of Continental Shelf Development: Rethinking International Standards* (Martinus Nijhoff, Leiden, 2013) 15–52. Also see, *inter alia*: European Wind Energy Association (EWEA), Wind In Power: 2012 European Statistics (Brussels: EWEA, 2013); European Environmental Agency (EEA), 'Europe's onshore and offshore wind energy potential: An assessment of environmental and economic constraints' (Luxembourg: EC, 2009) (hereinafter EEA Technical Report No. 6, 2009); Joint Research Centre, 'JRC wind status report—Technology, market and economic aspects of wind energy in Europe,' JRC Technical Reports, (Luxembourg: EC, 2012).

16 EWEA, 'Key 2013 trends and statistics' (Brussels, EEA, 2014). Available at: http://www.ewea.org/fileadmin/files/library/publications/statistics/European_offshore_statistics_2013.pdf; accessed 12 September 2014.

17 EEA (n 15), at p. 6.

18 EWEA (n 15), at p. 10.

19 See: www.londonarray.com; accessed 12 September 2014.

20 EWEA (n 15), at p. 10.

The technical and geographical parameters governing the deployment of turbines vary considerably. That said, the majority of farms are located in close proximity to the shore (less than 50 kilometres) and in water depths of less than 50 metres, with the notable exception of Norway, where plans are in place to deploy floating turbines in depths of 200 metres and greater.[21] The general trend is to locate farms further seaward in the exclusive economic zone (EEZ) and away from the coastal zone.[22] Overall, there is extensive variation in the geographical distribution of the industry, with more than half of the farms located in the North Sea by the end of 2013.[23] In stark contrast, no major projects were operational in the Mediterranean Sea and there is therefore a clear north/south divide regarding the geographical footprint of the industry.[24] This trend is unlikely to change as it is anticipated that 60% of European offshore wind power capacity will be located in the North Sea basin and a further 20% along the Atlantic coast by 2030.[25]

Caution should be exercised in drawing any conclusions about the strategic importance of the industry; offshore wind was only capable of generating a minuscule 0.7% of the EU's total electricity consumption in 2013.[26] This is a relatively insignificant contribution to the energy demands of countries such as Germany, Poland and the UK, which are both energy-intensive and major sources of GGEs.[27] On the other hand, the offshore wind sector is expected to grow close to 20-fold from 2.9 GW in 2010 to 42 GW by 2020[28] and capable of generating 3.5% of the EU's total electricity consumption by this target date, doubling to 7% by 2030.[29] In comparative terms, Europe is expected to remain well ahead of other coastal States worldwide, including China, where electricity generated from offshore wind is anticipated to reach 6 GW by 2020.[30]

21 COM(2014) 8, 20 January 2014, at p. 109.

22 EWEA (n 15), at p. 32.

23 COM(2014) 8, at p. 11.

24 *Ibid.*, at p. 15.

25 COM(2013) 133, at p. 15.

26 *Ibid.*

27 EEA, 'Annual European Union greenhouse gas inventory 1990–2012 and inventory report 2014' (Luxemburg: EU, 2014). Available at: http://www.eea.europa.eu/publications/european-union-greenhouse-gas-inventory-2014; accessed 12 September 2014.

28 COM(2014) 8, 20 January 2014, at p. 107.

29 *Ibid.*, at p. 115.

30 *Ibid.*, at p. 141.

TABLE 1 *Status of the European offshore wind energy industry in 2013*[31]

Country	BE	DE	DK	ES	FI	IE	NL	NO	PT	SE	UK	Total
No of farms	5	13	12	1	2	1	4	1	1	6	23	69
No of turbines	135	116	513	1	9	7	124	1	1	91	1082	2080
Capacity installed (MW)	571	520	1,271	5	26	25	247	2	2	212	3681	6,562

Factors Influencing Industry Growth

First and foremost, EU energy and climate change policies are influencing the growth of the offshore industry as they stipulate amongst other matters that the combined output of all renewable energy sources must contribute 20% of gross energy consumption in the Member States by 2020,[32] growing to at least 27% by 2030,[33] and possibly to an incredible 75% by 2050 on the basis of the most optimistic forecast.[34] Ultimately, the aim is to reduce GGEs to 80–95% below 1990 levels by 2050, as part of a concerted global cooperative effort by developed countries to address climate change.[35]

Many other factors influence the growth of the sector, including: the exclusive sovereign rights granted to coastal States to develop the resource in the EEZ under the United Nations Convention on the Law of the Sea (LOS Convention);[36] physical factors, including meteorology and bathymetric

31 EWEA (n 15), at p. 10.

32 Art. 3, Dir. 2009/28/EC. Also, COM(2006) 848, 10 January 2007.

33 The European Council will take a final decision on the 2030 targets for renewables in October 2014. See European Council Conclusions, 20–21 March 2014. Available at: http://www.consilium.europa.eu/uedocs/cms_Data/docs/pressdata/en/ec/141749.pdf; accessed 12 September 2014.

34 COM(2011) 885, 15 December 2011, at p. 4.

35 See Information Note, Council of the European Union, EU position for the Copenhagen Climate Conference (7–18 December 2009), Council conclusions, Brussels, 21 October 2009, para. 15. Available at: http://register.consilium.europa.eu/doc/srv?l=EN&f=ST%20 14790%202009%20INIT; accessed 12 September 2014.

36 Art. 56(1)(a), LOS Convention (Montego Bay, 10 December 1982, in force 16 November 1994) 1833 *UNTS* 396. Council Dec. 98/392, OJ L 179/1, 23 June 1998. On marine renewables, see, *inter alia*: M. Abad Castelos, 'Marine Renewable Energies: Opportunities, Law and

conditions in coastal waters, with the industry expressing a strong preference for locations with steady wind speeds and shallow waters; the availability of maritime space in sea areas under the sovereignty and jurisdiction of the Member States; the potential for conflict with other users of the marine environment, or clashes with other spatial designations, including those that provide for shipping and nature conservation; market considerations, including fossil fuel and carbon prices, allied with demand for energy both within and beyond the EU; as well as extraneous factors, such as social opposition to land-based wind turbines in several Member States.[37] The latter consideration is pushing wind farms further seawards in the Netherlands, Germany and the UK, who have all placed restrictions on the construction of wind farms within 12 nautical miles of the coast in order to mitigate, amongst other matters, the visual impact of the turbines on the human environment.[38]

Most notably, government policy and national regulatory measures in several Member States are influencing the development of the sector.[39] A multiplicity of political considerations is also at play, which vary from one Member State to another. A case in point is Germany, where government policy mandates a move away from nuclear power and greater reliance on renewable sources of energy, a policy decision that will cost an estimated $340 billion to implement and which has been influenced and accelerated by the Fukushima

---

Management' (2014) 45(2) *Ocean Development and International Law* 221–237; D. Murray, C. Carr, J. Jeffers and A. Núñez-Luna, 'Riding the Wave: Confronting Jurisdictional and Regulatory Barriers to Ocean Energy Development' (2011) 5(1) *Golden Gate Univ. Env. L.J.* 159–195; F. Galea, 'A Legal Regime for the Exploration and Exploitation of Offshore Renewable Energy' (2011) 25(1) *Ocean Yearbook* 101–129; J. Sterne, T. Jensen, J. Keil, R. Roos-Collins and D. Wand, 'The Seven Principles of Ocean Renewable Energy: A Shared Vision and Call for Action', (2009) 14(3) *Roger Williams University Law Review* 600–623; D. Leary and M. Esteban, 'Climate Change and Renewable Energy from the Ocean and Tides: Calming the Sea of Regulatory Uncertainty' (2009) 24(4) *IJMCL* 617–651. More specifically on wind power, see, *inter alia*; M. Esteban and D. Leary, 'Current developments and future prospects of offshore wind and ocean energy' (2012) 90 *Applied Energy* 128–136; B. Snyder and M. Kaiser, 'A comparison of offshore wind power development in Europe and the U.S.: Patterns and drivers of development' (2009) 86(10) *Applied Energy* 1845–1856.

37 EWEA, 'Wind Barriers: Administrative and grid access barriers to wind power' (EWEA, Brussels, 2010), 8 and 23. Available at: http://www.windbarriers.eu/fileadmin/WB_docs/documents/WindBarriers_report.pdf.; accessed 12 September 2014.

38 EEA Technical Report No. 6, 2009 (n 15), at p. 32.

39 ORRECA Project, 'European Offshore Renewable Energy Roadmap' (University of Edinburgh, 2011) at pp. 86–89. Available at: http://www.orecca.eu/c/document_library/get_file?uuid=1e696618-9425-4265-aaff-b15d72100862&groupId=10129; accessed 12 September 2014.

nuclear disaster in Japan.[40] In order to facilitate this switch to green energy, the German marine spatial plan provides for the deployment of 8,000 turbines in the North and Baltic Seas.[41]

Progress in other Member States has faltered, with some countries, such as Ireland, indicating that its substantial offshore wind resource will only be developed as an export opportunity if it is economically beneficial to do so.[42] Moreover, the European Commission has identified several regulatory reasons why EU Member States are slow to exploit the full potential of ocean energy, including wind power.[43] In particular, it appears that the absence of discrete licensing processes is impeding progress, with many Member Sates adopting a case-by-case approach using the laws that apply to petroleum, aquaculture or other offshore developments, for the purpose of evaluating and approving ocean energy projects, including offshore wind farms.[44] This is compounded by the utilisation of different consent processes for projects that are located in the territorial sea *vis-à-vis* those that are located in the EEZ, reportedly a feature of the licensing schemes utilised by Belgium, Germany and Sweden.[45] In some instances, the administrative costs associated with offshore project applications can amount to 14% of total project costs, which is far higher than similar projects on land.[46]

Apart from the inordinate cost associated with generating electricity from offshore wind power, challenges are posed by the subsea power transmission grid and its integration into the terrestrial network, as well as the completion of seabed inter-connectors between Member States to allow for the export and importation of electricity.[47] Remarkably, grid connections are designed to serve exclusively the national energy markets in individual Member States

---

40 L. Davies, 'Beyond Fukushima: Disasters, Nuclear Energy, and Energy Law' (2011) 6 *Brigham Young University Law Review* 1937–1990, especially at pp. 1947–1951.

41 See R. Long, 'Offshore Wind Energy Development in Germany: Actors, Legal Instruments and Decision-Making Procedures', in H. Koch and D. Könnig (eds), *Global Environmental Problems and the Globalisation of Environmental Law* (Martinus Nijhoff, Leiden, 2013) 227–240.

42 Department of Communications, Energy and Natural Resources, 'Strategy for Renewable Energy 2012–2020' (DCENR, Dublin, 2012). Available at: http://www.dcenr.gov.ie/NR/rdonlyres/9472D68A-40F4-41B8-B8FD-F5F788D4207A/0/RenewableEnergyStrategy2012_2020.pdf; accessed 12 September 2014. See also (n 196).

43 COM(2014) 8, at p. 14

44 *Ibid.*, at p. 15.

45 *Ibid.*

46 *Ibid.*, at p. 14.

47 ORRECA (n 39).

with little regard, up until recently, for regional cooperation or the direct transmission of electricity supplies between Member States.[48]

In the main, the principal over-riding factors shaping the industry are the high capital costs and the questionable profitability of offshore wind power. In this regard, although offshore wind speeds are higher than those onshore and are characterised by higher load hours,[49] the production and transmission of electricity from offshore sources is considerably more expensive than the cost of energy generated from fossil fuels or indeed from terrestrial wind farms.[50] The future of the offshore wind industry is thus highly dependent on fiscal and market support from public funds in the Member States in the form of feed-in tariffs, grants, subsidies, and tax credits. Moreover, fiscal subvention of the industry is very much contingent upon EU State aid approval and is closely linked with national renewable energy support programmes, which again diverge significantly across the EU.[51]

Constraints Arising from EU Primary Law

As is well known, the EU can act only within the limits of the competences conferred upon it by the Member States under the European treaties.[52] In this regard, a range of diverse and complex EU treaty provisions pertain to energy, the environment, the internal market, as well as on trans-European networks and infrastructure, are influencing offshore wind power development in the Member States.[53] Three brief points can be made about these provisions from the perspective of EU energy law more generally.

---

48 See (n 83).

49 EEA Technical Report No. 6, 2009 (n 15), pp. 35–49, and especially at p. 41.

50 The European Joint Research Centre estimated that the cost of electricity from offshore wind is €0.18 per kWh, from nuclear technologies €0.067/kWh, combined cycle gas €0.061/kWh, and coal without carbon capture and storage €0.052/KWh. See Annex 16, COM(2014) 8 final, Brussels, 20 January 2014.

51 For a summary of the various support schemes in operation in the UK, Scotland (which differs from the rest of the UK), Ireland, France, Italy, the Netherlands, Germany, Belgium, and Denmark, see Annex 8 of COM(2014) 8, 20 January 2014, at pp. 83–93. Also, J. Krzeminska, 'Are Support Schemes for Renewable Energies Compatible with Competition Objectives? An Assessment of National and Community Rules' (2007) 7 *Yearbook of European Environmental Law* 125–158.

52 Art. 5(2) TEU.

53 Arts. 112, 170, 194, 192 TFEU.

First, much of the difficulty in rolling out a coherent and integrated framework governing the offshore wind sector at a regional seas level appears to stem from the fact the EU and Member States share competence (responsibility) for the formulation and implementation of energy policy.[54] Accordingly, any EU legislative proposals concerning the future development of the sector must respect the dual principles of subsidiarity and proportionality.[55] Under the former principle, the EU can only act if and insofar as the objectives of the proposed action cannot be sufficiently achieved by the Member States, or if it can be better achieved at the level of the EU by reason of the scale or effects of the proposed action.[56] The principle of proportionality ensures that the content and form of EU action does not exceed what is necessary to achieve specific treaty objectives, such as the promotion of renewable energy.[57]

Second, the EU treaty objectives for energy are remarkably *avant-garde* from an offshore wind power perspective insofar as they aim to ensure the functioning of the energy market, the security of supply, the promotion of energy efficiency and savings, and to ensure the development of new and renewable forms of energy, together with the interconnection of energy networks.[58] The EU is obliged to take internal market and environmental considerations into account in the attainment of these objectives.[59] Elsewhere, the TFEU provides that the EU is obliged to contribute to the establishment and development of trans-European energy networks and infrastructures.[60] The latter is an absolute imperative for the completion of the subsea power grid at regional seas levels.

The third point concerns the remit and law-making powers of the European institutions. In the first instance, the European Parliament and the Council are tasked with adopting the measures necessary to achieve the treaty objectives on energy including the rolling out of an appropriate legislative programme within the European institutions.[61] They must follow the ordinary legislative procedure in the European Parliament and Council, with the latter body acting on the basis of a qualified majority of votes of the Member States.[62]

---

54 Art. 4(2)(i) TFEU.

55 Art. 4(2)(i) TFEU.

56 Art. 5(3) TEU.

57 Art. 5(4) TEU.

58 Art. 194(1) TFEU.

59 Arts. 112 and 194 TFEU.

60 Art. 170(1) TFEU.

61 Art. 194(2) TFEU.

62 Art. 238 TFEU.

At first sight, it may appear that EU primary law provides a legal basis for the adoption of EU harmonisation measures promoting the further development of offshore wind power. Crucially, however, Member States retain absolute discretion under the treaties in setting the conditions for exploiting energy resources, as well as in choosing between the different energy sources and the general structure of energy supply with a view to meeting their national needs.[63] Indeed, in the context of adopting measures that are primarily of a fiscal nature, or to advance environmental policy, the law-making powers of the European institutions are clearly fettered by the TFEU, which requires the Council to act with unanimity in accordance with a special legislative procedure if it is to adopt measures significantly affecting a Member State's choice between different energy sources and the general structure of energy supply.[64] Furthermore, the European Parliament, the Economic and Social Committee and the Committee of the Regions are only afforded a mere consultative role by the EU treaties in the law-making process regarding such measures and this undermines their capacity to influence the development of a common EU policy on energy.[65] What this means in practice is that the power to adopt EU legislative measures promoting a regional solution to the future development of offshore wind power rests firmly with the Member States, who must act collectively within the Council of Energy Ministers. The latter is a formidable hurdle to overcome in light of the divergent national interests that are at stake and the tendency of the Member States to guard rigorously their sovereign rights from further EU encroachment in a key industrial sector.

Fragmented Tableau of EU Secondary Legislation

In addition to EU primary law, a fragmented tableau of EU regulatory instruments is applicable to offshore wind power development, including legislation on the internal electricity market,[66] the Energy Security Directive,[67] the Renewable Energy Directive (the RES Directive),[68] the law related to the

63 Declaration 35 of the Intergovernmental Conference on Art. 194 TFEU, OJ C 83/349, 30 March 2010.

64 Arts. 192(2)(c) and 194(3) TFEU.

65 *Ibid.*

66 Dir. 2009/72/EC, OJ L 211, 14 August 2009, 55–93.

67 Dir. 2005/89/EC, OJ L 33, 4. February 2006, 22–27.

68 Dir. 2009/28/EC, OJ 2009 L 140, at p. 16.

EU Emissions Trading Scheme,[69] the rules on State aid and competition policy,[70] as well as a raft of legislation on the protection and preservation of the marine environment.[71]

Foremost is the RES Directive,[72] which provides a common regulatory framework for the promotion of energy from renewable sources, including offshore wind power. The RES Directive establishes mandatory national targets for the overall share of energy from renewable sources, as well as the rules relating to joint energy projects between Member States, guarantees of origin, administrative procedures, information and training, along with access to the electricity grid,[73] and the renewable energy targets that must be achieved by individual Member States by 2020.[74]

Although the wind resource could theoretically meet the EU's entire electricity needs if it is developed to its full capacity,[75] the RES Directive does not specify any preference for wind power or indeed require the Member States to have an offshore wind component in their national renewable energy action plans.[76] Moreover, by the end of 2013, the pace of implementation of this instrument was slow as demonstrated by the European Commission initiating infringement proceedings against 12 Member States for incomplete transposition of the RES Directive.[77] In addition, Member States have also shown a marked reluctance to establish joint or regional renewable energy projects between two or more Member States.[78] Having said that, they remain on schedule to meet their 2020 targets under their national policies and programmes.[79]

---

69 Dir. 2009/29/EC, OJ L 140, 5 June 2009, 63–87; Dir. 2008/101/EC, OJ L 8, 13 January 2009, 3–21; Dir. 2004/101/EC, OJ L 338, 13 November 2004, 18–23; Dir. 2003/87/EC, OJ L 275, 25 October 2003, 32–46; Dir. 2003/87/EC, OJ L 275, 25 October 2003, 32.

70 Community guidelines on State aid for environmental protection, OJ C 82, 1 April 2008, 1–33.

71 Long (n 15).

72 Dir. 2009/28/EC (n 68).

73 Art. 1, Dir. 2009/28/EC.

74 Art. 3(1). Dir. 2009/28/EC.

75 COM(2008) 768, at p. 3.

76 Art. 4, Dir. 2009/28/EC.

77 Austria, Bulgaria, Cyprus, Czech Republic, Finland, Hungary, Ireland, Latvia, Luxembourg, the Netherlands, Poland and Slovenia. COM(2013) 175, at p. 13.

78 COM(2013) 175, at p. 12.

79 COM(2013) 175, at p. 15.

Complementary to the RES Directive, the EU has adopted various legislative instruments that are aimed at facilitating cross-border trade in electricity.[80] Sizeable efforts have also been made to promote and integrate renewable energy sources in the Member States through the provision of financial support for their interconnection at the continental level by means of the development of trans-European energy infrastructure.[81] Not all of these efforts have been entirely successful and the European Commission has reported that significant obstacles remain concerning permits, regulatory and fiscal matters.[82] In order to redress some of these shortcomings, the European institutions and the Member States are in the process of adopting a comprehensive package of measures aimed at developing priority corridors and areas of trans-European energy infrastructure, including the Northern Seas Offshore Grid and the related interconnectors in the North Sea, the Irish Sea, the English Channel, the Baltic Sea and neighbouring waters.[83]

Legal Challenges and Policy Conundrums

In spite of the considerable progress that has been made in several of the Member States, two major impediments appear to be holding the industry back from evolving into a highly competitive and a well-integrated sector that contributes on a regional basis to security of supply in the European energy market.

The first difficulty stems from the EU regulatory approach to renewable energy in general, which is at odds with some central tenets of European trade

80 Dir. 2003/54/EC, OJ 2003 L 176, 15 July 2003; Dir. 2009/72/EC, OJ 2009 L 211, 14 August 2009; Reg. 1228/2003, OJ 2003 L 176, 15 July 2003; Reg. 714/2009, OJ 2009 L 211, 14 August 2009.

81 COM(2010) 677, 17 November 2010.

82 Arts. 34–37 TFEU.

83 Reg. 347/2013, OJ L 115/39, 25 February 2013; Commission Delegated Reg. 1391/2013, OJ L 349/28, 21 December 2013; Reg. 670/2012, OJ L 204/1, 31 July 2012; Reg. 1316/2013 OJ L 348/129, 20 December 2013. There is a regional agreement between 10 Member States and Norway to develop a super-network high voltage cable in the North Sea by 2030. See, Memorandum of Understanding on the North Seas Countries Offshore Grid Initiative signed by Germany, Belgium, Denmark, France, Ireland, Luxembourg, Norway, Netherlands, UK, and Sweden on 3 December 2010. Available at: http://www.ewea.org/fileadmin/files/library/publications/research-notes/MoU_definitief.pdf; accessed 12 September 2014.

law on the functioning of the internal market and the free movement of goods across the internal borders of EU Member States.[84] One patent complexity arises from the RES Directive,[85] which assigns individual Member States mandatory national targets formulated in quotas regarding the production of green electricity without specifying which if any of the sources ought to be prioritised.[86] Indeed, according to the Court of Justice, the scheme advanced by EU law enables Member States to "control the effect and costs of their national support schemes according to their different potentials", while maintaining investor confidence in the sector.[87] Key decisions in this regard, however, rest with the national authorities in the Member States who can meet their renewable energy targets using domestic resources, or through the transfer of guarantees of origin for renewables by means of international agreements between governments, or through a system of private trade.[88]

The second peculiarity relates to the manner in which EU policy on renewable energy deviates significantly from some of the core objectives of the EU's Integrated Maritime Policy.[89] Supposedly, the latter aims to harmonise national policies on maritime activities, including those pertaining to energy, with a view to achieving the right balance between the economic, social and environmental dimensions of sustainable development.[90] The absence of uniform regional rules on MSP up until recently undermined the capacity of Member States to attain this objective and did little for the orderly management and administration of offshore activities, or to lessen the trans-boundary impacts associated with placing thousands of turbines in relatively congested areas of the marine environment. This lacuna in EU law contributed to a putative dispute that arose between the Netherlands and Belgium in 2012 concerning the authorization of a wind farm by Belgium in an area that impeded shipping routes serving Dutch ports.[91] This was not an isolated incident, as a similar dispute arose between the Netherlands and Germany concerning the technical aspects of wind farm safety zones in the German EEZ.[92]

84 Arts. 26 and 34–37 TFEU.

85 Dir. 2009/28/EC (n 68).

86 Arts. 3(1), 5(1) and (3), Dir. 2009/28/EC.

87 Case C-573/12, para. 99.

88 Arts. 4, 7 and 9 Dir. 2009/28/EC.

89 COM(2007) 575 (n 14).

90 *Ibid.*, at p. 9.

91 SWD (2013) 65, at p. 34.

92 *Ibid.*

Although these disputes were settled amicably through bilateral diplomacy,[93] they nonetheless highlighted the pressing need for a common EU approach on MSP, characterised by close inter-Member State coordination and planning of offshore economic activities. Pointedly, the whole issue of uniformity and the diversity of national rules with respect to the operation of the internal energy market is also a theme that has been placed firmly on the EU's law-reform agenda, due to a landmark decision of the CJEU concerning renewable energy support schemes, which merits further consideration here.

Court of Justice Clears the Air on National Support Schemes

The definition of goods in EU law extends to electricity.[94] The free movement of goods across the internal frontiers of the Member States is a key feature of EU trade law.[95] Several important CJEU judgments in the field of energy[96] touch upon the compatibility of Member State law restricting trade in goods with EU climate change and environmental obligations.[97] Instructively, as far back as 1998, the Court upheld a German law on renewable energy on environmental grounds, even though the contested legislation required private companies to purchase renewable electricity at prices that were higher than the real economic value of this type of electricity.[98] Since then, the EU regulatory

93 Closing remarks made by Dr. René Lefeber, Netherlands Ministry of Foreign Affairs, at the final session of the conference, Energy from the Sea: An International Law Perspective on Ocean Energy, Utrecht, 19–20 February 2014, (contemporaneous note taken by the author).

94 Case 7/68, [1968] ECR 423.

95 Arts. 28–37 TFEU.

96 See *inter alia*: Case 72/83, [1984] ECR 2727; Case C-213/96, [1998] ECR I-1777; Case C-323/02, [2003] ECR I-9071; Case C-239/07, [2008] ECR 1-7523; C-264/09, [2011] ECR I-13693; Case C-2/10, [2010] ECR I-5031; Case C-219/12, 20.06.2013; Case C-347/10, 17.01.2012; Case C-198/12, 5.06.2014.

97 See, for example, Case C-2/10, [2010] ECR I-5031. The Court has also upheld discriminatory national measures in the field of air transport on the grounds of noise pollution in Case C-389/96, [1998] ECR 1-4473.

98 Case C-379/98, [2001] ECR I-2099. See *inter alia*: D. Fouquet and U. Prall, 'Renewable Energy Sources in the Internal Electricity Market: The German Feed-in Model and its Conformity with Community Law' (2005) 2(4) *Journal for European Environmental and Planning Law* 309–324; B. Müller, 'EC Legislation Concerning Renewable Energy Sources: Promotion at the Community Level and Implementation in Germany' (2005) 2(5) *Journal for European Environmental and Planning Law* 393–408.

regime applicable to renewable energy has undergone fundamental change in the form of the RES Directive, so it was only a question of time before many of the key issues remerged again in the Court's jurisprudence.[99]

Against this background, the *Ålands Vindkraft* case marks a new high point in EU energy and climate change law, insofar as it offered a Grand Chamber of the Court the opportunity to interpret the RES Directive and to clarify the precise relationship between EU trade law and environmental law relating to the production of energy from renewable sources, as well as the legality of the national renewable energy support schemes that restrict intra-Member State trade in electricity.[100]

The case came to the European Court by way of preliminary reference from the Administrative Court in Linköping in Sweden.[101] The gravamen of the reference arose out of the refusal of the Swedish Energy Agency to award an offshore wind farm located in the Finnish Åland archipelago tradable "green certificates", on the grounds that only installations located within Swedish territory were eligible for such an award under the national support scheme.[102] Among other matters, Ålands Vindkraft contended that the net effect of the refusal was to obstruct the importation of electricity from Finland into Sweden contrary to European treaty provisions on the free movement of goods.[103] As a consequence, they asserted that the producers of green electricity in Sweden had an unfair commercial advantage in that they could couple or package the sale of electricity with green certificates and thereby promote the sale of the latter to the detriment of producers in other Member States.[104] Both the RES Directive and Swedish law make provision for collaborative arrangements, whereby two or more Member States can coordinate their national support schemes.[105] Although such an arrangement applied between Sweden and Norway, there was no similar agreement between Sweden and Finland.[106]

99 See discussion on secondary legislation *infra.*

100 Case C-573/12, (n 9).

101 Art. 267 TFEU.

102 Case C-573/12, paras 23–24. The judgment is silent on whether the Swedish law also applied to installations in sea areas under national sovereignty and jurisdiction.

103 Art. 34 TFEU.

104 Case C-573/12, para. 28.

105 Art. 11 Dir. 2009/28 and Swedish Law (2011:1200) on electricity certificates (*lagen* (2011:1200) *om elcertifikat*), chapter 1, para. 5.

106 Case C-573/12, para. 22.

The Grand Chamber of the Court declined to follow the previous (non-binding) Opinion of Advocate General Bot,[107] and held that the RES Directive allows Sweden to operate a support scheme that is characterised by territorial restrictions on the award and forfeiture of green certificates.[108] Moreover, this restriction is permissible under EU law as it is aimed at promoting increased use of renewable energy in the production of electricity,[109] and is thus "in principle" capable of justifying trade barriers.[110] The Court seized the opportunity to clarify a long-standing issue that has clouded the precise interface between EU trade and environmental protection law for close to two decades.[111] Citing its own jurisprudence and Article 194(1)(c) TFEU,[112] the Court noted that one of the aims of renewable energy is to combat climate change through the reduction of GGEs and that this justified restrictions on the free movement of electricity between Member States.[113] The rationale underpinning the judgment and the Court's application of the proportionality principle are very much focused on the practical aspects of promoting the achievement of renewable energy targets at the production stage rather than the consumption stage,[114] as well as on promoting investor confidence in financing green energy.[115]

The CJEU has one other pending case on its docket concerning cross-border trade restrictions on green electricity in Belgium,[116] but a major *volte-face* in the Court's approach to the functioning of the internal energy market is highly unlikely. Accordingly, the reform of EU law on national support scheme now appears to be a task for the EU's legislator as it strives to establish a new Energy Union.

---

107 Opinion of Advocate General Bot delivered on 28 January 2014. Available at: http://curia.europa.eu/juris/document/document.jsf?text=&docid=146942&pageIndex=0&doclang=EN&mode=lst&dir=&occ=first&part=1&cid=370669; accessed September 12, 2015.

108 Case C-573/12, paras. 38–54, citing Article 2(2)(k) and Article 3(3) Dir. 2009/28/EC.

109 Case C-573/12, paras. 77–82.

110 Art. 34 TFEU; Case C-573/12, paras. 82, 94.

111 Case C-203/96, [1998] ECR I-4075; Case C-379/98, [2001] ECR I-2099; Case C-320/03, [2003] ECR I-7929; Case C-142/05, [2009] ECR I-4273; Case C-524/07 [2008] ECR I-187.

112 Case C-379/98, paras. 73, 75.

113 Case C-573/12, para. 82.

114 Case C-573/12, paras. 95–96. This judgment is difficult to reconcile with the previous decision of the Court concerning the importation of electricity from Swedish hydropower into Finland in Case C-213/96, [1998] ECR I-1777.

115 Case C-573/12, paras. 100–103.

116 Case C-208/12 (Joined Cases C-204/12, C-205/12, C-206/12, C-207/12, C-208/12). On the questions referred concerning the Flemish green certificates and guarantees of origin, see OJ C 227/11, 28 July 2012.

In marked contrast to the scheme advanced by the RES Directive and upheld by the Court in the *Ålands Vindkraft* case, the European institutions took a more innovative and European approach in the MSP Directive, which actively promotes cross-border cooperation and coordination in relation to the provision and management of offshore energy infrastructure.

A Partial Panacea: EU Directive on MSP

Many coastal States worldwide, including EU Member States, are implementing sophisticated planning systems governing the use of maritime space in sea areas under their sovereignty and jurisdiction.[117] Strategic environmental and project assessment combined with MSP can aid the process of wind farm site selection and conflict management.[118] The European Commission has nonetheless pointed out that the spatial planning procedures followed by the majority of EU Member States are not targeted specifically at marine renewable energy development or at resolving conflict between wind farms and other maritime activities.[119]

The European institutions are actively pushing MSP as a panacea to many of the problems encountered by the Member States in managing offshore activities including offshore wind farm development. This approach fully accords with international best practice and is a relatively new initiative on the landscape of EU law.[120] More specifically, the initial blueprint on the subject-matter was set out in two strategic policy documents entitled 'Roadmap for MSP:

117 These include Belgium, Germany, Portugal, Sweden, the Netherlands and the UK. See F. Douvere and C.N. Ehler, 'New perspectives on sea use management: Initial findings from European experience with marine spatial planning' (2009) 90 *Journal of Environmental Management* 77–88.

118 Long (n 15) at pp. 36–41.

119 COM(2014) 8, 20 January 2014, at p. 15. Also see, EWEA, 'Offshore Renewable Energy and Maritime Spatial Planning' (EWEA, Brussels, 2011) available at: http://www.seanergy2020.eu/wp-content/uploads/2011/11/111020_Seanergy2020_Deliverable3.2_Final.pdf; accessed 12 September 2014.

120 See, *inter alia*: D. Rothwell and T. Stephens, *The International Law of the Sea* (Hart Publishing, Oxford, 2010) at pp. 465–467; F. Douvere and C. Ehler, 'Marine spatial planning: identifying the critical elements for success', in E. Ciccotelli and C. Benigno (eds), *Spatial Planning: Strategies, Developments and Management* (Nova Sciences Publishers, Hauppauge, 2012) 233–250; F. Douvere, *Marine Spatial Planning: Concepts, Current Practice and Linkages to Other Management Approaches* (Ghent University, Ghent, 2010) 124.

Achieving Common Principles in the EU' and 'MSP in the EU—Achievements and Future Development', which were published by the European Commission in 2008 and 2010, respectively.[121] Subsequently, extensive stakeholder consultation revealed public concerns about the manner in which Member States were authorising offshore infrastructure development without the benefit of appropriate planning tools and processes.[122] In response, the European Commission adopted a Directive establishing a framework for MSP in July 2014.[123]

The MSP Directive aims to promote the sustainable growth of maritime economies, the sustainable development of marine areas and the sustainable use of marine resources.[124] The objectives of the instrument include contributing to the sustainable development of the energy sectors at sea, the planning and management of maritime transport, fisheries and aquaculture, and the preservation and protection of the environment, including improving resilience to climate change impacts.[125] The MSP Directive is also intended to facilitate the implementation of the many EU policies and strategies that are applicable to the marine environment.[126] The importance of MSP in this regard cannot be over-emphasised in light of the findings of a comprehensive environmental monitoring programme undertaken over a ten-year period in Denmark, which concluded that "proper spatial planning" can ensure that the construction of offshore wind farms does not lead to significant damage to biodiversity in the marine environment.[127]

Apart from establishing an appropriate framework for conflict avoidance and resolution, the normative methodology advanced by the MSP Directive is clearly aligned with applying an ecosystem-based approach to the sustainable use of marine and coastal resources, including the wind resource.[128] A particular focus is on the integrated planning and management of infrastructure and systems that traverse the maritime boundaries of the Member States,

121 COM(2008) 791, 25 November 2008; COM(2010) 771, 17 December 2010.

122 Summary report available at: http://ec.europa.eu/dgs/maritimeaffairs_fisheries/consultations/msp/summary-results-of-msp-questionnaire_en.pdf, accessed 12 September 2014.

123 Dir. 2014/89/EU (n 10).

124 Art 5(1), Dir. 2014/89/EU.

125 Art 5(2), Dir. 2014/89/EU.

126 Long (n 15).

127 Danish Energy Agency, 2013. 'Danish Offshore Wind. Key Environmental Issues—a Follow-up.'

The Environmental Group: The Danish Energy Agency, The Danish Nature Agency, DONG Energy and Vattenfal at pp. 12, 21–23, 28; available at: http://www.orbicon.dk/media/Havvindmøllebog.pdf; accessed 12 September 2014.

128 Recitals 1, 3, 13, 14 and 22, as well as Art. 5 (1), Dir. 2014/89/EU.

such as infrastructure associated with the production of renewable energy, seabed cables, and shipping routes and lanes.[129] At one level, this approach is foursquare with the EU's Integrated Maritime Policy, which identifies the integrated management of various sector activities as one of the main ways to promote growth of the maritime economies in the Member States.[130] Indicatively, in outlining the *raison d'être* underpinning the adoption of the MSP Directive, the European Commission noted that one of the greatest pressures on the use of maritime space arises from the construction of offshore wind farms following the implementation of the RES Directive.[131]

The MSP Directive goes a long way towards addressing some of the planning issues that are blighting offshore wind power development in the Member States to date. More specifically under the scheme advanced by the Directive, Member States must establish and implement spatial plan(s), as soon as possible, and at the latest by 31 March 2021.[132] The geographical scope extends to marine waters, that is to say the sea and subsea areas that are under the sovereignty and jurisdiction of the Member States, as defined in other EU instruments.[133] Other than infrastructure associated with energy installations, the plans adopted by the Member States must take into consideration: aquaculture areas, fishing areas, maritime transport routes and traffic flows, military training areas, nature and species conservation sites and protected areas, raw material extraction areas, scientific research, tourism and underwater cultural heritage.[134] Most importantly, Member States must cooperate on issues of a transnational nature and by means of the appropriate regional seas structures, and or networks or structures of Member States' competent authorities, and or by using methods that meet the requirements of the EU's sea-basin strategies.[135] Furthermore, every effort must be made to cooperate with third countries in the planning and management of offshore activities.[136]

The MSP Directive is therefore very much premised on the establishment and implementation of coherent planning mechanisms that apply across regional seas basins. As pointed out by the European Commission, the cross-border effects of economic activities undertaken at sea cannot be alleviated by

129 Art 8(2), Dir. 2014/89/EU.
130 COM(2007) 575 (n 14).
131 COM(2013) 133, 12 March 2013, at p. 15.
132 Art. 15(3), Dir. 2014/89/EU.
133 Art. (3)4, Dir. 2014/89/EU.
134 Art. 8(2), Dir. 2014/89/EU.
135 Art. 11, Dir. 2014/89/EU.
136 Art. 12, Dir. 2014/89/EU.

a planning system that is structured on a purely national basis and which pays little or no regard to trans-national impacts.[137] In addressing this shortcoming, the MSP Directive notes that the Preamble of the LOS Convention states that issues relating to the use of ocean space are closely interrelated and need to be considered as a whole.[138] Furthermore, MSP is the "logical advancement and structuring of the use of rights" granted under the LOS Convention and a practical tool that assists Member States to comply with their international and regional obligations.[139] Indeed, one distinctive feature of EU policies and many legislative instruments, such as the common fisheries policy and the Marine Strategy Framework Directive,[140] is that they apply a regional approach to the management and utilisation of marine resources and the protection of the marine environment.

Remarkably, however, the MSP Directive does not prescribe in detail how regional cooperation mechanisms on spatial planning should look or work in practice because of the differences between various marine regions, or sub-regions and coastal zones.[141] This oversight may well damage its effectiveness as a legal instrument in addressing the cross-boundary impacts of wind farms unless there is further legislative and policy action by the Member States and the third countries bordering the regional seas on this matter.

The Push to Get Europe to Stand on Its Own Feet on Energy Security

As far back as 2008, the European Commission pointed out the pressing need for additional legislation to facilitate stronger regional cooperation between energy regulators and between system operators, as well as to streamline the rules applicable to spatial planning and grid access in the Member States.[142] Since then, however, the harmonisation of the regulatory environment has evolved laboriously within the fragmented milieu of a broad span of EU policy and legislative initiatives, where the predominant interests at play are still driven by the strategic and economic concerns of individual Member States regarding their future energy needs, with little regard for many matters of

137 SWD (2013) 65, at p. 24.
138 Recital 7, Dir. 2014/89/EU.
139 *Ibid.*, Preamble and Art. 56(2) LOS Convention.
140 See (n 164).
141 Recital 20, Dir. 2014/89/EU.
142 COM(2008) 768, 13 November 2008, at p. 3.

common interest.[143] This in turn is undermining competiveness in the wind energy sector and the benefits that could derive from the offshore wind power as a European resource.

In light of the outcome of the *Ålands Vindkraft* case,[144] the time has come to expedite further EU law reform in this area with a view to ensuring greater convergence and harmonisation of EU policies and regulatory instruments applicable to renewable energy in general and offshore wind in particular. As a first step, a concerted effort ought to be made by both EU and European Economic Area Member States to use the cooperation mechanism under the RES Directive to establish joint or regional collaborative arrangements similar to the one in operation between Sweden and Norway.[145] Unpromisingly, negotiations on a bilateral inter-governmental agreement between Ireland and the UK concerning the construction of 2,300 turbines in Ireland to supply electricity in the UK energy were stood down in 2014 due to concerns about regulatory uncertainty and the fiscal benefits that could be derived from such an agreement.[146]

Looking at the EU legislative agenda in the longer term, however, the process of reform appears to be well underway. In 2013, for instance, the European Commission outlined its commitment to reforming the internal energy market and the further harmonisation of national support schemes through greater use of the European Regional Development Fund, the European Neighbourhood Policy Instrument, and the Horizon 2020 Research Programme.[147] Furthermore, it is pertinent to note that the Europeanisation of national support schemes is a central strand in the European Energy Security Strategy.[148]

In July 2014, Jean-Claude Juncker went one major step further by declaring that one of his ten priorities as the incoming European Commission President is to ensure that "Europe stands on its own feet when it comes to energy security" by establishing a new European Energy Union.[149] Apart from ensuring that Europe remains the world leader in renewables, he also highlighted in his

---

143 COM(2014) 8, 20 January 2014, at p. 13.

144 Case C-573/12, (n 9).

145 The bilateral agreement between Sweden and Norway was noted in Case C-573/12, para. 22.

146 *Irish Times*, 13 April 2014. Available at: http://www.irishtimes.com/business/sectors/energy-and-resources/deal-for-2-300-turbines-to-supply-uk-energy-by-2020-called-off-1.1760645; accessed 12 September 2014.

147 COM(2013) 175, 27 March 2013, at p. 10; Also, SWD (2013) 438, 5 November 2013.

148 COM(2014) 330 (n 12).

149 http://ec.europa.eu/about/juncker-commission/priorities/index_en.htm; accessed 12 September 2014.

initial policy programme the vital need for Europe to continue to lead the fight against global warming.[150] Moreover, moving from words to action, several of the key policy portfolios within the designated College of Commissioners have been reshaped under his direction to deliver on this mission, including the combining of the environment with the maritime affairs and fisheries portfolios with a view to fostering a sustainable future for Europe.[151] Similarly, the climate change and energy portfolios have been merged to ensure greater coherence in the EU approach to law reform in the energy sector.[152]

Rationale for a Regionalised Approach to Offshore Wind Power

At this important juncture in EU integration, as the European Commission strives to achieve a new European Energy Union, characterised by the "pooling of resources, the combining of infrastructures and the strengthening of negotiating power *vis-à-vis* third countries",[153] there are several compelling reasons why it should advance a regional seas approach to the future development of offshore wind power.

First, the introduction of a regional approach can make the production of offshore renewable energy far more cost-effective through the rationalisation and convergence of the disparate approaches to the support schemes pursued by the Member States, as well as by reducing restrictions on cross-border access to energy resources.[154] This in turn will ensure that the offshore wind industry attracts capital investment and that all EU coastal States have an equal opportunity to develop the resource.[155] In this context, one should keep in mind that the principal investors in the industry are public and private commercial bodies, which are very much open to pursuing trans-national investment opportunities at a pan-European level, provided that the regulatory environment is absolutely stable and uniform from competition and trade perspectives.[156] More fundamentally, a regional approach will bring the

150 Juncker (n 11), at p. 5.

151 European Commission Press Release, IP/14/984, 10.09.2014. Available at: http://europa.eu/rapid/press-release_IP-14-984_en.htm; accessed 12 September 2014.

152 *Ibid.*

153 Juncker (n 11), at p. 5.

154 SWD (2013) 439, at p. 23.

155 *Ibid.*, at p. 24.

156 According to the EWEA, the major European power companies financed 73% of the annual online capacity by the end of 2013, followed by specialist wind-energy companies and the banking sector. EWEA (n 15), at p. 22.

functioning of the internal energy market in relation to the production and transmission of electricity from offshore wind into line with EU treaty provisions on the free movement of goods.[157] However, the latter task is confounded by the requirement of achieving unanimity in the Council with respect to legislative proposals affecting different energy sources and supply in the Member States.[158]

Second, regionalisation will improve the technical capacity of the sector and make it far more resilient to the vagaries of wind energy, which often results in large and unpredictable oscillations in the amount of electricity fed into the grid across different geographical regions.[159] This difficulty will be mitigated substantially if the offshore wind industry has a much wider footprint at regional seas levels and through a sophisticated subsea transnational grid linking Member States.[160]

Third, a regional approach to MSP will help avoid and resolve conflicts concerning economic and recreational uses of the marine environment, such as the disputes that arose in the North Sea between the Netherlands, Germany and Belgium, regarding the location of and the parameters applying to wind farm development.[161]

Fourth and most critically, geo-political factors outside the control of the EU, such as regional tensions in the Middle East and the Ukraine, are forcing the EU institutions to re-consider the structure and dynamics of the European internal energy market. Ominously, all but 4 EU Member States, Portugal, Spain, Ireland, and the UK, are reliant upon the importation of gas from one external supplier, the Russian Federation.[162] In acknowledging the strategic implications of such a dependency, the European Commission has stated that the immediate EU priorities on energy are to "strengthen regional cooperation, diversify supplier countries and routes, strengthen emergency mechanisms, protect critical infrastructure, moderate energy demand, increase indigenous production, and further develop energy technology".[163] The development of

157 Arts. 34–37 TFEU.

158 Arts. 172(2)(c) and 194(3) TFEU. See discussion constraints arising from EU treaty provisions *infra*.

159 EEA Technical Report No. 6, 2009 (n 15), at pp. 20–24, 30–34.

160 *Ibid.*

161 SWD (2013) 65 (n 91).

162 Annex 1, Com (2014) 330, at pp. 2, 22.

163 Speech by Günther H. Oettinger, European Commissioner for Energy, 'The European Energy Policy for 2020 and beyond', Erasmus Energy Forum, Rotterdam School of Management, Rotterdam, 19 June 2014. Available at: http://europa.eu/rapid/press-release_SPEECH-14-478_en.htm. Accessed on 23 September 2014.

the offshore wind industry at a regional level can certainly contribute in some shape or form to all of these objectives and thereby reduce exposure to the volatility of international energy markets.

Finally, it ought to be recalled that the EU has made substantial progress in advancing an ecosystem-based approach under the Marine Strategy Framework (MSF) Directive with a view to achieving good environmental status of all EU marine waters by 2020.[164] Inherent within the ecosystem approach is that the planning and management of offshore activities is undertaken at eco-region or sub-regional levels within four European marine regions, namely: the Baltic Sea, the North-east Atlantic Ocean, the Mediterranean Sea, and the Black Sea.[165] What is more, two of the qualitative descriptors for determining good environmental status under the MSF Directive are aimed at ensuring that: (1) the introduction of energy, including underwater noise, is at levels that do not adversely affect the marine environment, and; (2) sea-floor integrity is at a level that ensures that the structure and functions of the ecosystems are safeguarded.[166] Surely, a regional seas approach to offshore wind power development will help the Member States meet their obligations in relation to these descriptors and achieve the sustainability objectives set out in the MSF Directive. In this context, it should also be recalled that the LOS Convention places an express obligation on States bordering enclosed or semi-enclosed seas to cooperate with each other in the protection and preservation of the marine environment.[167]

Conclusions

The Global Commission on the Economy and the Climate has reported that the type of infrastructure that we build over the next 15 years will have a major

164 Dir. 2008/56/EC of the European Parliament and of the Council of 17 June 2008 establishing a framework for community action in the field of marine environmental policy (Marine Strategy Framework Directive) OJ L 164, 25 June 2008, 19–40. See, *inter alia*: R. Long, 'Legal Aspects of Ecosystem-Based Marine Management in Europe' in A. Chircop, M. L. McConnell and S. Coffen-Smout (eds), *Ocean Yearbook* Vol. 26, (Brill Academic Publishers, Leiden, 2012) 417–484, at p. 24; R. Long, 'The EU Marine Strategy Framework Directive: A new European approach to the regulation of the marine environment, marine natural resources and marine ecological services' (2011) 29 (1) *Journal Of Energy And Natural Resources Law* 1–45.

165 Art. 1(3), Dir. 2008/56/EC.

166 Arts. 3(5), 9(1), 9(3) 24 and Annex 1, Dir. 2008/56/EC.

167 Art. 123(b), LOS Convention.

bearing on our capacity to combat climate change.[168] EU law and policy facilitates the pioneering of new technologies and the production of renewable energy has undoubtedly contributed to the improvement in energy security and the reduction in GGEs in Europe. Considerable difficulties have arisen in the offshore wind sector, nonetheless, because of the absence of harmonised rules applicable to the internal energy market, including most notably the operation of support schemes promoting the production and consumption of green electricity in the Member States. The national approach to the subvention of renewable energy has received the imprimatur of the Court of Justice in the *Ålands Vindkraft* case in a judgment that exposes the dysfunctionality of the internal energy market and does little to advance a common regional seas approach to the development of offshore wind power.

Hence, as part of the push to establish a new European Energy Union, and as we move towards the crucial climate change negotiations in Paris at the end of 2015, there is a pressing need for further EU law reform on industry support schemes in order to make the internal energy market work better from a European perspective. At the same time, the Member States and third countries need to press ahead and strengthen the cooperative mechanisms and structures under the MSP Directive so that they provide a solid legal basis supporting the regionalisation of the EU's renewable energy policy as it applies in the marine environment.[169] All told, much remains to be done if all EU Member States are to harness the full potential of offshore wind power for the benefit of the common good and to fulfil the words of a Gaelic proverb, *ar scáth a chéile a mhaireann na daoine*.[170]

---

168 Global Commission on the Economy and the Climate, Better Growth, Better Climate: The New Climate Economy Report (Washington, DC: World Resources Institute, September 2014) pp. 308, especially at pp. 131–168.

169 Arts. 11 and 12, Dir. 2014/89/EU.

170 *People live in each other's shadows.*

CHAPTER 7

Regulating Offshore Energy Sources in the North Sea—Reinventing the Wheel or a Need for More Coordination?

Hannah Katharina Müller
Researcher, Groningen Centre of Energy Law, University of Groningen, Groningen, The Netherlands

Martha M. Roggenkamp
Professor of Energy Law, Director, Groningen Centre of Energy Law, University of Groningen, Groningen, The Netherlands

Abstract

In this chapter we examine the legal frameworks for developing oil, gas and wind energy in the North Sea. We discuss whether there are parallels to be seen and lessons to be learned from these different sectors and suggest that experience in the offshore petroleum sector could be used to improve the evolving legal regimes for offshore wind energy. For this purpose, we first examine the legal basis for offshore activities under the international law of the sea. Subsequently, we discuss the regulation of oil and gas exploitation and the regulation of offshore wind energy. We focus in particular on the way in which energy sources are transported to shore via pipelines and cables. We consider whether comparable decisions have been made when establishing a legal regime for offshore wind and whether lessons could still be learned. This is particularly relevant for the future when the production of offshore wind energy and the production of petroleum need to be coordinated, and when sizable amounts of offshore wind energy will be integrated into the (offshore) transmission grid.

Keywords

energy law – oil and gas production – offshore wind – offshore grid – pipelines – infrastructure

---

* Hannah Müller LL.H., is a Ph.D. researcher, Prof. Dr. Martha Roggenkamp is a Professor at the University of Groningen.

 | DOI 10.1163/9789004303522_009

Introduction

The European Union (EU) aims at achieving a share of 20% of renewable energy in its energy mix by 2020.[1] Offshore wind energy is expected to make a significant contribution towards this objective. Whereas offshore wind energy exploitation is a new development, offshore oil and gas exploration and production have been taking place for decades. This chapter examines the legal frameworks under international law, EU law and national law for developing offshore oil, gas and wind energy. As coastal states are facing several comparable challenges when designing a proper legal framework for offshore wind energy, we will discuss whether there are parallels to be seen and lessons to be learned. Experience in the upstream petroleum sector could be used to improve the evolving legal regimes for offshore wind energy generation.

For this purpose, we focus on the North Sea, as this area is characterised by large-scale oil and gas exploration and production that has continued since the 1970s, and currently also by major developments in offshore wind energy. First, we analyse the legal basis for offshore activities under international law of the sea. Subsequently, we discuss the regulation of oil and gas exploitation. We then focus on the development of offshore wind and analyse the regulatory solutions. The analysis includes an assessment of the regulation of submarine networks and the development of cross-border infrastructure.

The Offshore Jurisdiction of Coastal States

For centuries, the offshore jurisdiction of coastal states was limited to one zone: the territorial sea. Beyond this zone, the offshore waters were considered as high seas and thus of common use.[2] Increased interest in the resources of the seabed, however, led to the negotiation of the 1958 Geneva Conventions.[3] Here, the Convention on the Continental Shelf is of particular relevance for oil

1 Directive 2009/28/EC of 23 April 2009 on the promotion of the use of energy from renewable energy sources, OJ L140/16.

2 Christos L. Rozakis, 'Continental Shelf' in Rudolf Bernhardt (ed), *Encyclopedia of Public International Law* (Vol. 1, North-Holland, Amsterdam, 1992) 783–792, at p. 784.

3 These were the Convention on the Territorial Sea and the Contiguous Zone, 29 April 1958, 15 *UST* 1606, 516 *UNTS* 205; Convention on the High Seas, 29 April 1958, 13 *UST* 2312, 450 *UNTS* 81; Convention on Fishing and Conservation of the Living Resources of the High Seas, 29 April 1958, 17 *UST* 138, 559 *UNTS* 285; Convention on the Continental Shelf, 29 April 1958, 15 *UST*. 471, 499 *UNTS* 311.

and gas exploitation as it recognizes that coastal states have sovereign rights over the continental shelf for the purpose of exploring it and exploiting its natural resources (= functional jurisdiction). It also affords coastal states jurisdiction over installations and other devices necessary for the exploration and exploitation.[4] Although the 1958 Conventions introduced a functional jurisdiction for oil and gas exploitation and consequently the right to establish all necessary installations and devices, it was not clear whether submarine pipelines were to be seen as an installation, a device or as a separate object.

In 1982, the UN Convention on the Law of the Sea (LOSC) was adopted.[5] It introduced a new offshore zone: the exclusive economic zone (EEZ), which provided coastal states with sovereign rights regarding economic activities such as "the production of energy from the water, currents and winds".[6] In order to exercise jurisdiction, coastal states are required to declare an EEZ. Coastal states with a continental shelf and an EEZ thus have exclusive rights regarding the exploration and production of oil and gas, as well as the production of offshore wind energy. They may authorize and regulate offshore drilling[7] and the construction, operation and use of installations and structures.[8] Furthermore, the LOSC confirms that coastal states have jurisdiction over cables and pipelines constructed or used in connection with exploration and exploitation activities on their continental shelf and the economic activities in the EEZ or connected to installations under the jurisdiction of the coastal state.[9] Cables or pipelines that are not linked to any of these activities, however, still fall under the general freedom to lay cables and pipelines. Thus the LOSC aimed at finding a balance between the interests of coastal states to exploit their energy resources and the freedoms and rights of all other states.

4 Arts. 2(1), 5(2) and (4) of the Convention on the Continental Shelf. Art. 4 provides that in exploiting the natural resources, the coastal states may not impede the laying or maintenance of submarine cables or pipelines on the continental shelf.

5 United Nations Convention on the Law of the Sea of 10 December 1982, Montego Bay, 1833 *UNTS* 396. As between state parties, the 1982 Convention prevails over the 1958 Geneva Conventions, Art. 311(1) LOSC. All North Sea countries are party to the LOSC.

6 Article 56(1)(a) LOSC.

7 Art. 77(1) LOSC.

8 Art. 60 LOSC. Although this Article is found in Part V (EEZ), Art. 80 extends it to natural resource activities on the continental shelf. The exercise of the rights of installations and structures must be linked with the purposes set out in Art. 56.

9 See Arts. 48(2), 76, Art. 79(4) and 87(1)(c) LOSC.

Exploitation of Oil and Gas in the North Sea

In Europe, the exploitation of offshore oil and gas mainly takes place in the North Sea. As the continental shelf underlies the whole North Sea, the coastal states may exercise jurisdiction over their respective parts of the North Sea. The starting-point for all coastal states were the 1958 Geneva Conventions and, in particular, the Convention on the Continental Shelf.[10] Denmark became the first of the four North Sea States to ratify the Convention in 1963, followed by the United Kingdom (UK) in 1964 and the Netherlands in 1966. Norway only ratified the Convention in 1971. A primary reason for Norway's late ratification was uncertainty as to whether the 200-m-deep trench off the Norwegian south coast could represent the outer limit to the Norwegian continental shelf[11] and uncertainty as to the extent to which the equidistance principle should be applied. Following the International Court of Justice ruling in 1969 that delimitation had to be effected by agreement in accordance with equitable principles, but also by taking account of all relevant circumstances in such a way as to leave as much as possible of these parts of the continental shelf to each country,[12] the other North Sea States could finally agree on delimitation.[13] The delimitation agreements provide a basis for the coastal states' functional jurisdiction over their respective parts of this continental shelf.

Offshore Legal Regimes

When developing their offshore regimes, the North Sea states were faced with the question of how to regulate the exploitation of oil and gas. The 1958 Convention on the Continental Shelf left the coastal states with considerable freedom as to how to design the exact legal framework. The choices made by the four main petroleum-producing North Sea states vary from applying their onshore legislation offshore to designing new offshore regimes.

Denmark clearly chose the first option. By a Royal Decree of 7 June 1963, it declared "sovereignty" over the continental shelf regarding the exploration for

10 See (n 4). However, not all North Sea states were party to it. Germany, for example, never ratified it.

11 Hans Jacob Bull, 'Norwegian Offshore Petroleum—The Legal and Administrative Responses' in Anders A. Victorinn (ed), *Scandinavian Studies in Law* (Vol. 25, Almqvist & Wiksell, Stockholm, 1981) 31–50, at p. 36.

12 *North Sea Continental Shelf Judgment, I.C.J Reports 1969*, p. 42.

13 The agreements were concluded between 1965 and 1972. For the delimitation agreements, see David Freestone and Ton IJlstra (eds), *North Sea: Basic Legal Documents on Regional Environmental Co-operation* (Kluwer, Dordrecht, 1991) 383–419.

and exploitation of natural resources. It further laid down that these exploration and exploitation activities are subject to a concession granted pursuant to the Act of 1950 concerning prospecting for and exploitation of raw materials, including hydrocarbons, in the subsoil of the Kingdom of Denmark.[14] The 1950 Act in turn aimed at preserving the legal regime that was first established by an Act of 1932 stating that the raw materials in the Danish subsoil belong to the State of Denmark and that its development is reserved to the State.[15] The Government may, however, grant to a party a concession conferring the right to prospect for and exploit such raw materials.[16] Consequently, the Danish government awarded a sole concession to search for and exploit raw materials throughout the whole of the Danish territory.[17] In October 1963, the concession was amended to extend to the entire Danish territorial sea and continental shelf.[18] The first field was discovered in the Danish continental shelf in 1966.[19] By 1976, a gradual process for relinquishment of the sole concession area began and in 1981 the Danish Government and the concessionaire agreed that the latter only retained fields already in production and a very limited part of the original concession area. Consequently, other oil companies have been able to apply for licenses to explore and exploit oil and/or gas from the Danish continental shelf.

Like Denmark, the UK decided in 1964 to extend its onshore regime to the continental shelf. The Continental Shelf Act of 1964 not only vested in the Crown the rights exercisable by the UK outside territorial waters with respect

14 Royal Decree of 7 June 1963 concerning the exercise of Danish sovereignty over the Continental Shelf, at http://www.un.org/depts/los/LEGISLATIONANDTREATIES/PDFFILES/DNK_1963_Decree.pdf; accessed 30 September 2014.

15 Anita Rønne and Michael Budtz, 'The Legal Framework for Exploration for and Production of Oil and Natural Gas in Denmark' (1985) 3 *Journal of Energy & Natural Resources Law* 153–168.

16 Articles 1–2, Act No. 181 of 8 May 1950 concerning prospecting for and exploitation of raw materials in the subsoil of the Kingdom of Denmark, at http://www.logir.fo/foldb/lov/1950/0000181.htm; accessed 30 September 2014.

17 The first sole concession was awarded for the period 1936–1958. In July 1962 a new sole concession was granted to a group of companies to explore for and recover raw materials from the Danish subsoil in all of Denmark for a period of fifty years.

18 See Danish Energy Agency, 'Home', 'OIL AND GAS', 'Licenses', 'Existing Licenses', at http://www.ens.dk/EN-US/OILANDGAS/LICENCES/EXISTING_LICENCES/Sider/Forside.aspx; accessed 25 August 2014.

19 Danish Energy Agency, 'Home', 'OIL AND GAS', 'Licenses', 'Agreement with A.P. Moller', at http://www.ens.dk/en/oil-gas/licences/agreement-ap-moller-maersk, and Danish Energy Agency, 'Home', 'Licenses', at http://www.ens.dk/en/oil-gas/licences; accessed 25 August 2014.

to the seabed and subsoil and their natural resources,[20] but also extended the application of various provisions of the earlier Petroleum (Production) Act of 1934, including the provision vesting in the Crown the property in all petroleum *in situ* in the territory of Great Britain, together with the exclusive right to search and bore for such petroleum and the provisions relating to licensing.[21] In addition, it also adopted the Petroleum (Production) (Continental Shelf and Territorial Sea) Regulations 1964, describing further the system for licensing offshore petroleum activities on the continental shelf. An exploration or production license could be awarded to persons resident or companies incorporated in the UK. The UK Government issued the first oil and gas licenses for the North Sea in 1964,[22] and the first field discovered shortly thereafter was brought into production in 1967.[23]

The Netherlands decided to pass a special law governing exploration and production on the continental shelf: the Continental Shelf Mining Act of 1965 (CS Mining Act).[24] The reason for this approach was that onshore production of oil and gas was based on the Napoleonic Mining Act of 1810,[25] which, after the Netherlands regained independence in 1814, has been applied provisionally in its original language. The legislator further considered that the concession regime of this Act was not suitable to deal with modern petroleum activities. The CS Mining Act therefore established that the minerals present in or on the continental shelf were the property of the Dutch State[26] and forbade the exploration or exploitation of minerals in or on the continental shelf without a

20 Subsection (1) of section 1 of the 1964 Act, at http://www.legislation.gov.uk/ukpga/1964/29; accessed 30 September 2014.

21 The 1964 Continental Shelf Act did not, like the 1934 Act, expressly state that the Crown had the exclusive right of searching and boring for and getting petroleum. Nonetheless, this is the effect of vesting in the Crown the rights exercisable by the UK on the continental shelf under international law and application of the licensing provisions of the 1934 Act to exploration and exploitation of the continental shelf.

22 See Richard Young, 'Offshore Claims and Problems in the North Sea' (1965) 59(3) *American Journal of International Law* 505–522.

23 Oil & Gas UK, 'Economic Report 2013, at p. 15. Available at http://www.oilandgasuk.co.uk/2013-economic-report.cfm; accessed 25 August 2014.

24 Act of 23 September 1965, Stb. 1965, 428. The Act entered into force in March 1967.

25 Loi concernant les Mines, les Minières et les Carrières, April 1810. Bulletin des Lois No. 285. For an English translation see Martha Roggenkamp, *Oil & Gas: Netherlands Law and Practice* (Chancery Law Publishing, London, 1991).

26 See Article 22 CS Mining Act (n 25).

license.[27] The Minister granted licences for a specific period of time to natural or legal persons situated in the Netherlands. Further rules were included in Royal Decrees.[28] The first offshore (gas) field was discovered in 1970 and many discoveries, although small in size, followed.[29]

Norway distinguishes itself from the other North Sea states because it had no onshore oil and gas production and therefore had to establish a special offshore petroleum regime. Already in May 1963, Norway proclaimed that the seabed and subsoil comprising the submarine areas off the Norwegian coast were under Norwegian sovereignty as regards the exploitation of and exploration for natural resources.[30] The legislation vested the right to the natural resources of the submarine areas in the State, with the authority vested in the King to grant exploration and exploitation rights to Norwegian or foreign persons, subject to conditions, and to issue further regulations governing these activities.[31] The 1965 Regulations provided that exploration and/or extraction licenses could be granted for specific periods of time to foreign companies if a local branch or subsidiary was established in Norway. This regime was amended by the Petroleum Act 1985 that provided for a similar licensing regime and a codification of government practice.[32] Norway is now the largest oil and gas producer in Europe. Given the absence of a large domestic market, most of its production is exported.

The above shows that the approach towards legislating offshore exploration and production differs. Whereas Denmark extended its onshore regime to its continental shelf almost without any changes, the other North Sea countries adopted directly (Norway and the Netherlands via their offshore petroleum

27 Such a license was either a reconnaissance license, a prospecting license or a production license.

28 See Royal Decrees of 1967 (Stb. 1967, 24), 1976 (Stb. 1976, 102) and 1996 (Stb. 1996, 199).

29 Currently about 50% of the Dutch continental shelf is under exploration and production. However, large discoveries offshore failed to materialize. The smaller finds have nevertheless been attractive following rising oil prices after the 1973 oil crisis.

30 Royal Decree of 31 May 1963 relating to the sovereignty of Norway over the sea-bed and subsoil outside the Norwegian Coast, at http://www.un.org/depts/los/LEGISLATIONANDTREATIES/PDFFILES/NOR_1963_Decree.pdf; accessed 30 September 2014.

31 Articles 2 and 3 of the Act of 21 June 1963 relating to exploration and exploitation of submarine natural resources, at http://www.un.org/depts/los/LEGISLATIONANDTREATIES/PDFFILES/NOR_1963_Act.pdf; accessed 30 September 2014.

32 See further Finn Arnesen, Ulf Hammer, Per Håkon Høisveen, Knut Kaasen, and Dagfinn Nygaard 'Energy Law in Norway' in Martha Roggenkamp, Catherine Redgwell, Anita Rønne, and Iñigo del Guayo (eds), *Energy Law in Europe: National, EU and International Regulation* (2nd ed., Oxford University Press, Oxford, 2007) 885–895.

laws) or indirectly (the UK via its Regulations) specific legislation for the offshore. Except for Denmark applying a traditional concession regime, all other coastal states chose to apply licensing regimes with certain variations, which involved at least two kinds of licenses: (non-exclusive) exploration licenses and (exclusive) production licenses.

Licensing: Location and Timing

The states were further confronted with deciding how the permitting would take place; i.e., whether the government would identify certain areas or whether the potential producers were allowed to choose any area not used for navigation or other activities. Except for Denmark opting for a sole concession, the majority of the coastal states chose to identify specific offshore areas as available for licensing. The UK[33] and Norway[34] granted licenses to private companies to explore for oil and gas in specific areas. By doing so, the government could control the activities and possibly cluster them in specific parts of the North Sea. The Netherlands applied a different approach and made the entire Dutch continental shelf available for exploration and production, except for those areas in use as military defence areas, for navigation and development of other resources.[35]

Similarly, a decision had to be made as to whether a permit could be applied for at any time or only during a specific period of time (a licensing round). All coastal states opted for a regime of licensing rounds but these were not necessarily designed the same way. By contrast to a 'normal' licensing round used in Norway and the UK (and later Denmark), where governments officially proclaim a specific period in which licenses for specific areas can be applied for, the Netherlands opted for an opposite (negative) approach by publishing in the Official Gazette the periods where a license could not be applied for. The end result is the same, as it limits licensing to a specific period.[36]

---

33 Stephen Dow, 'Energy Law in the United Kingdom' in *ibid.*, 1169–1261, at p. 1194.

34 Arnesen (n 33) in *ibid.*, 881–975 at p. 897.

35 Roggenkamp (n 26) at pp. 60–65.

36 Apart from this, the licensing regimes have another feature in common, involving the principle that development of natural resources should benefit society. Such benefits could be derived from requiring licensees to use domestic personnel and services, and by including the principle in the national petroleum law or in individual licenses, by obliging the licensees to bring all petroleum produced offshore to the national coast for domestic consumption.

The EU Hydrocarbon Licensing Directive, adopted in 1994,[37] has directly or indirectly brought about changes to the above regimes. Explicitly acknowledging the sovereignty of EU Member States over their natural resources and thus allowing them to determine the areas in which exploitation of energy might take place and to whom they might grant the right to produce energy, it strove to establish an internal market, increase competition and improve security of supply. It therefore established common rules providing for non-discriminatory access to the exploration for and production of hydrocarbons, which ultimately should prevent single entities from having exclusive rights for huge areas where the exploitation by several entities would be more effective. Member States may choose between a licensing-round system or an open-door system (i.e., a regime where the request for or the grant of authorization is available on a permanent basis at any time.)[38] License conditions should be transparent and non-discriminatory. Domestic content requirements and national landing obligations[39] are no longer permissible, as they are contrary to the basic EU principles of free movement of goods and services. Although most North Sea states already applied a licensing regime based on competitive elements, the Directive did lead to changes in all petroleum laws.

In 1995, Denmark amended the Subsoil Act substantially, as it needed to abolish the preferential status of the State and national oil companies, as well as the State's special purchase rights for oil and gas produced in its territory. The amendments also changed the licensing regime, as Denmark opted for the more flexible system of licensing via the open-door regime instead of the previous licensing rounds. Norway also adopted a new Petroleum Act (1996), introducing a more flexible licensing regime and expanding petroleum activities to new areas further north. Two years later, the UK issued a new Petroleum Act as well, taking into account basic requirements of the Directive. In 2003, the Netherlands promulgated a new Mining Act, which implemented the Directive and especially affected the onshore regime. The legislator opted for a

37 Directive 94/22/EC of the European Parliament and of the Council of 30 May 1994 on the conditions for granting and using authorizations for the prospection, exploration and production of hydrocarbons, OJ L 164, pp. 3–8.

38 Article 3, paras. 1–3 of Directive 94/22/EC, *ibid.*

39 Such explicit landing obligations applied in the Netherlands (Article 25 of Article III of Royal Decree of 1967 (Stb. 1967, 24) and Royal Decree of 1976 (Stb. 1976, 102) of the CS Mining Act and in the onshore concessions), the United Kingdom (Article 30 of Schedule 4 of the Petroleum (Production) (Seaward Areas) Regulations, S.I. 1987, no. 1270) and Norway (Article 26 Petroleum Act 1985, Act of 22 March 1985, no. 11).

complete new mining regime covering both the onshore and the offshore and all subsoil resources.[40]

Regulating Offshore Pipelines

The 1958 Geneva Convention on the Continental Shelf provided that states had the right to "construct and maintain or operate on the continental shelf installations or other devices necessary for its exploration and the exploitation of its natural resources, and to establish safety zones around such installations and devices and take in those zones measures necessary for their protection".[41] However, uncertainty existed as to whether the wording 'installations' and 'devices' referred to different kinds of objects. Are pipelines connecting an offshore installation to shore to be classified as an 'installation' or a 'device'? A parallel discussion occurred about the exact meaning of the word 'exploitation', and more particularly whether exploitation is limited to production activities or also included bringing the petroleum products to shore via pipelines. Although discussed by the International Law Commission whilst drafting the Convention, a clear definition did not find its way into the 1958 Convention.[42] Even though the LOSC brought an end to any uncertainty, as it clearly established that pipelines connecting fields to shore are part of a coastal state's jurisdiction and that these states have the right legislate on their construction and use,[43] national laws still bear marks of the initial uncertainty on this issue.

The Netherlands has taken the approach that the word 'exploitation' needs to be considered broadly and also covers the transportation of oil and gas by pipeline to shore. This does not mean, however, that a pipeline is automatically considered to be part of an offshore installation. Neither the CS Mining Act nor the current 2003 Mining Act provide for a separate pipeline license, as the development of offshore pipelines is considered as part of the *jus communicationis* and regulation should be limited to environmental and safety protection issues.[44] Norway, Denmark and the UK, however, introduced a specific

40 See further the chapters on EU, Denmark, Netherlands, Norway and the United Kingdom in Roggenkamp *et al.* (n 34).

41 Art 5(2) Convention on the Continental Shelf (n 4).

42 It appears from the Yearbook of the International Law Commission of 1953 that France was in favor of a broad meaning of the word 'exploitation'. See *YbILC* (1958) part II, 24. On the same note the *Yearbook of the International Law Commission* of 1958 shows that pipelines connecting several installations within one field should be considered as part of the installation. See *YbILC* (1958) part VI, 81.

43 Article 79(4) LOSC.

44 However, in the further Mining Regulations of the 2003 Mining Act, Stb. 2002, 604, a limited licensing requirement has been introduced.

licensing regime for offshore pipelines.[45] Although the content and extent of the regulation differ, it is clear that these coastal states consider the construction and operation of offshore pipelines as a separate activity, albeit subject to their functional jurisdiction.

Initially, all offshore oil and gas fields were connected by a single field-to-shore pipeline. In order to avoid an increase in such individual pipelines, most governments began facilitating third-party access to offshore pipelines. The British, Danish and Norwegian legislation provided for a regime of third-party access based on negotiations between the licensees of the field and the pipeline operator.[46] In addition, these governments could further influence third-party access via provisions in the pipeline licenses stipulating requirements regarding the size of the pipeline and the rate of return of the pipeline company. Given the absence of a pipeline license and a general third-party access regime, the Dutch government had to rely on general competition law in cases where access negotiations failed. As a large number of small fields exist, a connection to an existing pipeline has usually been preferred. These connections are governed by a 'tie-in agreement'.[47]

Cross-Border Pipelines

Domestic landing requirements imposed by most North Sea states resulted in the development of several national pipeline systems without cross-border connections. The only exception was Norway. Due to the size of its offshore petroleum reserves and limited local demand, licensees were exempted from bringing the produced oil and gas to shore. Norway consequently exported most of its oil and gas to continental Europe. The decision to export necessarily brought with it the construction of cross-border pipelines. By contrast to the situation onshore, these transnational pipelines were all based on an agreement between the "sending" state (Norway) and the "receiving" state (Germany, the UK, Belgium, France) without any involvement of the transit state.[48] The Ekofisk agreement seems to have served as a legal framework for all subsequent

45 Paragraphs 1–5 of the Norwegian Petroleum Act (n 40), Article 17 of the Danish Subsoil Act (n 17) and Article 20 of the UK Petroleum and Submarine Pipelines Act 1975, at http://www.legislation.gov.uk/ukpga/1975/74/contents; accessed 30 September 2014.

46 See chapters on Denmark, Norway and the UK in Roggenkamp *et al.* (n 34).

47 On this, see also Ruven Zeuschner, 'Pipelines and cables: the offshore transportation of oil, gas and renewable energy' (2011) 29(8) *International Energy Law Review* 311–326, at p. 322.

48 Norwegian/German Ekofisk Treaty, St.prp.nr. 88 (1973–1974), Norwegian/UK Ekofisk Treaty, St.prp.nr. 110 (1972–1973), Norwegian/UK Frigg Treaty, St.prp.nr. 183 (1975–1976), Norwegian/Belgium Zeepipe Treaty, St.prp.nr. 148 (1987–1988), Norwegian/German

agreements. These agreements contain provisions on the nationality of the pipeline company and the pipeline, the route of the pipeline, co-operation between both states with regard to laying and operating the pipeline, the safety and fiscal regime, and dispute settlement procedures.[49] All agreements state that the Norwegian Petroleum Act applies to the entire pipeline, which means that the pipeline agreements provide for concurrent jurisdiction over the part of the pipeline situated on the continental shelf of the "receiving" state.

Conclusions on the Classification of Offshore Pipelines

Since the 1960s an extensive pipeline system has been developed in the North Sea. These systems consist of field-to-shore pipelines, inter- and intra-field pipelines, and pipelines crossing the continental shelf of a third state (transit pipelines). Whereas field-to-shore pipelines are considered as separate objects and regulated as such, other pipelines are considered as being part of the installation (such as intra-field pipelines). Given the absence of any clear guidance in the Law of the Sea Conventions (1958 and 1982) and the Hydrocarbons Licensing Directive, it is up to each coastal state to decide which regulation applies and the extent to which these pipelines are regulated. The only common element is that these pipelines usually are labelled as 'upstream' pipelines, which in EU law is defined as "any pipeline or network of pipelines operated and/or constructed as part of an oil or gas production project, or used to convey natural gas from one or more such projects to a processing plant or terminal or final coastal landing terminal".[50]

Europipe Treaty, St.prp.nr. 60 (1992–1993), Norwegian/French NorFra Treaty, St.prp.nr. 44 (1996–1997).

49 Despite the similarities between most agreements, some differences can be noted with newer agreements as well. First, the older agreements like the Ekofisk agreements contain more detailed provisions. Second, whereas the older agreements refer to the piped transportation from a particular fields like Ekofisk and Frigg (i.e., field development agreements), the more recent agreements are more general in scope; they provide for the construction of (present and future) pipelines from the Norwegian continental shelf to the receiving state. A typical example is the development of the Europipe between Norway and Germany. As the Ekofisk agreement between Norway and Germany was limited to the development of the Ekofisk field, both parties had to enter into a new agreement in order to develop the Europipe. This so-called Europipe agreement is broader in scope and covers the construction of future pipelines (Europipe II) as well.

50 Art. 2(2) of Directive 2009/73/EC of 13 July 2009 concerning common rules for the internal market in natural gas and repealing Directive 2003/55/EC, OJ L 211/94.

Generation of Offshore Wind Energy in the North Sea

As noted in the introduction, the EU has established the so-called 20-20-20 targets, which aim at a 20% reduction in EU greenhouse gas emissions from 1990 levels and a 20% increase of renewable energy sources (RES) in the share of EU energy consumption by 2020.[51] In order to achieve the latter, Directive 2009/28/EC introduced binding national targets for the individual Member States.[52] Although the targets are binding, each Member State is free to decide how to reach its target. Most of the North Sea countries expect that offshore wind energy will make a substantial contribution towards reaching their targets.[53]

The development of offshore wind energy in Europe only started in the 1990s.[54] The first offshore wind farms were all built as demonstration projects and were located in the territorial sea. Then the North Sea states all established an EEZ, which also gave them the sovereign right to generate offshore wind energy outside the territorial sea.[55] As laws need to be explicitly declared applicable to the EEZ, the coastal states had to decide whether to extend existing laws or to adopt a new legal regime for offshore wind.

In doing so, the North Sea states were faced with a comparable situation as when they were developing offshore oil and gas.[56] Both energy activities require the construction of installations and connections to shore. The coastal states therefore had to decide how to design the permitting regime and how to classify the cables connecting the offshore wind farms to the shore. Among the North Sea states, Denmark, the UK, the Netherlands and Germany have

---

51 Directive 2009/28/EC (n 2), which also aims at a 20% increase in EU's energy efficiency.

52 These national targets are contained in Annex I of Directive 2009/28/EC (n 2).

53 See, e.g., their *National Renewable Energy Action Plans*, at http://ec.europa.eu/energy/renewables/action_plan_en.htm; accessed 30 September 2014.

54 The first offshore wind farm was constructed in Denmark in 1991. Since then, a total of 69 wind farms have been installed in European waters by the end of 2013, with a total capacity of 6,562 MW, see European Wind Energy Association (EWEA), 'The European offshore wind industry: key trends and statistics 2013' (January 2014) 3, at http://www.ewea.org/fileadmin/files/library/publications/statistics/European_offshore_statistics_2013.pdf; accessed 30 September 2014.

55 Germany has established an EEZ in 1995, Denmark in 1996, the Netherlands in 2000. The UK followed in 2004 by declaring first a Renewable Energy Zone, which was turned into an EEZ in 2009.

56 As in the case of oil and gas, offshore wind exploitation depends on the existence of a specific offshore zone (EEZ) and the legal regimes are subsequently limited to a functional jurisdiction. See section on coastal states' competences above.

gathered the most experience with offshore wind exploitation and rank amongst the EU countries with the highest potential for offshore wind energy.[57] Therefore, their legal regimes will be examined below.

Offshore Legal Regimes

When examining the legal frameworks applied to offshore wind development in these countries, two different approaches can be identified. They have classified offshore wind farms either as installations requiring some sort of construction permit, or as an activity aimed at producing electricity and falling under the relevant national electricity legislation.

The Netherlands and Germany both chose the former and decided to regulate the construction of offshore wind farms on the basis of existing laws governing the construction of installations in waters. The permitting of offshore wind farms in Germany was mainly based on the *Marine Facility Acts*,[58] whereas the permits for the first offshore wind farms in the Netherlands were issued on basis of the *Public Works and Water Management Act*.[59] The UK took a slightly different approach: it decided to extend the onshore Crown Estate Act so that a lease from the Crown Estate would be required for developing offshore wind farms.[60] Denmark, however, decided to apply its *Electricity Supply Act* offshore.[61] In the last couple of years, the North Sea states have all gradually moved towards a more distinct legal regime governing offshore wind installations, as discussed below.

Licensing: Location and Timing

The coastal states also needed to decide how to allocate the permits: by a competitive tendering regime or by a 'first come, first served' regime. They further

57 European Environment Agency (EEA), 'Europe's onshore and offshore wind energy potential. An assessment of environmental and economic constraints' (Technical report No 6/2009) 21, at http://www.energy.eu/publications/a07.pdf; accessed 30 September 2014. Regarding the installed number of wind turbines, the UK is leading with 52%, followed by Denmark with 24.6%, Belgium (7%), the Netherlands (6%) and Germany (6%), see EWEA (n 55) at p. 11.

58 *Seeaufgabengesetz*, BGBl. 1965 II S. 833, last amended by BGBl. I S. 3836 and the *Seeanlagenverordnung*, BGBl. 1997 I S. 57, last amended by BAnz. 2013 AT 30.08.2013 V1.

59 *Wet beheer rijkswaterstaatswerken* (*wbr*), Stb. 1996, 645.

60 See Sec. 3 of *The Crown Estate Act*, *http://www.legislation.gov.uk/ukpga/Eliz2/9-10/55/contents*; accessed 30 September 2014.

61 Art. 13, para. 1 and Art. 17 of the *Electricity Supply Act 1999, at https://www.retsinformation.dk/Forms/R0710.aspx?id=12196; accessed 30 September 2014.* Developing offshore wind energy requires an electricity supply license and usually also a construction permit.

had to determine the extent to which they would identify specific offshore wind areas.

Despite earlier attempts to introduce a competitive bidding regime, the Netherlands opted for a 'first come, first served' regime, in which stakeholders could apply for a permit to construct wind turbines in all available locations.[62] A permit would thus be awarded to the first party to have fulfilled all criteria. From the beginning, there were doubts about the adequacy of this regime, as it resulted in a flood of applications without any means of funding them.[63] Several permitting moratoria were applied. In 2009, it was decided, once again, that no new permits would be awarded until an adequate legal framework was developed.[64] As a first step, a new *Water Act*[65] was adopted and wind energy areas were identified in 2009.[66] It has yet to be decided how these areas will be allocated, but it is most likely that the government will opt for a tender procedure.[67]

In the UK, the Crown Estate invited potential offshore wind farm developers in 2000 to apply to explore and then develop sites. As in the Netherlands, the developers could freely choose the offshore areas. The Crown Estate assessed the bids on the basis of specific criteria.[68] However, the process for obtaining

62 On the development of the Dutch regime, see Martha Roggenkamp and Hannah Katharina Müller, 'De regulering van offshore windenergie sinds 2008. Een offshore processie van Echternach?' (2013) 2 *Nederlands Tijdschrift voor Energierecht* 84–94.

63 Of the 79 initiatives, 19 parties requested a permit, of which 12 also received a permit. However, only 3 projects were granted a subsidy. See the explanatory notes: Ministerie van Economische Zaken, '*Memorie van Toelichting: Ontwerp-wetsvoorstel windenergie op zee: internetconsultatie maart 2014*' (19 March 2014), at http://www.internetconsultatie.nl/wetwindenergieopzee; accessed 30 September 2014.

64 See Article 3, para. 2 of the Beleidsregels inzake de toepassing van de Wet beheer rijkswaterstaatswerken op installaties in de exclusieve economische zone, Stcrt. 2009, 19704.

65 Waterwet, *Stb.* 2009, 107 and 2009, 490. Art. 6.5 forms the basis of permits for offshore wind farms, in connection with Art. 6.13 of the Water Ordinance, Stb. 2009, 549.

66 The policy regarding spatial planning for offshore wind has mainly been laid down in the 'Nationaal Waterplan', at http://www.rijksoverheid.nl/documenten-en-publicaties/rapporten/2009/12/01/nationaal-waterplan-2009-2015.html; accessed 30 September 2014.

67 See the explanatory notes to the draft bill on offshore wind, see (n 64) at pp. 13–14. The draft Bill also suggests combining a permit application with a request for a subsidy (based on a feed-in tariff).

68 These were, for example, the financial situation and the expertise in offshore and wind turbine development. Department of Trade and Industry (DTI), 'Future offshore: a strategic framework for offshore wind energy' (2002) 32, at http://tethys.pnnl.gov/sites/default/files/publications/A_Strategic_Framework_for_the_Offshore_Wind_Industry.pdf; accessed 30 September 2014.

planning consent proved to be difficult and the Government decided to renounce this regime. It thus identified three strategic areas and introduced a tender process for locations within these three areas.[69] In doing so, the UK Department of Trade and Industry referred to experience in the oil and gas sector.[70] Since 2010 the approach has slightly changed; Round 3 focussed on tendering larger zones instead of smaller sites.[71] Within these zones, the developer determines the most suitable sites.[72]

A comparable development took place in Germany. Offshore wind permits were awarded on a 'first come, first served' basis and developers could initially also freely choose locations. Several construction permits have thus been awarded.[73] As this approach was not perceived as efficient, a spatial plan identifying offshore wind areas in the EEZ was adopted in 2009[74] and a more detailed offshore plan was developed in order to establish specific wind energy clusters.[75] Although the procedure for allocating permits has not changed, a developer who receives a permit is no longer guaranteed a connection to the grid. In 2014, the government decided to limit, until 2020, the amount of offshore wind energy to be connected to the grid to 6.5 GW.[76] If requests

---

69 *Ibid.*, at p. 26. Also Renewable UK, 'Consents: Lessons Learned: An offshore wind industry review of past concerns, lessons learned and future challenges (2011), at http://www.renewableuk.com/en/publications/reports.cfm/Offshore-Wind-Consenting-Lessons-Learned; accessed 30 September 2014.

70 DTI (2002), (n 69) at pp. 38–39.

71 For the exact process, see Catherine Caine, 'The Dogger Bank Offshore Wind Farm Proposal: A Study of the Legal Mechanisms Employed in the Construction of an Offshore Wind Farm' (2014) 2(1) *North East Law Review* 89–128, at pp. 97–99. Also The Crown Estate, 'Round 3 offshore wind site selection at national and project levels' (2012), at http://www.thecrownestate.co.uk/media/5644/ei-round-3-offshore-wind-site-selection-at-national-and-project-levels.pdf; accessed 30 September 2014.

72 For the exact process, see Caine, *ibid.*

73 For the permits, see http://www.bsh.de/de/Meeresnutzung/Wirtschaft/Windparks/; accessed 25 August 2014.

74 *Verordnung über die Raumordnung in der deutschen ausschließlichen Wirtschaftszone in der Nordsee* vom 21. September 2009 (BGBl. I S. 3107). The spatial plan also included the connecting cables, Annex to the Spatial Plan, *Anlage zur Verordnung über die Raumordnung in der deutschen ausschließlichen Wirtschaftszone in der Nordsee* (AWZ Nordsee-ROV) vom 21 September 2009, p. 3.

75 Bundesfachplan Offshore, see § 17a German Energy Supply Act (EnWG), BGBl. I S. 1970, 3621, lastly amended on 21 July 2014 by BGBl. I S. 1066.

76 § 17d para. 3, *ibid.*

exceed available capacity, capacity will be allocated on the basis of competitive tenders.[77]

In Denmark, offshore wind farms can be developed on the basis of a government-led tender or a developer's own initiative.[78] In the latter case, a developer can apply for a permit to develop offshore wind in all available areas, but not in the areas specifically selected by the government as being suitable for developing offshore wind energy. When issuing a tender, the regulatory authority will make use of these pre-selected areas.[79] The first Action Plan on Wind Turbines issued in 1997 identified four offshore wind areas.[80] More areas for the development of large-scale offshore wind parks were identified in 2005.[81] Except for some wind parks very close to shore, all offshore wind parks have been developed on the basis of a tendering procedure.

The above shows that the four North Sea states now all aim at pre-selecting suitable wind energy locations and, except for Germany, offer these locations to developers via some sort of a tendering regime. The size of the locations and tendering processes may still differ.

Regulating Offshore Cables

When the North Sea countries developed their first offshore wind farms, barely any attention was paid to the cables connecting the wind farms to shore. As wind farms are increasingly built further away from shore and available cable routes are scarce, the question of how to best connect them to shore is gaining

77 § 17d para. 4, *ibid.*

78 Danish Energy Agency, 'Wind turbines in Denmark' (2009) 18, at http://www.ens.dk/sites/ens.dk/files/dokumenter/publikationer/downloads/wind_turbines_in_denmark.pdf; accessed 30 September 2014.

79 § 23 Danish Promotion of Renewable Energy Act, at https://www.retsinformation.dk/forms/r0710.aspx?id=159159; accessed 30 September 2014.

80 Elselskabernes og Energistyrelsens Arbejdsgruppe for havmøller, 'Havmølle-Handlingsplan for de danske farvande' (Juni 1997), at http://www.ens.dk/undergrund-forsyning/vedvarende-energi/vindkraft-vindmoller/havvindmoller/miljopavirkninger/baggrund; accessed 30 September 2014. Jens Bengtsson, 'Offshore Wind Farms in Denmark' in Martha Roggenkamp and Ulf Hammer (eds), *Energy Law Report I* (Intersentia, Antwerp, 2004) 137–138; Danish Energy Authority, 'Offshore wind power: Danish experiences and solutions' (October 2005), at http://ec.europa.eu/ourcoast/download.cfm?fileID=984; accessed 30 September 2014.

81 The Committee for Future Offshore Wind Power Sites, 'Future Offshore Wind Power Sites—2025' (2007). This plan was updated in 2011, see Danish Energy Agency, 'Stor-skala havmølleparker i Danmark. Opdatering af fremtidens havmølleplaceringer April 2011' (2011) 7, at http://www.ens.dk/en/node/418; accessed 30 September 2014.

importance. A first question is how to classify these cables. By contrast with oil and gas pipelines, there is no concept of 'upstream cables,' thus these cables must be classified as part of the installation or as a transmission line.

In the Netherlands, the cables between the offshore wind farms and the onshore system are considered as part of the production installation simply because only the provisions of the *Electricity Act 1998* governing production have been extended to the EEZ.[82] The transmission system operator (TSO) therefore has no obligations in the offshore area and thus wind farm developers have to construct the offshore cables to the onshore connection point.[83] As mentioned above, the Netherlands is in the process of establishing a new legal regime. If the bill as it stands is enacted, the TSO will be responsible for extending the transmission grid offshore and for connecting the offshore wind farms to the offshore grid.[84]

Offshore wind farm developers in the UK were initially also responsible for constructing the cables between the offshore wind farm and the onshore grid.[85] The *Energy Act 2004*, however, introduced the concept of the Offshore Transmission Owners (OFTOs) as the entity responsible for developing, operating and owning the connecting offshore cables. These OFTOs are appointed via a government-led tender.[86] Although the initial approach was that the OFTOs would also construct the connection cables, developers still have the possibility to construct the transmission lines themselves and to transfer them to an OFTO after they have been commissioned.[87] As these cables are classified

82 This provision is applied offshore in 2000 in order to give offshore wind park developers the possibility to benefit from renewable energy subsidies. It also means that the permit includes the construction of the offshore cables.

83 Art. 23, para. 1, Electricity Act *1998* in conjunction with Art. 16 (1)(e), Stb. 1998, 427.

84 See the Bill providing for a new integrated Electricity and Gas Act, 'Voorstel van wet houdende regels met betrekking tot de productie, het transport, de handel en de levering van elektriciteit en gas (Elektriciteits- en gaswet), 31 July 2014, at http://www.internetconsultatie.nl/stroom1; accessed 30 September 2014.

85 Renewable UK, 'Consenting Lessons Learned: An offshore wind industry review of past concerns, lessons learned and future challenges' (2011), at (n 70) p. 5. Also Electricity (Competitive Tenders for Offshore Transmission Licences) Regulations 2010, at http://www.legislation.gov.uk/uksi/2010/1903/contents/made; accessed 30 September 2014.

86 DECC and Ofgem, 'Offshore Electricity Transmission: A further Joint Ofgem/DECC Regulatory Policy Update' (2008) 15, at https://www.ofgem.gov.uk/ofgem-publications/51140/offshoreelectricitytransmission-ajointofgemdeccregulatorypolicyupdate.pdf; accessed 30 September 2014.

87 The Electricity (Competitive Tenders for Offshore Transmission Licences) Regulations 2013, at http://www.legislation.gov.uk/uksi/2013/175/schedule/9/made; accessed 30 September 2014.

as offshore transmission grids, generators are not allowed to own them and must transfer them to the OFTO after commissioning.[88]

Also in Germany, wind farm developers were initially responsible for constructing the cables connecting the wind farm and the onshore grid.[89] Although the first permit was granted in 2002, no wind farm was constructed under this regime. Due to geographical conditions, the German offshore wind farms are situated far away from shore and would thus require lengthy cables. Moreover, many parts of the German coast are classified as nature protection areas and the prospect of many separate connections was soon considered as undesirable, if not impossible. Consequently, the TSOs became legally obliged in 2006 to construct the offshore connection cables as it was expected that they would be in a better position to develop these connections in the most efficient way.[90] The regime was further amended in 2011 to oblige the TSOs to connect several offshore wind farms to one submarine cable.[91] Developing such huge connections posed challenges to the responsible TSOs and delays occurred. In response the German government has tried to align the development of the offshore wind farms with the offshore transmission lines and possible joint connections; since 2013 the TSOs have developed the *Offshore Grid Development Plan*.[92] This plan includes all offshore infrastructure projects planned for the next ten years and allows the TSOs to start building the infrastructure before construction of the wind farm begins.[93] By contrast to the other coastal states, the connecting (transmission) cable is thus already built in anticipation of the development of future offshore wind farms designated as such in the *Offshore Grid Development Plan*.

Denmark has chosen to apply a combination of the two approaches above. In a government-led tender, the Danish TSO is responsible for the construction and financing of the offshore cable, i.e., the transmission grid is extended to

88 Sec. 6C-6D Electricity Act 1989, at http://www.legislation.gov.uk/ukpga/1989/29; accessed 30 September 2014.

89 § 17 para. 2a German Energy Supply Act (n 76), version valid until August 2011.

90 For historical reasons four TSOs are operating in Germany. The connection obligation applies to the TSO responsible for the relevant coastal area.

91 See § 17 para. 2a German Energy Supply Act in its version applying from 5 August 2011 on, changed by Art. 2 G of 28 July 2011, BGBl. I S. 1690. Also Dieter Sellner and Frank Fellenberg, 'Atomausstieg und Energiewende 2011: das Gesetzespaket im Überblick' (2011) *Neue Zeitschrift für Verwaltungsrecht* 1025–1035, at p. 1033.

92 § 12a and § 17d para. 2 of the German Energy Supply Act (n 76). Here, the TSOs take into account the government's energy targets and the offshore wind capacity that has been approved by the regulatory authority.

93 § 17d German Energy Supply Act (n 76).

the offshore area.[94] However, if the developer takes the initiative to develop an offshore wind farm outside the tender procedure, the cable connecting the wind farm to the onshore grid has to be constructed and financed by the wind farm developer.[95] Given the additional costs of developing a connecting line, this approach has rarely been applied.[96]

The above shows that so far most cables are still considered as a park-to-shore activity and that these cables are not necessarily operated by TSOs. As most wind parks are situated relatively close to shore, the need for third-party access has yet to be addressed. This is different when compared to oil and gas development, where the sharing of infrastructure was common. Germany is so far the only country that requires the connection of several wind farms via one connection point. This is due to the long distances between the wind parks and the coast.

Cross-Border Cables

Given the parallels in regulating the offshore wind energy and oil and gas sector, we now discuss the possibilities for cross-border cable connections. The incentives for exporting offshore wind energy are limited. As outlined above, Norway was the only North Sea state to construct cross-border pipelines offshore due to its huge resources and limited national demand. There will be little need to export offshore wind energy because of sufficient national demand, as all EU Member States need to meet their 20-20-20 targets. Furthermore, currently an important obstacle to developing cross-border cables exists, which is that renewable support schemes are national in scope, as these schemes require the electricity produced to be fed into the national grid.[97]

94 See § 5 para. 1 of the Notice of grid connection of wind turbines and the surcharge for wind generated electricity, etc., at https://www.retsinformation.dk/Forms/R0710.aspx?id=133266; *accessed 30 September 2014*. The offshore cables need to have a separate permit, see § 16 *Electricity Supply Act*.

95 § 6 para. 1 of the Notice (n 95). This applies to all projects, which are not within the defined wind energy areas, see § 5 and 6. See further Deloitte, 'Analysis on the furthering of competition in relation to the establishment of large off-shore wind farms in Denmark: Background report 1: Analysis of framework conditions in key EU countries' (April 2011) 63–64, at http://www.ens.dk/sites/ens.dk/files/info/news-danish-energy-agency/cheaper-offshore-wind-farms-sight/deloitte_background_report_1_-_analysis_of_frame work_conditions_in_key_eu_countries.pdf; accessed 30 September 2014.

96 It is limited to four small projects close to shore: Samsø (23 MW), Rønland (17 MW) Middelgrunden (40 MW) and Avedøre/Hvidovre (7.2 MW). See also Deloitte, *ibid*.

97 The Court of Justice of the European Union recently confirmed that the EU Member States are allowed to limit their support schemes to the national territory. The Court ruled

Nevertheless, cross-border cables may be developed in the future if circumstances change. Perhaps electricity prices will rise and subsidies will decline,[98] or the subsidy regimes may be amended to facilitate cross-border connections and/or the construction of cross-border cables may be cheaper given shorter distances to another national grid. Moreover, a large number of submarine cables will be necessary if the current plans for offshore wind energy are implemented. Due to the costs of submarine cables, limited available space and the intermittency of offshore wind energy, the need for cross-border connections and the sharing of existing infrastructure (via third-party access) will grow in importance. This would also be in line with the EU's objective of an internal energy market.

When developing such cross-border cables, the coastal states could benefit from the experience in the oil and gas sector where cross-border pipelines have been established on the basis of specific pipeline agreements between the governments of the sending and receiving states. Here, the experiences with these pipeline agreements could be used to develop an adequate framework for offshore electricity infrastructure.

Conclusions

In this chapter, we have analysed the development of oil and gas and offshore wind energy. Although both sectors have faced comparable development stages, we note that legislators rarely expressly draw on experience in the oil and gas sector when drafting legislation for offshore wind energy.

As with the development of oil and gas resources, it has been necessary to classify offshore cables. Given the absence of 'upstream cables', the cables could be classified as part of the installation or as a separate activity. Although most North Sea countries are still in the process of developing their offshore regime, we note that they are increasingly classifying the cables as transmission

that the objective of promoting the use of renewable energy sources is in principle capable of justifying barriers to the free movement of goods; see Case C-573/12, *Ålands Vindkraft AB v. Energimyndigheten* [2014] not yet published.

98 The European Commission expects that support levels will decline and eventually be phased out. See Commission (EC), 'European Commission guidance for the design of renewables support schemes: Accompanying the document Communication from the Commission Delivering the internal market in electricity and making the most of public intervention' (Commission Staff Working Document), 5 November 2013, SWD(2013) 439 final, 6.

cables. In consequence, transmission system operators (TSOs) are increasingly involved in developing offshore transmission grids, which is usually not the case in the petroleum sector. Due to this extension of transmission grids offshore, coastal states need to assess whether all obligations of the TSOs should apply offshore. This includes the need for third-party access. Germany requires the TSOs to provide for a joint grid connection for several offshore wind farms. However, it is too early to say whether the other North Sea states will follow this approach, as the geographical circumstances differ.

We further note the need for more coordination and planning. Germany initiated this coordination between wind park development and offshore transmission, and even requires the construction of the offshore cable infrastructure before the offshore wind farm is constructed. It is not yet clear to what extent other coastal states will increase that coordination. The increasing competition for marine space might further require the coordination of offshore wind energy and petroleum.

We conclude that in order to develop the range of offshore energy sources now becoming available, coastal states need to be actively involved in regulating these activities and to use the possibilities they have as part of their functional jurisdiction. Currently, it is not clear yet whether more cross-border cables will be laid, but considering the current disincentives, it may be necessary for the EU to intervene in order to facilitate such a development. Here, a broader perspective should be applied so that lessons can be learned from the offshore petroleum sector and decisions about offshore energy developments are no longer taken in isolation.

Index